The Evolution of Consciousness

D1564514

The Evolution
of Consciousness

Edited by

KISHORE GANDHI

PARAGON HOUSE
NEW YORK, NEW YORK

Published by Paragon House
2 Hammarskjold Plaza
New York, New York

First Published by National Publishing House, New Delhi, India, 1983

0718-92 / Amity "Gandhi" / fd 2 / Second Proof

Library of Congress Cataloging-in-Publication Data

The Evolution of consciousness.

    1. Consciousness.   2. Genetic psychology.
I. Gandhi, Kishor.
B105.C477E96   1986   126   86-91502
ISBN 0-913757-50-0

First American publication in 1986 by Paragon House.

Contents

The Contributors

GEORGE WALD is a Nobel Laureate and a Professor in the Biological Laboratories, Harvard University.

B.R. SESHACHAR is a Professor at the Indian Institute of Sciences, Bangalore.

R.M. VARMA is Director of the National Institute of Mental and Health Sciences, Chandigarh.

DAVENDRA SINGH is a Professor of Psychology at Austin University, Austin, Texas.

E.C.G. SUDERSHAN is a Professor of Physics at Austin University, Austin, Texas.

RAVI RAVINDRA is a Professor of Physics and Religion in Canada.

ROBERT ARTIGIANI is an Associate Professor at the U.S. Naval Academy, Anapolis, Maryland.

JOEL COLTON is Director of Humanities of the Rockefeller Foundation, New York.

ALASTAIR M. TAYLOR is a Professor at the University of California, at Berkeley.

KISHORE GANDHI is Editor of this book, the author of many books, and has directed many international seninars under the joint sponsorship of the Jawaharlal Nehru University, the University of Delhi and the Sri Aurobindo Center.

M.A. SINACEUR is Chief of the Philosophy Division, UNESCO, Paris.

SISIRKUMAR GHOSE is Professor of English at Vishva-Bharati, Santiniketan.

PREM KIRPAL is former Educational Adviser and Secretary to the Government of India.

KARAN SINGH is a Member of Parliament.

ARYMURTHY is an Indonesian Professor and mystic.

D.S. KOTHARI is Chancellor of Jawaharlal Nehru University, New Delhi.

FRITJOF CAPRA is an Associate Professor at Lawrence Laboratories, University of California, at Berkeley. He is the author of *Tao of Physics*.

Preface

This collection of essays, by experts in various disciplines and perceptive thinkers, touches upon the major ambivalent theme of our times, the choice between suicide and an increased level of consciousness. The crisis of man and civilization, at every level, is too real to be ignored. Looking in depth, it is traceable to a crisis of consciousness. This is a subject deep and dark, but full of promises.

The present fluid situation in the world is partly the result of our inability to achieve a balanced development between the unique scientific and technological breakthrough of the twentieth century and the growth of human consciousness. Consequently, the human species has been brought to the verge of self-destruction, and it is now an open question as to whether or not man will be able to survive his own technological ingenuity. In such a situation, nothing is more important than our search for viable alternatives for the human race to live in global harmony, with norms of its own, based on a holistic and evolutionary world view. It is only through actualizing the total potentiality of the human mind and enlarging our areas of awareness that we will be able to contain our societal and psychological conflicts which threaten to explode as we move towards the twenty-first century.

While much of contemporary thought has engaged itself in the problem of man and society, no subject has been so neglected as the evolution of consciousness. Perhaps no one fully knows the total potentialities of the human mind and our awareness of human nature (including the nature of human systems) is selective, shaped by our explicit and implicit images. True, man is the product of millions of years of evolution. From the first unicellular organisms, evolution has developed a race which has crossed terrestrial barriers and landed on the moon. Spectacular though this development has been, there is no valid reason to assume that human consciousness is the final product of evolution. Indeed, a strong case can be presented—on the basis of a variety of writings—to show that man is an intermediary creature and that there is a distinct

x   THE EVOLUTION OF CONSCIOUSNESS

possiblity of a new leap in evolutionary consciousness. Man is more a project, a possibility and a promise rather than an achievement. The seed of this idea is to be found in many ancient texts, but in our times the remarkable writings of Teilhard de Chardin in the West and Sri Aurobindo in the East have thrown a great deal of light on the evolutionary possibilities that lie ahead.

Once it is accepted that consciousness of this planet is still evolving, the question arises as to what the next step in evolution will be. If the hope of a new order—the new age consciousness in which man will evolve and finally exceed himself—is not a fiction, then the evolution from now will be more significant in the realm of consciousness than in any biological and physiological changes. The human brain is still a largely unexplored area. Neuroscientists have shown that at present we are using an average of ten per cent of our existing brain cells. Could it be that the evolutionary process will now direct itself towards an increase in the use of brain cells, with a corresponding expansion in the field of consciousness? Also, as man continues his evolutionary adventures on this planet, will he move towards an optimum utilization of the billions of cells in his brain?

If these twin propositions are accepted as a possibility, the next question that arises is regarding the time span involved in the process. The past processes of evolution have taken billions of years, and if the same time-scale is to be continued, there will be hundred of generations before any perceptible change. However, we have a number of fascinating theories which present the possibility that man is the first creature to be self-conscious and able to enjoy the unique possibility of actively cooperating with the evolutionary process and thus speeding it up. One of the major theories at present in the field revolves around the *Kundalini*, a power that is believed to reside at the base of the human spine and which can, under certain circumstances, travel up the spine and finally to irradiate the brain, thus triggering off a quantum leap in consciousness. For example, consciousness researchers in the West are now learning how to combine new tools (biofeedback training and learning theory) with older techniques (meditation and autosuggestion) for unlocking more rapidly the vast untapped potentials of the human mind, especially its power of creativity. This brings us to the nature of the new consciousness that may be expected to emerge.

A parallel theory could revolve around the fact that whenever any species is in danger of extinction, some evolutionary urge within the race itself pushes towards a new mode of consciousness which would enable it to overcome the danger. This survival mechanism has in fact been largely responsible for evolution so far. Since the development of nuclear weapons, the human race has found itself in a constant threat of extinction. Could it be that in response to this factor, among others, the beginning of a new consciousness can be discerned which transcends barriers of race, religion, ideology and nationality? It is fascinating to note that in our times the evolution of consciousness has acquired a new and added significance. One even perceives a new trend towards convergence between the perennial philosophy and recent researches in physics, biology, pedagogy and psychology, if not social reconstruction.

In the *Tao of Physics*, Fritjof Capra has eloquently worked out the parallels between modern physics and Eastern mysticism and they are so striking that often one "encounters statements where it is almost impossible to say whether they have been made by physicists or by Eastern mystics." He writes: "Quantum theory and relativity theory both force us to see the world very much in the way a Hindu, Buddhist or Taoist sees it, and how this similarity strengthens when we look at the recent attempts to combine these two theories in order to describe the phenomena of the sub-microscopic world: the properties and interactions of the sub-atomic particles of which all matter is made." He further observes that: "Although these parallels have not, as yet, been discussed extensively, they have been noticed by some of the great physicists of our century."

Perhaps it is relevant to note the comment of Julius Robert Oppenheimer on this subject. He writes that ". . .the general notions about human understanding which are illustrated by discoveries in atomic physics are not in the nature of things wholly unfamiliar, wholly unheard of, or new. Even in our own culture they have a history and in Buddhist and Hindu thought a more considerable and central place. What we shall find is an exemplification, an encouragement, and a refinement of old wisdom."

Niels Bohr, another distinguished scientist, speaks about the need for convergence between science and mystical insights, which is the need of the hour for the sheer survival of biological life on this planet and also for another adventure in the evolution of consciousness. Only a quantum jump in this area will enable the human being to live in harmony with himself, community, laws of nature and the cosmos. Bohr writes that: "For a parallel to the lesson of atomic theory . . . [we must turn] to those kinds of epistemological problems with which already thinkers like the Buddha and Lao Tzu have been confronted, when trying to harmonize our position as spectators and actors in the great drama of existence."

It is not for us to speculate on the nature of the convergence and integration; but perhaps the hope of mankind lies in this direction.

Our loyalty to this emerging idea will be the measure of our responsiblity to the race and reality; that will determine the fate of mankind and the curve of culture. Voices past and present mingle, raising the hymn of humanity to new heights. There may be a new definition of man, reality and consciousness: some unachieved unified field lies before the dreamer, the enquirer, the lover of mankind.

I am greatly indebted to the contributors of this volume who promptly responded to my invitation and enriched this publication with their scholarly and perceptive essays. Included also are some of the updated presentations made in the international seminar directed by me under the joint auspices of the University of Delhi, Jawaharlal Nehru University and Sri Aurobindo Centre, New Delhi. The author expresses his gratitude to all the contributors once again, especially to Professor D. S. Kothari and Professor Fritjof Capra for permitting their published lectures to be included in this book.

The book is dedicated to Sri Aurobindo and the Mother and the post-Einsteinian scientists who are working relentlessly for the survival of the human race on this beautiful planet.

KISHORE GANDHI

Life and Mind in the Universe

"As the hand held before the eye conceals the greatest mountain, so the little earthly life hides from the glance the enormous lights and mysteries of which the world is full, and he
who can draw it away from before his eyes, as one draws away
a hand, beholds the great shining of the inner worlds."
—*Rabbi Nachman of Bratzlav*

A LIFE-BREEDING UNIVERSE

We seem to find ourselves in a universe permeated with life,
in which life arises, given enough time, wherever the conditions
exist that make it possible. How many such places are there?
At least one billion, apparently, in our own home galaxy, the
Milky Way; and with about one billion such galaxies now visible through our most penetrating telescopes, the number of
such places in the already observed universe should be of the
order of at least 10^{18}—one billion.[1]

So a universe that breeds life; and yet, were any one of a
number of properties of our universe other than it is—some
of these properties basic, others seeming trivial, almost accidental—that life, which now seems to be so prevalent, would
become impossible here or anywhere.

For example, the proton and electron, though altogether
unlike in every other dimension, have an opposite yet numeri-
cally identical electric charge. If that were not so, all the matter

in the universe would be charged, and in the same sense. Hence all matter would repel all other matter. That in itself could account for an expanding universe. Yet a difference in charge of only 2×10^{-18} e—two billionths of e—in which e is the charge on either the proton or the electron, while enough to bring about the expansion, would also suffice to overwhelm the forces of gravitation that bring matter together.[2] Hence no galaxies, stars or planets—nor physicists to observe them.

An afterthought: it seems clear that life, wherever it arises, must be composed primarily of the same four elements, hydrogen (H), carbon (C), nitrogen (N) and oxygen (O), for only these among the natural 92 element share the properties upon which life depends. There are many such properties, observable yet hardly predictable, and not shared by any other elements. For example, only C, N and O can form multiple bonds, double and triple bonds. Carbon dioxide, for example, is formed by the combination of carbon and oxygen by a double bond relationship, and it issues as an independent molecule in the air and dissolves in all the waters of the earth—providing essential carbon to living organisms all of which need water to survive. In contrast, take silicon dioxide (SiO_2) which cannot make double bonds, which can retain four half-formed bonds, and hence combines with itself over and over, ending in yielding such a rock as quartz.[3]

Water is the strangest molecule in all chemistry; and its strangest property is that *ice*, the solid state of water, *floats*. Everyone knows that, on cooling, virtually all materials contract and so grow denser. So does water, down to 4 °C; but between 4° and 0 °C, where it freezes, it expands and so rapidly that ice is lighter than water and floats. Almost nothing else behaves that way. Yet this special property of water enables life to be maintained in water even in the most severe winters or in a veritable ice age because the low temperature on earth can at most freeze the temperature of the waters. The frozen "crust" or ice floats and shields the rest of the watery mass from the hostile cold. As the sun grows warmer, the ice quickly thaws, liberating again the aquatic creatures. If ice did not float, I think there would be little if any life in the universe.

In 1837 Heinrich Olbers stated what came to be known as Olbers's Paradox. On the wholly reasonable assumption that space extends infinitely in all directions, and contains everywhere about the same density of stars (our present cosmological principle), he pointed out that hence every planet in the universe should receive light not only from its sun but from all the stars, and as much from distant shells of stars as from those nearby. Therefore the sky over every planet should be ablaze with light night and day.[4] And every planet in the universe should have long since been heated to a state of incandescence, in which it reirradiated light as fast as absorbed. Why is the night sky dark? The most widely accepted explanation is that this is one consequence of an expanding universe.[5] But by the same token only an expanding universe should support life.

Here I have only sampled a much more extensive argument, meanwhile quite intentionally ascending the scale of states of organization of matters: from elementary particles to atoms, molecules, and star systems. At every level we find special properties that foster life. It takes no great intelligence or imagination to think of other universes, perfectly workable as such, yet lifeless. All that one has to do is to choose differently any of the properties mentioned, or any one of a number of others, and out would come a possible universe, yet no life.

How then does our universe "happen" to have just that complex of properties which breeds life? A silly question?—after all, if it didn't breed life, we wouldn't be here to ask. But that's a silly answer for we *are* here, and strangely inclined to ask that question.

ONE WITH THE UNIVERSE

I do not need spiritual enlightenment to know that I am one with the universe. That is just good physics.

The hydrogen, carbon, nitrogen and oxygen that compose 99 per cent of living substance compose also 99 per cent of such a star as the sun. The first generation of stars began as hydrogen, of mass 1 (H^1), and lived by fusing it to helium, of mass about 4 ($4H^1 \rightarrow He^4$). The helium has a slightly smaller mass than 4 hydrogens. This loss of mass, converted to energy according to Einstein's formula $E = mc^2$, generates enormous energy that keeps the star from collapsing, and is also the source of sunlight.

Eventually this process runs every star short of hydrogen. Generating less energy, it begins to collapse; and that raises its temperature to the point at which its helium fuses. Two atoms of helium fuse to yield the highly unstable beryllium ($2He^4 \rightarrow Be^8$). This captures another helium to make carbon ($Be^8 + He^4 \rightarrow C^{12}$). That is how carbon enters the universe. Carbon can add two hydrogens to make nitrogen ($C^{12} + 2H^1 \rightarrow N^{14}$), or can add another helium to make oxygen ($C^{12} + He^4 \rightarrow O^{16}$). That is how nitrogen and oxygen come into the universe. So are generated the elements that will principally compose living organisms.

These new processes yield a new outpouring of energy that puffs the star up to an enormous size. It becomes a *red giant*, a dying star. By distillation, and in such stellar catastrophes as flares, novae and supernovae, red giants spew their substance into space to become part of the mass of gases and dust that fill all interstellar space. Over aeons of time new stars aggregate out of the gases and dust. But such latecomers, unlike the first generation of stars made wholly of hydrogen and helium, contain also carbon, nitrogen and oxygen. Hence their planets can support life. We know that our sun is such a later-generation star because we are here.

But composition only begins the story. Stars and organisms must metabolize to live. Stars live by fusing hydrogen to helium, the source of sunlight. That sunlight comes to provide all the components for how we live: by burning hydrogen with oxygen to water. That burning of hydrogen to water—so-called *respiration*—is superimposed upon an anaerobic substrate of *fermentation* shared by all living cells that recalls the long initial period of almost two billion years in which the earth's atmosphere lacked oxygen. Oxygen first entered our atmosphere and is now maintained there as a byproduct of photosynthesis performed by plants—the process by which, using the energy of sunlight, plants convert carbon dioxide and water to sugars (the organic molecules from which ultimately all our other organic molecules are derived) and oxygen. It is from those sugars that we pluck the hydrogen that we burn with oxygen to have water. Hence all life on earth now runs on photosynthesis, on sunlight: the fusion of hydrogen in the sun generates all the components for the burning of hydrogen here.

We tend to think of the earth's physical environment as something given, that sets the tune to which life must dance. But some of the main features of the physical environment are products of life. All the oxygen in our atmosphere comes out of photosynthesis and goes into cellular respiration and so is completely renewed about every two thousand years. All the carbon dioxide in the atmosphere and dissolved in all the waters of the earth goes into photosynthesis and comes out of respiration and is completely renewed every three hundred years. All the water on the earth goes into photosynthesis and comes out of respiration, and so is completely renewed every two million years—still only a day in geological time. These main aspects of our environment have been in and out of living organisms many time over.

The salts in our blood are virtually the same in composition and proportion as those of the ancient seas in which marine vertebrates first closed off and stabilized their circulations hundreds of millions of years ago. Sea water has grown more concentrated since; but even now a frog heart will keep beating for hours in sea water diluted with three volumes of distilled water.

Stars must die before organisms can live. In their deaths they generate the elements that come to compose the sun, its planets, and ourselves. The sun's metabolism powers our metabolism. The salts of ancient seas run in our blood.

We see this universe not from outside but from inside; its history is our history, its stuff our stuff. Much of the past of the galaxy, of our sun and of this planet comes together in us. *Over the ages other persons traveling other paths have come to similar perceptions of unity with the cosmos.* Here we have done so through physics. One can add this discipline to the others, or take it by preference. It hardly matters for they all come together in the end.

MAN, THE ANIMAL WHO KNOWS

In that universe of which we are so integral a part, we—

and our like elsewhere—have a special place. We are the animals who know and who create. Our knowing is epitomized in science, our creation in the arts, and both in our technology. We are animals who not only occupy worlds, but seek to understand them and transform them.

In that sense we are a kind of culmination. In our knowing, the universe comes to know itself. I have heard it said that a hen is only an egg's way of making another egg. In the same sense a physicist is the atom's way of knowing about atoms, the star's way of knowing about stars. It has taken a long time—on our planet, three billion years!

Do systems of life elsewhere in the universe evolve such contemplative and creative, science-art- and technology-making creatures? They probably do. The main counters in the game of evolution are to be possible, and to be successful. Clearly we are possible, though if we did not exist we'd be hard to imagine. As for our success, not only does our species dominate the earth, but we have achieved the heady eminence of being able to exterminate ourselves, taking much of the rest of life on earth with us—the first self-extinction of a species of which we know.

So I suppose that elsewhere in this universe other such creatures exist, in many places probably far ahead of us in their development—unless, as is now sometimes suggested, their technology inevitably turns as suicidal as has ours, and they extinguish themselves, as we are now threatening to do, when they reach about our stage. That however is an inference I entirely reject; it is making altogether too much of the present organization of our society to imagine that all other social systems in the universe need function so disastrously. Indeed, I still cling to a hope for our own species.

THE PROBLEM OF CONSCIOUSNESS

It is always better in science to have a problem force itself upon one rather than to seek it out. For then one can be sure that it is real and not a *Scheinproblem*, not an escape or perhaps a vehicle for self-display or aggrandizement. If it enters forcibly there is nothing left but to try to come to terms with it—unless instead one throws it out and locks the door upon it.

I have spent most of my scientific life studying mechanisms of vision. When I started, it was a lonely enterprise. Now this field has exploded. An annual meeting in Sarasota, Florida, draws upwards of two thousand workers.

One can put together everything that we have learned, and add to it everything that workers in this area hope to learn; and none of it comes anywhere near, or even aims in the direction of *what it means to see.*

That is the problem of consciousness. Come at from this direction, it was hardly to be avoided. I have been aware of it for many years, but held it in the background. I had other, easier, things to do. Now I have stopped doing these other things and it is in the foreground.

Seeing—the event in consciousness—seems to lie in another universe, unapproachable by science. I know that I see. You tell me that you see; and you are enough like me to make me willing to believe it, even to be reassured by it that I am not hallucinating. Extending that analogy, I believe that apes, monkeys, dogs, cats and other mammals see. The trouble is that I can do nothing whatever to verify those suppositions. Does a frog see? Certainly it reacts to light, with behavior, with chemical changes in its retina and electrical responses in its nervous system, all of which I can measure—and all of which resemble responses I can measure in human eyes. But does it see?—does it *know* that it is responding? I can do nothing about that!

After all, I can make any number of mechanical devices that respond to light chemically (a camera), electrically (a photocell), behaviorally (a photoelectrically-activated garage door); and with special trouble can design devices that mimic closely the photic responses of animals.[6] Do they see?—in the sense that I see? I feel quite sure that they do not; yet not *entirely* sure, for there is nothing I can do about that either!

Science offers no way of testing for the mere presence or absence of consciousness, let alone its content. At most, we guess by analogy, with greater assurance the closer another organism is to ourselves, with stronger doubt the more remote, but with no way whatever of shoring up our guesses.

Let even another human being, whose consciousness we

are quite ready to concede, claim to hear something that we fail to hear or see, or feel something that we fail to perceive— such as an otherwise normal person at a spiritualistic seance, for example—and we cry delusion, illusion, mass hypnosis, fakery! We have a whole armory of terms with which to deny to other persons elements of consciousness that we do not share. And if someone insists upon having such perceptions in ordinary circumstances, as part of their ordinary waking existence, we declare them insane. They are hallucinating, we say—hearing voices, having visions, all to us symptoms of psychic disorder.

It is curious to what degree such attitudes are culture-bound. One has only to go from the United States to England, for example, to find a distinct relaxation, notably among natural scientists, involving the belief in ghosts. Americans reject ghosts out of hand; the English rather enjoy them. To an American scientist the entire structure of science would shake were one to admit a single ghost. The English scientist, asked for an opinion, and a little uncomfortable if it is an American who asks, is likely to reply, "Well, we don't know, do we?" A famous Cambridge ethologist, whom I once approached on this matter, expressed a special interest in poltergeists. But, he said, you had to be careful not to be taken in; the observations had to be well authenticated. To an American, this is obvious nonsense, musty with the smell of old attics, and not at all like UFOs, with their whiff of space travel and still-unrealized mechanical devices.

I doubt that there is any Eastern culture in which I would fail to be congratulated if I were to announce that I could hear what other persons were thinking. "How fine!" they might say. "Were you always that way, or did you have to learn? If you learned, would you tell me how?"

However we in the West insist that for communication to occur there must be an exchange of energy: to see demands that light has passed, to hear there must be a transfer of sound. I remember many years ago in Berlin hearing Hans Spemann lecture on embryonic development. How is it that a single cell, a fertilized egg, by its repeated divisions ends up with a highly differentiated, beautifully integrated living organism? (That, by the way, is still a major biological problem.) In the discussion that followed Spemann's lecture, an old gentleman rose to ask why Spemann did not consider some extraphysical organizing force that might govern such phenomena? Spemann replied that for communication among cells, as among persons, energy must be exchanged. In this case the gentleman had spoken and he had heard. "If I were an insect," he said kindly, "I might be able to *smell* what you are thinking." The audience loudly applauded.

To return to our problem: science has no way of dealing with consciousness, nor even to identify its presence or absence. Take the matter of pain. In the course of my work I have had to kill many animals and work with many kinds of living tissues; and I have tried hard not to inflict pain. Which animals, which parts of animals, can feel pain? When I lop the head off a frog, I assume that the headless body is beyond pain. But the head? Is the brain surviving to feel perhaps intolerable pain? I hastily destroy the brain, and hope that now I have disposed of the problem. But have I? If I cut off a frog's head just behind the eyes, at the angle of the jaws, all the forward parts of the brain that I hope are needed to have sensations are gone. Pinch the toe of such an animal, and the leg is withdrawn. A reflex, I say; no implication of pain. If I lay a bit of filter paper wetted with vinegar on its back, shortly it raises one or both hind legs and very expertly wipes the paper away. A more complicated reflex, I explain, full of admiration for reflexes. But no unpleasantness because that frog cannot feel. Can an intact frog feel pain? A neurophysiologist assured me that it cannot; one need worry only about warm-blooded animals, mammals and perhaps birds. The struggling and escape behavior of cold-blooded animals are not accompanied by sensations; they are "just reflex". This view has been widely accepted by physiological societies and journals. The U.S. national Eye Institute in 1979 announced a first break when it asked its workers, who were doing experiments with cold-blooded animals, to try to avoid giving them "unnecessary pain". So physicians performing circumcisions without anesthesia assure mothers that human infants cannot feel pain: the nervous system is not yet sufficiently developed, they explain.

In my own work I long ago decided that if I did something to any animal that would be painful if done to me, and it responded by writhing and struggling as I would do, I preferred to assume that it felt pain—provided that it still had a brain, or what makes do for a brain in a higher invertebrate. But almost any piece of a worm squirms and writhes on being pinched. I have without great emotion strung a writhing worm on a fishhook. How high can one ascend in the scale of writhing and struggling creatures and assume that they feel no pain?

The only point of this discussion is to illustrate how completely arbitrary is any decision involving another creature's consciousness or lack thereof.

Since consciousness presents us with no identifying signals, nothing mensurable, no apparent energy expenditure, it would be a comfort for a scientist to deny that it exists, or to declare it irrelevant. I have known distinguished scientists to take both positions. I remember the physicist P. W. Bridgman speaking of consciousness as "just a way of talking". He made an operational definition his criterion of reality; and since there are no operations that define consciousness, he excluded it. B.F. Skinner, in the same discussions, dismissed consciousness as irrelevant to science in that it must remain a private experience, whereas science is a social, public activity.[7]

Unfortunately for such attitudes, all that I know is in my consciousness. Consciousness is not just a curious epiphenomenon, a trivial concomitant of our muscular and neural activity ("the brain secretes thought as the liver secretes bile"), which we project onto physical reality. On the contrary, we know how livers secrete bile, and are learning about muscular and nervous activities, yet only through our consciousness. No consciousness, no science, public or private.

So consciousness is not to be sought in the superstructure, but in the foundations. Scientists should be among the last to push it aside, since it underlies all science, is all that makes science possible. Does it also underlie all physical reality? This is a question to which we shall return. The essential condition of all science is that science has no way to approach consciousness. It lies in another sphere from what we call physical reality, congruent in part with it, yet distinct from it, and projecting far beyond: beyond physics into metaphysics, intuition, emotions, imagination, dreams, perhaps much more.

Science tells us nothing about consciousness, nor does it promise ever to do so. I used to make the brave assertion that we would keep on trying, but in reality we are not trying because we have not found a way to begin.

There is a point here that needs some further statement, to prevent misunderstanding. That science tells us nothing of consciousness does not involve any limitation within its own sphere. There science expands without limit, each answer breeding new questions, facing in all directions an ever-widening horizon. As has often been said, it is an endless quest. For what? To bring more and more of the material world to consciousness; to recognize—hence make conscious—more and more subtle and detailed aspects of Nature.

That recognition is a kind of creation of distant galaxies, quasars and pulsars, elementary particles and genes. We say that they were all there, ready to be discovered. But until discovered they did not exist *for us*. In that sense science does not only discover, but creates and makes real what it asserts to be real.

So the limitation of science we speak of here is no limit to its endless expansion within its own horizons. The limitation is only in crossing over *as science* to that other sphere, the realm of consciousness, congruent in part with material reality, yet distinct; and itself endless, outside space and time, always encompassing yet extending endlessly beyond science. Metaphysics is the sky over the sea of physics; said differently, it is the territory always beyond physics, not only what we know in physics, but what we are likely ever to find out *as physics*.

The mistake—made all too frequently—is to go to metaphysics without physics; for until one has explored the physics of one's time to its boundaries, how find one's way beyond? It is mainly in this sense that science becomes a Tao, a Way to the boundaries. This is a particularly relevant consideration as we approach the twenty-first century; for there is a new sense of drawing together of modern physics in its furthest reaches—in relativity theory and quantum dynamics—and particularly in Eastern modes of mysticism.[8] The approaches are mutual, physics having foregone much of its earlier materiality, and the mysticism now increasingly recognized as being—in what I think are its most relevant forms—whole *empirical*, whole experiential, an invitation to explore, without any preconception of where it will lead, or what one will find.[9]

EPISODE IN THE GARDEN

The encounter between God and the first human beings in the Garden of Eden has been much misunderstood. Had that been a Greek myth, the tree which yielded the forbidden fruit would have been the Tree of Knowledge. But it was a Jewish myth; and hence that tree was the Tree of Knowledge of Good and Evil. It was the entry into the creation of freedom of choice, of what we call Free Will. Before that, Adam and Eve had lived like and among the other animals, cared for as were they, sharing with them one system of communication, talking with them as they talked with God. But now they knew good and evil, and so had to leave the Garden, were cut off to shift for themselves.

Judeo-Christian theology speaks of this as the Fall of Man. But God took a different view of it. "Behold!" he said. "The man has become as one of us, knowing Good and Evil. And now, that he not eat also of the Tree of Life, and so live forever. . ." Man like a god, exercising choice, picking his way as do the gods, lacking only immortality.

I thought at first that that reference to Good and Evil marked the Jewish obsession with Justice. But in fact the story says nothing of *judgment*. It says only *knowing* Good and Evil, God and Satan, the creative and destructive aspects that in all Eastern theologies consitute one godhead.

I think that what this myth means most is that human beings, far beyond all other animals, have left the guardianship of instinctive behavior and so are free, for good or ill, to choose their paths. In "Murder in the Cathedral," T.S. Eliot speaks of

> . . .the greatest treason:
> To do the right deed for the wrong reason.

Other animals tend to do the right deed because that has

been for ages the condition of their survival; because what is essential in their behavior has been selected in the struggle for existence and built into them. They are not asked what to do; they are told. And it has to be right or they would not be here or will shortly be gone.

It is peculiarly the human condition to be able to make mistakes. We seem just now to have reached the brink of the ultimate mistake. We have only to release the nuclear weapons that are already stored to wipe ourselves out and much of the rest of life on earth.

I once was startled to hear Niels Bohr speak of the eel migrations. All the eels of the Atlantic Ocean come to the same area of the Sargasso Sea, in the South Atlantic, to spawn. They have grown up in fresh water; but now, as the time for spawning approaches, the mature eels migrate to the deepest and saltiest part of the Atlantic, and there spawn and die. The larval eels must find their way back alone. It takes the American eels some fifteen months to reach our shores, metamorphose, and ascend our rivers. It takes the European eels—a different species—about three years to get home. There is no record of the mistaken entry of a European eel into an American river, or the other way around.

No one has any idea how the larval eels find their way back. Niels Bohr said this wonderful thing: "It is just because they do not know where they are going that they always do it perfectly."

Our earth is an old organism. It has experienced many changes, many upheavals, and much rearrangement before settling down to its present state. That is the wisdom of the planet. Life arrived on the earth some three billion years ago. Many a star—indeed any star twice or more the mass of our sun—stays on the Main Sequence a shorter time than life has survived and flourished and occupied every possible niche upon the earth. If one conceives of the topography of the earth as a free energy surface, then every mound has some organism that lives by sliding off it. Hence we find organisms adapted to live on mountain tops and in the depths of the seas in hot springs, and in iron and surfur deposits. That is the wisdom of life. The planet and its life form one dynamic system, not in equilibrium, not even in a steady state, but evolving together in one great, dynamic balance, one communication system speaking its own quiet language.

That is the Garden of Eden. And we? We are those strange excluded creatures who have been liberated from the security and constraints of instinctual life. For good or ill? We who know where we are going are now heading rapidly toward self-extinction, toward removing humankind from the cosmic scene, and for the most trivial of reasons: profit, the rivalry of the United States and the Soviet Union, the momentum of the military-industrial complex in both nations. The cosmic drama will go on elsewhere, ignorant of our demise, caring nothing; but we will have no further part in it.

Does that matter? It matters to us.

MORE CULTURE OR LESS

It is clear to many thoughtful persons by now that our society has taken a wrong turn. In our thirst for knowledge, we have cut ourselves off from wisdom. In our pride in science, we have come to despise and reject intuitive and instinctual perceptions that have heretofore animated and given perspective and hope and meaning to human existence. By now the problem is not transcendence, but survival. If we are to survive there must be fundamental changes in direction, not only organizationally, but in our ways of thinking. We have to think different thoughts and to want different things.

Here we encounter a curious paradox. Though it is precisely what are commonly regarded as the top levels of our society —the most highly educated and technologically advanced and affluent elements—that have turned most threatening and seem most lost, it is frequently suggested that the cure, indeed our only hope, lies in more of the same: longer education, more and better schooling, higher learning. All the mystics through the ages have agreed that to achieve wisdom one must quiet the brain, stop using it as a tool, put aside knowledge and learning, try indeed to free one's consciousness, empty one's mind, and in quiet see what enters. One hopes then to connect directly with Nature, with the universe of which we know ourselves to be an intrinsic part, and to hear and perhaps even begin to express its endless exuberance and wisdom, to which we may once have been attuned, as the eels and salmon find their way home, as the birds know where to go with the march of the seasons, as newborn young know how to suckle; and the joy, the endless play: the bees and crickets and cicadas, the birds and whales and frogs, not just acting in the world, but singing. Why singing?

I should like to propose that what we seek—call it what you will, Primordial Consciousness, Suchness, That, Universal Mind—lies not before us but behind. It lies behind us individually and racially: individually in our early childhood, and racially in what we tend to regard as more primitive cultures, past and present.

I rather think that young children are connected up, that they are in touch with that universal instinctual, intuitive presence, communicating more or less freely with it, talking with and touching and tasting everything living and otherwise about them; and playing: dancing, singing, just making noise, like puppies, kittens, lambs, young deer, horses (young girls and horses have a special affinity) and porpoises (young children and porpoises get along famously). Where would it end if we just let it happen?

A few days ago I had a strange experience. My wife and I were returning on the ferry from an island off the coast. Seagulls flew along beside the boat. Then some children came to the railing, holding up pieces of bread. The seagulls swooped out of line, one by one, and took the bread. But seagulls are carnivores with great, cruel beaks. Why did they spare the fingers? If a child, altogether relaxed, were to offer a tiger a lump of meat, would it take the meat gently and go its way? I rather think it might. If it were not too hungry.

Once I saw a film called *African Lion*. There was a prairie with a large herd of antelopes grazing. A pride of lions came through, males, females, and young, walking among the antelopes. And the antelopes paid no attention, never stopped grazing. They knew and *we* knew, watching those lions, that none of them was hunting. If one of them had crouched, tensed up, and straightened out its tail, the antelope would have been off in a flash. There is a universal language, of signals and sometimes sounds, that all creatures recognize—and we do too, at least the grosser portions of it: rage, fear, pain, hunger; fleeing and attack.[10] Children from early infancy seem at home with that language, understand and indeed use it.

But the connections, I suspect, go much deeper.

When my daughter was nine years old, she and her brother were playing one day in her room. My son picked a piece of paper off the floor, looked at it, and said, "That's a pretty good poem, Debbie," and showed it to my wife. Otherwise I doubt that we or anyone else would ever have seen it.

The poem read as follows:

  If you ever get to infinity
  You will find me there
  For tomorrow I will climb
  The elementary stair.
  I will climb to the very top
  Open up the door
  Look at all the ages
  Lying on the floor.

To me that is not just a good poem; it is a revelation. How could a little, middle class, nine-year-old American girl, living a carefully nurtured life, going to a select private school—how could such a child write such a poem? And that was it: there never was another like it and I doubt that there ever will be. I don't really understand how that poem happened; but I think that at that time in her life an intuitive wisdom which distilled into those words was connected with what we should like to be connected, but have lost contact with and would have to work hard and change very much to reestablish it. And I am afraid that by now, nine years later, she too may have lost contact.

For in any of our developed countries, shortly after the age of nine if not before, the whole social structure—parents, teachers, schools, churches—go to work on a child to force the process spoken of as "growing up", to make that child into what Carlos Castaneda has called a "member". That child, all of whose life had been free, exploratory, whose potentials were limitless, whose play was highly imaginative to a degree permitted in adult life only to schizophrenics—who drew and painted and sang and shouted in pure enjoyment, who often

mixed experience in the waking world with those in dreams—
that child is put on a track by society to cast its life into a linear
progression. For when one is on a track, one is going somewhere, there are stations and a schedule. To be sure, one is prevented thereby from going anywhere else; but that's the point.
One may go somewhere else later; now we're going *there.* And
it's time to stop playing and learn to work—to be not only
trained but rated. And so the contact is lost. That wonderful
young inhabitant of the universe is domesticated into a useful
cog in an industrial society, someone with skills that can be
sold.

Many years later, often toward the end of life, a few such
persons try hard to achieve a state of awareness, of connectedness, that by then they have forgotten that they possessed
as children.

I had the joy of knowing Albert Einstein, Niels Bohr, and
Alfred North Whitehead. They were at once the greatest and
the most childlike persons I have ever known. There were no
tracks, no fences; they were interested in everything interesting. I thought of a man walking a young dog: he walks in a
straight line, while the dog is off in all directions, sniffing into
every corner, into everything. Most of us are trained to go
linearly, like the master. These celebrities went like the puppy.

How many of us have had—or can remember having had—
transcendental childhood experiences? I can remember just
one. I was six or seven years old and sick in bed, not in pain
or any great discomfort, but bored, isolated in an upstairs
bedroom. So I was glad to hear a hurdy-gurdy begin playing
down the street. The sound was easily localized; it was down
the street, below the big avenue, just within easy earshot. The
song was popular at the time and familiar to me: "Lily, lily of
the valley, . . ." It ended, "Be my lily-O, be my lily-O-daa-da-
da-dum-dum-daa." I heard it coming to the end with regret; I
wished it would go on. So I was surprised and pleased when
it started right over again. And then, a little later, I realized
that I was in control. I could make it do anything I wanted.
And I did until my mother appeared and broke the spell. I
think I told her what had happened; and that she listened in-
dulgently, and a little impatiently, to the rambling of a sick

child who had mixed up dreaming with waking, . . . And here I am, 65 years later, remembering a unique experience.

My son Michael at about the same age had imaginary friends with whom he reported close and intimate companionship and conversations. They had wonderful names: Panistro, Hambarner, and a particularly portentious one called Person. Our Michael was a somewhat insecure child who had been through a big illness and was being bullied on the street by some youthful viragos. Those imaginary friends meant a lot to him. And we?—amused, indulgent, knowing he would grow out of it. For what is permitted to a child, particularly when ill, would be taken as psychopathological—a symptom of schizophrenia—in a Western adult.

Is it *that* rejection by our society which makes us erase so efficiently our childhoods? What an astonishing process! That childhood, which is so filled with events, response and learning, and deep, stormy emotion! A child of two, four, six is a whole person, with a command of language, active in the world, full of experience awake and asleep, with vivid dreams hardly to be told from waking experiences; and then all of it is erased, so that frequently the only residue is an occasional, usually meaninglesss and emotionless vignette, like a casual snapshot.

Childhood and our dreaming as grownups are alike in this regard. The most interesting thing about our dreams as adults is the efficiency with which they are erased. For most of us and most of the time they fade to nothing as we awaken, slipping away even as we try to put them into words—gone irretrievably.

Much has been written about these things—much that I have not read. Our lives as children and our dreaming are both wiped out of memory, forgotten, and (I think) actively suppressed probably because they are inappropriate to our programmed lives, because they might take us off that track that we were so painstakingly trained to pursue.

This is part of our heritage of high culture. I have the idea that those gaps do not exist—surely not to such a degree—in what we regard as more primitive societies, both in earlier stages of our own society and in other preindustrial societies that still survive.

An example: *the vision quest of the American plains Indians.* A young boy, under the advice of one or several older men, goes off alone to a hilltop, or perhaps just a burrow on the open prairie, and is left alone, fasting, for several days, in the course of which every thought, dream, and occurrence is carefully noted and considered. He may indeed have a major vision, an illumination. All of that is told to his advisers on returning; and based upon his reports he is given his adult name, and perhaps carries a significant object or shield which symbolizes that experience throughout the rest of his life. The Oglala Sioux, Black Elk, had such a messianic vision at the age of nine. The tragedy of his life was his feeling that he had not fulfilled that mission.

Among the plains Indians, such crying or lamenting for a vision is a ritual experience that a man or woman can invoke at any critical time throughout life. Black Elk as an old man described the ritual in detail:

> Every man can cry for a vision, or 'lament'; and in the old days we all—men and women—'lamented' all the time. What is received through the 'lamenting' is determined in part by the character of the person who does this, for it is only those people who are very qualified who receive the great visions, which are interpreted by our holy men, and which give strength and health to our nation. It is very important for a person who wishes to 'lament' to receive aid and advice from a holy man, so that everything is done correctly. . . There are many reasons for going to a lonely mountain-top to 'lament'. . . But perhaps the most important reason for 'lamenting' is that it helps us to realize our oneness with all things, to know that all things are our relatives; and then in behalf of all things we pray to *Wakan-Tanka* (the Great Spirit) that he may give us knowledge of him who is the source of all things, yet greater than all things.[11]

Childhood visions and adult dreams, far from being rejected and erased, are cultivated and treasured in other societies than ours as precious connections with the universal and primordial mind-stuff. The road we have been taking has broken those connections. To reestablish them we must first of all recognize that they lie not ahead, in some further refinement of the way we have gone, but behind us. We will have to find our way back to the connectedness that was ours as children, and that belonged to our species and races when younger and freer.

The Eastern mysticisms have a particular attraction for the lost and lonely Westerner in that they have maintained such connections. The American Indian "lamenting" is the Hindu *samadhi*, the Hindu or Buddhist or Zen meditation and its hoped-for vision, the Buddhist enlightenment, the Zen *satori*. But in the end all mysticisms come together, those of the West with those of the East. What we now lack is wisdom: we have lost wisdom only lately, mainly in the last two centuries, as an outcome of too narrow a view of science and of an exploitative industrialization. Our need is to go beyond: not to more of those things, but to less.

What lies most in our way is a lack of respect, indeed a contempt for the age-old intuitions and traditions that once animated our culture. When they appear as new insights in some of our greatest savants—physicists!—they are dismissed as regrettable weaknesses, vagaries, if not evidences of senility. When I was a young graduate student, I encountered and to a degree shared what I came to think of as the "last chapter syndrome". There was a stereotyped comment that ran: "Have you read Eddington's *Nature of Physical Reality*—or Jeans' *The Universe Around Us* or Schrodinger's *What is Life?* Too bad about his last chapter!" That last chapter was in each case going from physics to philosophy, considering metaphysics, a religious perspective.

That kind of thing has been going on for a long time. I hardly know of a top physicist since Newton who has failed at times to go over the boundaries, from physics to metaphysics, in some instances with greater or less attachment to religion in the institutional sense. Thomas Young, James Clerk Maxwell, and Erwin Schrodinger in the epilogue on *What is Life?* raise such a question as, "Are we perhaps mistaken in assuming that there are as many minds as bodies? Clearly there are many bodies, but perhaps many fewer minds; perhaps indeed only one mind." Wolfgang Pauli explored Jewish mysticism, the Kabbalah. If one comes to the boundaries of physics, how is it that one does not look beyond?

And there are surprises. Not only the ancient intuitions

of atomism; the sphericity of planets; Pythagoras's recognition that the essential scheme of things is in numbers; the "music of the spheres" realized in Bode's Law of the distances of the planets from the sun, almost all expressible as simple ratios of whole numbers, as are musical tones—there is an occasional invasion of a province that seems offhand to be peculiarly in our modern scientific domain.

One such instance involves our cosmic chronology. The Hindu view of human history, going back before written records, agrees with Greco-Roman mythology in dividing it into four epochs, declining step-wise from an initial state of perfection. In the Greco-Roman scheme there were the four Ages: Golden, Silver, Bronze and Iron. In the Hindu chronology there are similarly four *yugas*: *Krita*, *Dvapara*, *Treta*, and *Kali*, this last named for the goddess of destruction and dissolution —not, to be sure, our Second Law of Thermodynamics, yet mythical concepts of a running-down universe. I have seen a computation—I must confess that I do not yet know its basis —of the beginning of the Kali Yuga, that puts it at 3100 B.C., not far from our present estimates of the beginnings of human civilization. The four yugas together make a mahayuga; the same calculation estimates that the present mahayuga began about 4 million years ago, close therefore to our present estimates of the age of humanoids. One thousand mahayugas make a kalpa, a day of Brahman: hence about 4 billion years, close therefore to the age of the Earth, now taken to be about 4.7 billion years. The strange thing is that, if these computations can be trusted, prehistoric Hindus seem to have arrived at a terrestrial chronology involving orders of time recognized by modern science only within the last few decades.

How did they know?

WHY THIS UNIVERSE?

The first section of this paper propounded a riddle. We find ourselves in a universe peculiarly adapted to support life. It takes no great ingenuity to imagine other universes, differing in one or another property from ours, that would seem possible and workable—even to possessing much the same physics—

yet would lack life. *If* the proton and electron did not have exactly the same numerical charge; *if* hydrogen, oxygen, nitrogen and carbon did not possess the exceptional properties they do; *if* ice did not float; *if* the night sky were not dark—*if* any one, or any combination of other such changes applied—those might all make fine universes, yet without life.

With so many other options, how did this come out to be a life- and mind-breeding universe? That is the riddle.

I have approached this theme in the past by making a mystique of *knowing*. Lacking such contemplative creatures as we, the universe could be, but not be *known*. Through such as we, the universe of matter comes eventually to know itself. Just as it is said that a hen is the egg's way of making another egg, etc., man and his like elsewhere become a kind of culmination in cosmic history that exalts both him and the matter that bred him.

That has been for me the most moving thought I know: that begin such a universe as this with hydrogen, and billions of years later, I think inevitably and in many places, creatures such as we will be making science, art and technology; yes, and exploring beyond, into metaphysics and religion; and will weep and pray, dance and sing and *play*. Start with hydrogen, or neutrons, and I think that inevitably, given enough time, those things will come; and come in forms that endure: for life begets life, societies and cultures perpetuate themselves and beget further societies and cultures. Because all those things can occur in this universe, as our own experience shows—and given enough trials, enough time in a sufficient variety of places— everything that is possible happens.

Those are still among my most moving thoughts. Yet they evade the main problem. For a universe that in any way can breed minds and so begin to know itself, one must concede to be at its core, from its inception, in some sense if only potentially, a *knowing* universe.

That thought has led me to take the next step. It came to me quite lately, as a new and extraordinary idea, both tempting and repellant, since it shocked my scientific sensibilities. Then I realized with some embarrassment that many others had been there before—not only many mystics, over past millennia, but also quite recently a few thoughtful physicists.

It is the view (just the contrary of consciousness first appearing as a late outgrowth of the evolution of life on this and other planets) that this universe breeds life and consciousness because consciousness is its source, because the stuff of this universe is ultimately mind-stuff. What we recognize as the material universe, the universe of space and time and elementary particles and energies, is actually an *avatar*, the materialization of primal consciousness. In that case there is no waiting for consciousness to arise. It is there *always*, at the beginning as at the end. What we wait for in the evolution of life is only the culminating *avatar*, the emergence of self-conscious *bodies* that can articulate consciousness, that can give it a voice, a culture, literature and art, and science.

IS IT GOOD PHYSICS?

How have physicists of late talked about the origins of the material universe?

The more prudent among them start our universe with hydrogen; some with neutrons, since within about 12 minutes half of them would have disintegrated into protons, electrons and radiation, and thereby would provide all the requisite particles. Of course hydrogen, or even neutrons, beg for something *prior*; but one has to begin somewhere!

Then there is *space*. An ancient recourse is: "Wherefrom do all these worlds come?" [*Chandogya Upanishad* (I:9, 1)]. "They come from space, and into space they return: space is indeed their beginning, and space is their final end."[12] This is the underlying impulse in Einstein's persistent effort to derive all physics from geometry, from the non-Euclidean geometry of space-time. In that context material bodies—elementary particles—appear as perturbations, wrinkles in the multidimensional curvature of space-time. Wheeler reminds us that this view was expressed very clearly by the mathematician W.K. Clifford, who in 1870 proposed in a paper before the Cambridge Philosophical Society that a material body is a "hill" built out of the geometry of space rather than a foreign object embedded in that geometry.[13]

Einstein, however, gave the *field* precedence over the

geometry of space-time. "There is no such thing as an empty space," he said, "i.e., a space without field. Space-time does not claim existence on its own, but only as a structural quality of the field . . . It requires the field as the representative of reality. . ." And later: "It is common to all these attempts, to conceive physical reality as a field."[14]

Lately Wheeler, impressed by gravitational collapse in its ultimate consequence, the black hole, has proposed "primordial chaos" as the source of our present reality. A black hole need possess only one property, gravitational mass. It is pure, fluid mass, containing no particularities, no particles. Wheeler believes that our universe has slowed down in its expansion, and will eventually go into a phase of collapse, ending in something like a cosmic black hole. In that state all the laws and constants of physics will have gone; and from that state, through the next Big Bang, a new universe will start expanding, presumably with new constants and laws. He calls for a "'pregeometry' that is primordial chaos, and law built upon this chaos". What law? "There is no law except the law that there is no law; or more briefly, ultimate MUTABILITY is the central feature of physics."[15]

I think that the most interesting physical theory for the origin of the material universe is to derive it from *nothing*. That was a feature of the Steady State model of the Universe proposed by Bondi and Gold, and Hoyle in 1948.[16] The model had much to offer. It extended the Cosmological Principle to time as well as space. The Principle holds that wherever one is in the Universe, things are about the same: there is no call for a different physics. In a *steady state universe* that would hold also for time: whenever one examined such a Universe one would find the same physics. That is a desirable feature. The Big Bang cosmology has big troubles, to be overlooked only by the thoughtless.

The trouble was that this Steady State hypothesis accepted the interpretation of the red shift, that this is an expanding universe. In that case, how can it stay the same? Why does it not thin out and eventually empty itself? For at some 15-20 light years from wherever one is, astronomical bodies approach the speed of recession of light. Hence no signal can ever pass between us again: they have in effect left our Universe, as we have left theirs.

To meet this problem Bondi *et al.* proposed the theory of *continuous creation*: that at a rate sufficient to replace those lost masses, hydrogen is slowly but continuously being created out of *nothing*; not out of energy, but out of *nothing*. And since hydrogen is all one needs to make a universe such as ours, that means making and continuously remaking it from *nothing*.

I have asked myself why it is that a physicist may feel more comfortable deriving the material universe from *nothing* than from consciousness. There are two reasons: *nothing* is in the same category as something, i.e., as *things*. It is the absence of *things*—elementary particles, fields, space itself—and hence representable by a *number*, zero, the most useful number we have; and a familiar origin, first in the series of ordinal numbers, positive and negative; and the origin of Cartesian coordinates.

So to close this summary, let me first counter the question, Is it good physics?—with a reciprocal question: Is it really better physics to say that in the beginning there was hydrogen, or neutrons, or space, or the field, or primordial chaos, or *nothing*—is any of those really better physics than "In the beginning was the Word?"

And then, let me answer: No, it isn't physics at all. It encompasses physics, it is the precondition for physics, it makes physics possible, both by marshalling the experiences of physicists, those late outgrowths of the evolution of life in this universe; and—as I am now coming to think—by providing its substrate, the material world of space and time. For our experience of reality contains physics and much else that lies beyond, and always will lie beyond the small, special part of it that we—those amongst us who try hard enough—can measure and turn into numbers. That science can make nothing of consciousness, even to identifying its presence or absence, much less measure it—that is no disability in the notion that the universe originates in consciousness. On the contrary, that is of the essence; for the part cannot contain the whole. And if, as considered here, consciousness provides the matrix, the whole, then it isn't any kind of physics, but—as should have been so obvious as not to need saying—all physics lies within it.

NOTES

1. G. Wald, "Fitness in the Universe: Choices and Necessities," *Origins of Life* 5 (1974): 7.

2. R.A. Lyttleton and H. Bondi, "On the physical consequences of a general excess of charge," *Proc. Roy. Soc. London*, A252 (1959): 313.

3. G. Wald, "Origins of Life," *Proc. U.S. Natl. Acad. Sci.*, 52 (1964): 595.

4. H.W.M. Olbers, *Ueber die Durchsichtigkeit des Weltraums, Astronomische Jahrb. fur 1826*, J.E. Bode, ed. (Berlin: Spathen), p. 110.

5. Cf. D.W. Sciama, *Modern Cosmology* (Cambridge: Cambridge University Press, 1971).

6. W. Gray Walter, *The Living Brain* (New York: Norton, 1953).

7. Both Bridgman's and Skinner's views are discussed in P.W. Bridgman, *The Way Things Are* (New York: Viking Press, 1961), Ch. 6.

8. F. Capra, *The Tao of Physics*, Berkeley, CA: Shambhala Press, 1975). R. Weber, "The good, the true, the beautiful: are they attributes of the universe?" *Main Currents* 32: Nos. 2-5; also 31: 4.

9. Satprem, *Sri Aurobindo, or The Adventure of Consciousness* (Pondicherry: Sri Aurobindo Ashram Press, 1968; New York: Harper and Row, 1970).

10. C. Darwin, *Expression of the Emotions in Man and Animals* (London: John Murray, 1872).

11. Recounted in *The Sacred Pipe* 2, recorded and edited by Joseph Epes Brown (Oklahoma: University of Oklahoma Press: 1953; Penguin Books: 1971).

12. *The Upanishads*, J. Mascaro, trans. (Penguin Books: 1965), p. 113.

13.   W.K. Clifford, *Lectures and Essays*, vol. 1 (New York: Macmillan, 1879), pp. 244, 322. Cited in J.A. Wheeler, *The Physicist's Conception of Nature*, ed. by J. Mehra (Reidel: 1973), p. 234.

14.   A. Einstein, *Relativity: The Special and General Theory*, 15th edition, R.W. Lawson, trans. (New York: Crown: 1961), pp. 155-156.

15.   J.A. Wheeler, op. cit., pp. 242-243. See also C.W. Misner, K.S. Thorne and J.A. Wheeler, *Gravitation* (San Francisco: W.H. Freeman: 1973): Ch. 44.

16.   H. Bondi and T. Gold, "The steady-state theory of the expanding universe, *Mon. Not. Roy. Astron. Soc.* 108 (1948): 252. F. Hoyle, "A new model for the expanding universe," ibid.: 372.

Biological Foundations
of Human Evolution
and Consciousness

Consciousness is a primary datum of human existence. It cannot be fully defined. It presupposes knowledge at *three* levels:

(a) *Knowledge* and awareness *of the external world* by exteroceptors: organs of sight, hearing, etc.

(b) *Inner sensing*, not directly derived from sensory data but triggered by them; e.g., emotions, intentions, memories, dreams, imagination, etc. Perhaps internal body states like hunger, pain, thirst, pleasure, etc. may be included in this category.

(c) *Knowledge of one's self* (other than the body), characterized by the recognition of the present from the information of the past and a projection of the future, providing a continuity in one's lifetime. The belief that there is an "I", the self who does the perceiving in man, makes possible the creation of the ethical, aesthetic and spiritual values regarded as unique to man.

Of these three levels, it is possible that only the first is present in lower animals, while in some higher mammals there is perhaps an element of the second. But the absence in them of language, which has been termed the "Organ of Consciousness", makes it difficult for them to express, to compare and to evaluate these experiences, and for us to make a valid assessment of the extent to which this inner sensing has been developed in these animals.

There is, however, hardly any doubt that the third level of

consciousness is exclusive to man. A fusion of the totality of impressions and experiences makes the consciousness of man a unique attribute and has given rise to concepts like *Atman*, Soul Ego and so on, indicative of the level to which man's consciousness has risen, during the course of evolution.

THE MIND-BODY PROBLEM

Thanks to a great deal of recent work on the physiology of the nervous system, we have a fairly adequate understanding of the nature of perception of the external world, from the biological point of view, the working of the sense organs, their relationship with the brain, the physical and chemical processes involved in perception of the external world. To be sure, there are still some vital gaps in this understanding but with the advance in science it is possible to bridge these gaps soon. And thanks again to advances in the medical sciences, we have some knowledge of the physiology of pain, hunger, etc. We have, however, little understanding of the processes of memory, imagination, emotions and intentions; and in spite of the enthusiastic claims of biologists, neurologists and psychologists, involving RNA, proteins, hormones, and so forth, no working hypothesis has yet emerged in regard to the biology of memory, learning process, storage and retrieval of information, either in man or in lower animals. The mind-body problem remains as baffling as ever. The theory of psycho-physical *monism* dominant in Western theory and philosophy has not been found satisfactory. That man is solely a physical organism and that everything which happens in him, all that he experiences, is explainable by physical, chemical and electronical events in the brain, which operates as a physical mechanism, has been found to be largely wanting. That all thoughts, feelings, and perceptions are mediated through electrochemical events in the brain has now been found to be inadequate by neurologists and neurophysiologists. Consciousness with all its powers of imagination and creative insights is not a mere product of physical forces.

This has brought Cartesian dualism back into vigorous discussion. Science discarded it in the early euphoria of the nineteenth and twentieth centuries but the recognition of the inability of science to reduce consciousness to physical, chemical and physiological dimensions has both intrigued as well as humbled many an enthusiastic student of brain processes. In the words of a great biologist, C.H. Waddington, "The nature of self-awareness completely resists our understanding. It is essentially mysterious." To quote another biologist, J. Z. Young, whose work on the brain and learning processes in animals is well known, "Lot of material about the chemistry of the brain especially concerning learning and RNA is speculative. Hyden's work as well as that of McConnell is of no importance."

The result has been a coming together of scientists and philosophers in order to understand better the processes and phenomena associated with consciousness. One such notable association is between physiologists J.C. Eccles and K.S. Lashley and philosophers Polten and Karl Popper, which has already promised new insights of consciousness. Eccles speaks of the "Experiencing Self" of man from which have arisen all his unique attributes: imagination, art in all its forms, sense of values, morality, philosophy, and religion, concept of soul, knowledge of death and sense of the infinite.

INDIAN PHILOSOPHICAL THOUGHT

Indian philosophical thought has always concerned itself with these problems. Every great work, from the Vedic era to the modern day, has dealt with the nature of the self and its relation with the external world. The search for identity, correspondence between *Atman*, the true essence of reality, and *Brahman*, the true essence of reality without, has been perennial in Indian tradition. The dynamic interpenetration of these two realities is basic to human living and more than one philosophical treatise is directed towards it. The *Upanishads* are deeply concerned with it; the *Bhagavad Gita* speaks of it constantly and the three great Acharyas of the South, Shankara, Ramanuja and Madhwa, all have made this their theme.

Indeed, the concept that human life involves much more than mundane living, that it has a purpose, a meaning, a goal, is the central theme which continually recurs in Indian philosophical thought. Man's life is unique; he is endowed with faculties meant for a higher purpose; he should continually bend his energies towards the attainment of this higher purpose: this has penetrated into the philosophical literature of India. Even our musical composers like Purandara Dasa and Thyagaraja constantly sang about this.

BIOLOGICAL AND CULTURAL EVOLUTION

That biological evolution has reached its near culmination in man is the view of most biologists today. Natural selection, which played such a dynamic role in organic evolution, has almost, if not entirely, come to an end. A new and a different kind of evolution is now operating in man. A nonbiological mechanism, involving his new faculties and operating on their employment—his culture—ensures a totally different line of his evolution.

Sure enough, man's abilities to perceive external phenomena will improve; his exteroceptorial understanding of nature will become keener, especially aided by tools which he himself is able to devise. His appreciation of his own body states and his accounting of them will also be attenuated. Physical, chemical and biological methods will be so refined and sophisticated that they will enable man to apprehend these states better and more efficiently.

However, it is my view that the most significant changes in the man of the future will come at a totally different level, of the comprehension of himself (outside his body states). The new image of man will be one of self-realization, placing the highest value on development of the individual to attain higher levels of human awareness. The vast untapped potentials of the human mind will be open to him, and new efforts directed towards a refinement of his consciousness will result in greater creativity and the emergence of a new paradigm.

THE BIOLOGY OF THE BRAIN

Biological research in recent years has brought to light two sets of important discoveries: (1) Man's brain is complex and composite and incorporates in it elements representing his evolutionary history; (2) The two halves of man's brain—left and right—are different from each other.

That mammals, including man, had their origin from reptiles which flourished about 200 million years ago has now been proved. That several relics of his reptilian ancestry still persist in man is also well known. Among these are parts of the reptilian brain which exist today as important constituents of the mammalian and human brain. These reptilian components which consist of the brain's stem, the reticular system, the midbrain, and the basal ganglia, have been bequeathed to man with little or no change. They account for certain fundamental instinctually determined functions, such as establishing territory, finding shelter, hunting, homing, mating, breeding, imprinting, forming social hierarchies, choosing a leader, etc. If man exhibits these instinctual characters and faculties, they are largely accountable to the presence in him of these reptilian brain components.

During the course of 200 million years of organic evolution, other components have been added to his brain, other traits to his behavior. The limbic system, the hypothalamus, the hippocampus, etc. and their connections are additions during this long period, endowing him with a "thinking cap" and rescuing him from the consequences of inappropriate, irrational and stereotyped behavior. The limbic system is similar, with structually primitive functions at an animalistic level, in all mammls and man. It has a basic role in emotional expression and viscero-somatic behavior. Indeed, it is the "emotional" brain of man.

But man's crowning glory is the development of yet another part of the brain, almost exclusive to him. The *neocortex* has reached a truly astonishing development in him. Incipient and rudimentary is some other mammals, the neocortex in man accounts for much of his brain volume. It is thrown into deeply folded convolutions. Unlike the brain of the rat and some other lower mammals, most of the human cortex is neither sensory in function nor motor. Uncommitted to either of these functions, the human cortex can come to assume the greatest significance, marking man as the most unique mammal. We do not know when this evolved; but it appears possible it is a comparatively recent addition, perhaps even during the past ten or twenty thousand years, long after the lineaments of man began to be shaped around two million years ago. With about 10,000 million cells, each communicating with the others by contacts (synapses), and each cell receiving thousands of contacts from other cells and in turn establishing contacts with others by axons, the human cortex assumes a complexity beyond understanding.

Man's unique faculties, his language, his superior consciousness, his creativity and all the highest expressions of his intellect, are located in the neocortex. It is the neocortex that makes him rational, wise, *Homo sapiens*.

The second set of discoveries in brain research is of even greater interest. It was first described by A.J. Akelaitis in 1944, and during the past ten years or so R.W. Sperry and his colleagues have shown that the brain of man (and of some higher mammals), and particularly the cerebral hemispheres, show a bilateral asymmetry which was never suspected before and which indeed has thrown a flood of light on the role of brain on behavior. Without entering into detail, it can now be said that the left cerebral hemisphere (including the neocortex) is different from the right and that the two have a complementary role in man's mental functions. Known as the dominant hemisphere, the left cerebrum controls speech, language, word intoxication, sequential thought, analytical and rational functions, science, architecture and mathematics. On the other hand, artistic vision, music, emotional and poetic insights, meditative and contemplative faculties are the province of the right (minor) hemisphere.

While these findings are being closely examined and analyzed, and as further work in this excitingly new field of "split-brain" studies is reported, it is clear that the two hemispheres of the cerebrum (made up largely of the neocortex) are different from each other and largely serve two different but complementary functions.

The two halves are connected by a band of nervous tissue, the corpus callosum, containing about 200 million nerve fibers, which permits transmission of nerve impulses from one hemisphere to another, providing thereby a unity to the cerebrum.

Consciousness in the Dominant Hemisphere

Among the most important findings of these split-brain studies is that consciousness is largely a matter of the left hemisphere. It is remarkable that speech and consciousness are associated with each other in one hemisphere, the left. Recent work has shown that anatomically also the dominant hemisphere is different from the minor. It weighs more. A seven-month human foetus has already a hypertrophied left cerebrum, especially the speech areas. Clearly it is genetically determined, but it does not seem to be irrevocable. If speech centers in the dominant hemisphere are damaged, they develop in the minor hemisphere.

From this account of the differentiation of the human brain, both vertically as well as horizontally (in a manner of speaking), it is clear that:

(a)   The brain of man has reached a state of enormous complexity during its evolution from the reptilian stage, unparalleled in any other animal, living or extinct.

(b)   The complexity is not only quantitative in that there is more brain matter, but it is also, and indeed primarily, qualitative, in that new brain stuff has been added.

(c)   Somewhere along this evolution of the human brain, "the rubicon has been crossed" and man has acquired newer and different attributes, like language, imagination, sense of values, concepts of soul, etc., unique to him.

CONSCIOUSNESS AND REDUCTIONISM

I must make myself clear here about one matter. When I say consciousness is located in the left half of the cerebrum (or for that matter, when I speak of the location of any factor in one part of the brain or the other), I am not being reductionist at all. I am of the view that consciousness has other dimensions than the physical (at least as we know physics now). I do not subscribe to the tenet that there are no other states in man than brain states (or body states, to put it generally) and that all phenomena of man can be understood by an analysis of his brain states. I think it is highly absurd to talk of brain states providing an adequate or satisfactory description of themselves.

Therefore, physiology is not the *cause* of anything mental, but that the physiological state of the *brain*, more than that of any other part of the body, *conditions* it. There is a great difference between causing and conditioning. When I say that consciousness lies in some part of the brain, I simply mean that the brain, of all parts of man's body, is the one that conditions his consciousness; no more.

THE FUTURE OF CONSCIOUSNESS

I must now deal with some aspects of what I believe is the future of man's consciousness. Here one is not as out on a limb as one appears to be, and it is possible to reasonably predict the lines on which the future of man's consciousness may be expected to evolve.

Both Western scientists and Oriental philosophers have thought of the problem: the scientist from the point of view of neurology, physiology and psychology, both subjective and objective; the Oriental thinkers from the point of view of contemplative empiricism. It is good to admit here that Western science has provided some insights into the future of consciousness, but they are of limited value. The possibilities of Eastern spiritual practices are only being appreciated now.

It is by and large scientifically understood that the level of consciousness is genetically determined and while it is, like other genetically determined characters, influenced by the environment, consciousness is largely governed by the genetic condition.

On the other hand, much of Eastern thought permits the honing and attenuation of consciousness during one's lifetime and prescribes methods and practices for its unfolding and development. Sri Ramanuja, the Visistadwaita philosopher, speaks of enlargement, perfection and Divinization of the consciousness. Consciousness is not something immutable or changeless. It can be improved upon, perfected, made keener, wider, deeper and more inclusive to contain more things, greater things: not merely in perceiving and comprehending the external world but also embracing a whole range of impersonal and nonmaterial things and directing it towards goals quite unique to man.

The future evolution of man would lie in the direction of the fuller development of his consciousness, especially of himself. Biologically (and scientifically) speaking, it would promote the growth, development, cultivation and amelioration of his neocortex, which would lead, not only to better use of his uniquely human qualities, but also to the suppression of his emotional and animalistic tendencies resident in the limbic system. Human evolution would also involve a more harmonious and balanced integration of the two halves of the cerebrum assuring the totality of human development and man's personality.

THE HINDU TRADITION

Hindu tradition speaks of the *Arishadvargas*, man's six enemies, which inhibit his full development and which, if suppressed, would bring him closer to Divinity: *Kama* (Desire); *Krodha* (Anger); *Lobha* (Greed); *Moha* (Passion); *Mada* (Pride, Arrogance); and *Matsarya* (Envy). While perhaps elements of the above are present in some of the higher subhuman animals, their fullest expression is attained in man. The contribution made by the three parts of his brain to the development and accentuation of these traits is not clear; that they attain their most sophisticated and effective development in man leads one to believe that the neocortex is not entirely blameless. It is also not clear when, during the course of man's evolution, they first made their appearance or attained their effective deployment; but it would appear, again, that they are coeval with the development of his culture, about 10,000 years ago.

However, ancient Indian (Buddhist, Hindu, Jain) exhortations were directed towards the suppression and elimination of these undesirable qualities in man, in the pursuit of perfection and the attainment of a higher state of human living. Buddha's central theme was "desire is the cause of all pain".

Sri Ramanuja outlines four ways to attain the goal of human living: *Gnana* (Knowledge); *Karma* (Action); *Bhakti* (Devotion) and *Prapatti* (Surrender to the Lord). These constitute his *Hita*, and are the means of attaining the ultimate Truth (*Tattva*). These are not mutually exclusive of one another; indeed, they are parts or phases of the same process, one leading to the other, finally culminating in *Prapatti* or *Saranagati*. This is the cornerstone of Ramanuja's concept of the essence of human living. Man's evolution should be along these lines and the ultimate goal, *Purushartha*, is attainable only by these means.

CONCLUSION

Western thinkers agree that at the lower levels of the evolutionary scale, consciousness, if it exists, must be of a generalized, unstructured kind. And that "with the development of purposive behavior and a powerful faculty of attention, consciousness associated with expectation will become more and more vivid and precise" (Thorpe). To the Eastern mind, this view of the future evolution of consciousness is far from satisfactory. "Greater purposive behavior"—to what end? This is important. Purposive behavior may be directed towards wrong ends, for the annihilation of the good and enthronement of the undesirable. Similarly, "*Faculty of Attention*" and "*Expectation*" are inadequate and unsatisfactory as the goals of consciousness and development. Evolution of consciousness should be towards some positive ends; it should be directed towards the "good" of man, towards his refinement and elevation. It should include a value system. Indeed, it should cease to be neutral and pursue a vigorous path of positive progress.

The perennial search for self-realization is the essence of human living in the highest sense. This, in the Oriental tradition, is the attainment of the highest consciousness, *Brahmajnana*. According to Ramanuja, it is not achieved by book knowledge. Study of the Veda does not provide it. It is a divine dispensation, sedulously developed through self-effort and experience. It is not mere intellectual excellence or brilliance in debate or even devotional or religious fervor. It is the development of total personality where consciousness shines forth with self-luminosity (*Swayam Prakasha*). It is the stuff of which our seers, *archaryas* and *alwars* were made. It is the superlative ability to see things beyond the ordinary (*Divyachakshu*) that distinguishes higher consciousness.

Two Sides of the Brain

Modern-age man reflects within himself the imprint of millions of years of evolutionary exercise and the potential for many millions of years to come. Any approach towards understanding him should take into consideration his own present equipment and capabilities.

One of his unique evolutionary acquisitions has been his "mind". Evolutionary experts say that the brain, which is the most sophisticated part of his physical equipment, has reached its biological limit in development and the next phase in evolution is psychological. The human mind, thus, is poised to play a very dominant role. Here is an entity, the crowning glory of our evolution, the nature of which eludes our understanding, yet the presence of which is very much felt, an entity capable of vast sweeps through time and space and yet fluctuating between freedom and thraldom, heralding human greatness or threatening human doom, elevating man to heavenly bliss or dragging him down to disease and misery; here is an entity that becomes the dramatist as well as the drama. It is significant to note that it is with this "mind" that we are attempting to understand the "mind".

When we proceed *to understand the mind with the mind*, it is of paramount importance to avoid the pitfalls involved in such an endeavor. There are several factors to be considered here. The very first question that comes up is regarding the definition of the mind. A definition may well be a comfortable tool to handle, but it abridges a dynamic entity and grossly limits the possibilities of an open exploration. If at all a definition is found to be necessary as an accessory aid, it should emerge at the end and not proclaimed at the beginning.

The impressive record of the expressions of the human mind in almost all fields of life provide ample evidence to show that the functioning mind occupies a junctional position in the universe on several counts. It has a fascinating memory system behind it, a dynamic interacting present and a projective or visionary future. It has a physical and biological substrate, it has its own qualities, and it has an environment that is unfathomed.

It has its ordinary working range of consciousness, a hierarchy of subconscious processes below it, and a transcendent dimension above it which is as gloriously affiremed as it is fanatically rejected. Is it any wonder that "the mind", so placed, is enigmatic, ill-understood, debased or mystified? Though there are several studies on the many facets of the functioning of the mind and several descriptions of it from various angles, the field is strewn with broken fragments and raging controversies as well as holistic glimpses. Yet it is gratifying to note that a body of knowledge is slowly emerging with possibilities of an integrated understanding, through experience, insight, interpretation, organization and action, marked by a degree of cohesion and openness which had practically disappeared from human deliberations in the recent past. Let us have a closer look at this trend and survey some relevant available material before considering the implications of the mind in health and disease.

THE MULTIDIMENSIONAL INTERACTION

When a multidimensional organism transacts with a multidimensional environment, maximum synchronization and resonance with the respective laws of each dimension is an absolute precondition to integration, understanding and harmony. Nonrecognition of this and cross-application of laws by man, endowed with a certain degree of choice, have created and are creating several problems in the world. Fortunately, the human mind has the unique capability of functioning in all the dimensions. But unfortunately the differential growth of competence in each dimension, in different stages and periods of evolutionary history, has often resulted in sad confrontations. Proficiency in handling and spectacular achievements lead to undue allegiance to one dimension and a gross distortion or outright rejection of the others.

There are four distinct dimensions discernible:

1. Matter-Obeying Physical Laws
The approach here is basically that of mathematics, physics and chemistry.

2. Life-Obeying Biological Laws
Here, for the understanding of biological systems, the methods of mathematics, physics and chemistry are not enough. The inadequate recognition of this additional dimension of "life" not only resulted in raging controversies in the academic world, but also retarded the growth of sciences like ethology and ecology. The "Two Cultures" that Snow wrote about, the "Two Biologies" described by Pringle and even the suggestion of the "two ethologies" from Schneila and Barnett are obvious examples of this. Driver brings out this point well: "It has been pointed out by Slobodkin that current mathematic techniques cannot cope with the description and elucidation of biological phenomena of higher levels such as those studied by ecologists." He says further, "I contend that there exist sciences whose present significance lies in the formulations of new thought patterns rather than in the prediction of events in terms of the more traditional mathematical and logical systems." I believe that this contention applied to both ecology and ethology, the sciences which are based upon the study of complex interrelationships between total organism and total environment, and I see no precedent for the tacit assumption that the total organism and its interrelations with environment can be understood in the same terms as those used for the study of parts of the whole.

3. Mind-Obeying Psychological Laws
If there was so much problem in moving from the field of physical sciences to that of biological sciences, one can well imagine

the difficulties encountered in rising to the psychological plane. In this discussion, it is important to note that each successive plane involves an additional dimension and not a mere replacement. In the physical and biological approaches, the maintenance of objectivity is of paramount importance. In the psychological plane, the release of subjectivity comes in as an important additional dimension. Nonrecognition of this dimension will result in controlled, manipulated, ordered, stereotyped subhuman behavior. Full recognition will result in a creative interpersonal interaction with unfoldment and enrichment of both.

4.   Spirit-Obeying Spiritual Laws
The added dimension transcends the objective-subjective complex. The real role of faith and the spiritual dimension will never be understood if one restricts oneself merely to any one of the other planes.

The approaches in any one of these planes can be real or unreal. A mere transposition of one set of laws in one dimension to the other will also produce distortion and unreality. The foregoing linear, successive presentation is made only to bring out the distinctive features of each dimension. In practice this multidimensional approach will immediately transform itself into a holistic approach, which is the only way of comprehending totality. Detailed examination and investigation of any part of any plane within this aspect of totality will certainly yield relevant, valuable, significant knowledge, retaining its cohesiveness and openness. The error all along has been the primary investigation of these parts either without relevance to totality or entering and generalizing totality from the knowledge derived therefrom.

Since time immemorial the human mind has expressed itself through science, art, philosophy and religion. The tremendous growth of science and technology, while conferring equally spectacular boons to mankind, has brought in some collateral crises in human perspectives. Values can remain and grow only in a multidimensional system, by virtue of its inherent openness. A unidimensional deviation has always the danger of closing up and consequent drainage of values. If values drain out of religion, it becomes religious superstition, which is well known to everyone. But, what is not so well known is the situation when science starts closing its doors under the guidance of a phantom referee and starts rejecting everything that does not fall within its own dimensional framework. Science, which is intrinsically open, can retain neither its openness nor its values in isolation. The scientific superstition poses the greatest threat to the world today.

THE NEURAL SUBSTRATE OF THE MIND

The human brain, which is the neural substrate of the mind, has about ten billion neuronal units, woven together into a highly organized functioning network. This neural network, which has direct or indirect contact with every point in the body, is interposed between receptor and expressor tissues facilitating environmental inputs, organismal integration and behavioral outputs. Some features in this remarkable neural substrate that make it a unique structure are:

1. Anatomical
There is an extensive relay system whereby information gets relayed from neuron to neuron. A neuron may establish connections with several neurons. Several neurons may establish connections with one neuron. Feedback neuronal units are also provided. Extensive connections are also established between structures, areas and hemispheres. Each neuron or neuronal pool has capabilities of participating in different functions. The whole arrangement is ideally suited for a wide variety of specific coordinating and integrating tasks.

Another anatomical feature is the localization of function in structures. It is interesting to note that in the study of brain and behavior, the pendulum has been swinging to and fro between those who attributed specific functions to specific parts ("localizers") and those who considered the brain as a whole. In the first half of the nineteenth century the phrenologists under the leadership of Franz Joseph Gall inferred man's character and ability from the superficial structure of his skull, postulating an association between brain structure and personality. Experimental evidence of the role of the brain in mental processes was first provided by Pierre Flourens in 1824–25, who conducted extirpation studies and assigned functions to various divisions of the central nervous system—cerebellum, medulla and corpora quadrigemina. The second half of the nineteenth century witnessed a reaction against localizers and the view to consider the brain as a whole gathered momentum. Even the experimenter Flourens emphasized the point that the localized regions studied, far from functioning independently of one another, interact in a complex manner. While each portion served a specific function, it also participated in other functions that represented integrated activities of the whole brain.

Nearly a century later, Lashley, after extensive study, highlighted the inexact and temporally variable nature of cerebral localization. However, several approaches were made, ultimately directed towards localizing particular functions within specified components or processes of the nervous system. Gross behavioral correlates with reference to changing demands in evolution showed birds needing quick relfexes in flying possessing relatively large cerebella; mammals with acute olfactory sense having well developed olfactory lobes; the visually-oriented frogs equipped with large optic lobes; and man with superior learning abilities endowed with gigantic cerebral hemispheres. The nature of nervous activity and information storage and control, the effects of brain damage on behavior, particularly learned behavior, and localized chemical events that could be correlated with overt behavioral or electrical changes—were all studied for the same purpose. The work on different wavelengths of light mediated by quantitatively different photo receptors by Young and Helmholtz in 1852, description of Broca's center for speech by Paul Broca in 1861, demonstration of limb movements by Fritsch and Hitzig and specific sensory centers by Munk, meticulous cerebral mapping of areas during operations by Wilder Penfield and the extensive knowledge gained during open as well as stereotaxic psychosurgical proceduress done for relief of symptomatology in behavior disorders in man are all significant landmarks in localization.

The most significant advance in localization that has occurred in recent years is the one that has demonstrated the functional localization of the highest human mental faculties differentially in the two cerebral hemispheres. The findings of

Robert Grustein, that the verbal, rational, discrete, logical, linear thinking functions are located in the left cerebral hemisphere of a right-handed individual and the visuo-spatial, holistic, intuitive, artistic and creative functions are located on the right, have far-reaching consequences though the full implications have yet to be explored. For the first time in the history of modern science have those higher faculties of man like art, intuition and creativity, which have all along been mandate of literature, philosophy and religion, come under the field of scientific enquiry. This holds out the bright promise of a holistic understanding of the human mind.

2. Bioelectrical and Biochemical Mechanisms

The junction of each neuron with another neuron is marked by a synoptic cleft across which highly organized bioelectrical and biochemical systems operate. Open to very selective conditions, the system provides for an enormous flexibility of function over a spectrum of manifestations from the crudest to the most refined.

3. Developmental Hierarchy

Irrespective of the rumbling controversies about the precise nature of the origin of man and the evolutionary process, the fact remains that the human brain has in it the coded treasure of a rich evolutionary past, along with a highly selective and refined mechanism to subserve the rapidly growing capabilities and potential of the human mind.

(a) The evolutionary process conserves and is highly economical. Though the functional dynamism is maintained by a continuous recycling of its structural ingredients within itself and through the environment, evolutionary progress is achieved by reinforcement, reemployment and refinement of systems rather than removal and replacement.

(b) A hierarchy is evident in the neural organization, where the latest developed function with its concomitant substrate exercises a control over the relatively older system in evolution.

(c) When faced with any adversity, be it accident, disease or old age, the latest developed function is the first to suffer. This would result in the loss of its own function and a release of the older function that was held in check.

Let us see the implications of these remarkable observations made by Sir Charles Sherrington. A fish in its aquatic milieu has to move over long distances by the alternate movements of its fins. This is provided with ease through a mechanism controlled by the extrapyramidal system of the brain. Man's propagation is through a different mechanism and hence the persistence of the older mechanism is embarrassing and not required. A higher system has therefore evolved in man which keeps the older system in check. However, a release of this alternate movement (tremor) can occur in old age, after some accidents or in what is known as Parkinson's Disease. Other types of rhythmic involuntary movements like choreoathetosis can also manifest themselves in certain disease states. A functional adversity like "fear" can also release a similar manifestation, so familiar to students in front of ominous examiners.

These are examples of release. Voluntary retrieval of built-in rhythmic movements are also possible. Perhaps the guided "letting go" phenomenon of dancers and drummers for artistic expression are examples of retrieval.

4. Rhythm
The importance of rhythm as one of the mechanisms in man's transaction with the envrionment is increasingly being recognized. Of the innumerable rhythms of the universe, from stellar rhythms to the biochemical and psychological rhythms, man is equipped to live optimally within a certain range. The nervous system is geared to support a certain range of conscious functions, the rest being delegated to autonomic mechanisms. Built-in rhythms are the mechanisms through which the system delegates its functions. These are the ones that are available for release, retrieval and recruitment. Rhythms are also the mediating mechanisms through which one transacts with the environment.

Recent work on memory also lends support to this. The bioelectrical circuitry and biochemical and macromolecular processes, coded and delegated to several levels of functioning with possibilities of release, retrieval and recruitment, offer fascinating prospects of bringing out unmanifest human potential.

In this context, it is worth mentioning that Rtm (Rta) referred to in the Rigveda as a state of absolute order, encompasses in one word the physical, physiological, existential and ecological movements of the present day.

These are some of the brain mechanisms available to us to serve as a substrate for our functioning mind.

HEALTH AND DISEASE

Health is not merely the state of absence of disease. The state of health results from a state of dynamic harmony between the individual and the environment at his physical, biological, mental and spiritual planes. A disharmony results in a disease in any or all of these planes.

It is unfortunate that science has so far been concentrating on the processes of breakdown and disease. Even the prophylactic attempts have been for the prophylaxis of known diseases. Our conception of health stems from that of ill health. It is encouraging to note that a shift towards looking primarily at health and states beyond it by positive and promotive health efforts is already occurring.

The second misfortune has been the ignorance on the part of the healing profession regarding the human dimension. In any general medical therapeutic situation, doctors invariably talk of a case of a particular disease occupying a bed number with recorded age, height and weight requiring the prescribed dose of medicine calculated accordingly—with no mention of the person who is suffering! We are, therefore, practicing veterinary medicine on human beings! Even the medical curriculum sadly lacks this dimension. In the preclinical stage are taught anatomy and physiology. Psychology and sociology, which are essential to give the human dimension over and above the mere structure and function of the body, do not even form part of the curriculum. The study of the mind in its individual and social interactive aspects is an absolute necessity.

In the holistic approach (Angyal) towards health, understanding the mind in its qualitative and interactive modes is vital. If the perspective of total health is to be appreciated, the understanding of a holistic approach to understanding the mind is of paramount importance. Under this approach, the human personality should be looked upon as a unified dynamic organization. It is important that a part should not be viewed in isolation. Every organismic part process is a manifestation of the dynamism of the whole organization. The part processes gain their meaning from the general pattern of functional organization. It is an open system. There is the input from the environment and behavioral and other outputs from the organization. While considering the totality of the personality organization, three trends are noticeable:

Autonomy
The self-governing process expresses itself in spontaneity and self-assertiveness, striving for freedom and mastery.

Homonomy
Here the human personality reveals a distinctly different trend. He seeks a place for himself in a larger unit of which he strives to become a part. He strives to surrender himself willingly to seek a home for himself in, and to become an organic part of, something that he conceives as greater than himself. Experiencing others as coparticipants in a larger whole brings another facet of his nature into manifestation. This basic relation is love.

Heteronomy
The organism lives in a world in which things happen according to laws which are heteronomous-foreign to the organism.

In a well-integrated personality the self-determination and self-surrender manifest themselves in varying degrees complementary to each other without conflicting. One or the other gets partially obliterated in unhealthy states.

Modes of Interaction with the Environment

In all the interacting situations, irrespective of the elements of interaction, one or more of the following may occur:
Escapism—When no interaction occurs.
Confrontation—This is a common mode in a competitive society. It may help in consolidation or success but not growth. Morbidity and energy wastage is also great. The operating system tends to close up whether there is success or failure.
Conformity—This is a submission to the behavioral determinants of the society and one lives on comparison and negation of individuality.
Containment—This might give mastery without conflict. But

what is mastered remains as a "foreign body" within. Since it is control without growth, the process still tends to be a closed one.

Creative Interaction—This is the most open interaction with maximum expression and growth. It involves tuning into the environment. It enriches both the organism and the environment.

THE INDIVIDUAL

The biological equipment has a fine homeostatic mechanism for adaptation and adjustment to the environment. Physiological needs, drives and instincts function at this level. Disruption of harmony at this level produces physical illnesses referred to in various systems according to the focus of breakdown.

The evolution of the mind in humans has brought in two distinct modes of functioning at the highest level. One is the logical reasoning (left brain) part which has helped man to acquire knowledge and gain increasing mastery over the environment. The other mode is the artistic, creative (right brain) one related to the higher human values of love, tenderness, freedom, etc. Creative imagination is one of the highest endowments of this mode.

Because of the success gained by the reasoning, thinking part, the other part was relegated to a subsidiary role in actual everyday transactions.

It is important that the reasoning, thinking mode should support and not lead the value-perceiving, creative part. The approach towards mental health is shifting from too much preoccupation with the roots of mental disorder and adjustment, to positive states of health and growth. For this a dynamic orientation and a holistic understanding of the mind is vital.

How can a "mind" understand "the mind"? The logical reasoning part of the mind can understand the same part of another mind, and with a little difficulty one's own mind, by the established and growing capabilities of the discipline of science. But the other part of the mind can be understood only by experience. Experience is transforming in character, and total in its dimension. It is this part of the understanding gained by experience that lends meaning to the knowledge gained by observation and interpretation. It is again this part of understanding that gives insight, cohesion and openness. It is this part that links up creatively with the corresponding parts of other minds and resonates with the whole of creation.

What we mean by "experience" needs a closer look. From the framework of the observer-observed, the logical mind can, at best, view it only as a close approximation to nonduality, i.e., it always retains the position that there has to be an experiencer to experience. Therefore the word experience is used in a variety of situations to describe many partial "experiences". On the other hand, from a holistic framework, the world experience connotes a state of total merger between the experiencer and the experienced. There is the merger of the components of three axes into the totality of an event—

    Subject—Object
    Individual—Environment
    Matter-Life-Mind—Spirit (Transcendental Dimension)

The steps may be described thus:

The observer and the observed move closer to each other to participate in an event, as the experiencer and the experienced. At the moment of experience, the identities of both get merged into the totality of the event.

The experiencer, transformed, emerges out of this event and describes authentically with varying degrees of capability and communicability about his experience. The phenomenon is the same, whether it is ordinary or extraordinary.

Much exists in this universe which would be wholly impossible within the framework of one's present philosophy. Fortunately, these things do not require one's knowledge or belief in order to exist. If we will but listen, have patience, and maintain a scientific openmindedness, we will profit immeasurably. All things will eventually yield to full understanding, but we must devote our lives to that end.

The Phenomenology of Mind
and Consciousness

The term, *mind*, is used in two principal senses: (1) as the *individual mind*, i.e., the self or subject which perceives, remembers, feels, imagines, conceives, reasons, and wills and is functionally related to an individual corporeal organism, and (2) as the *generic mind*, i.e., a metaphysical substance which pervades all individual minds and which is contrasted with matter.

Phenomenology has been called an expression of various concepts. Hamilton in *Lectures on Metaphysics* said: "If we consider the mind merely with the view of observing and generalizing the various phenomena it reveals . . .we have . . .one department of mental science, and this we may call the *Phenomenology of Mind*." Moritz Lazarus in his *Labender Scele* (1856–57) distinguished "Phenomenologie" from "Psychologie"—the former describing the phenomena of mental life, the latter seeking their causal explanation. Edmund Husserl (1859–1938) applied the name "Phenomenologie" to a whole philosophy. His usage has given the current sense to this term. In the beginning he defined it, much as Hamilton and Lazarus had done, and emphasized that "pure" phenomenology distinguished the subjective from the objective and refrained from looking into either the genesis of subjective phenomena or their relations to somatic or environmental circumstances. Later, however, he redefined phenomenology as the *eidetic* science of the material essences exemplified in subjective processes *qua* pure possibilities. He saw *intentionality* as the fundamental character of subjective processes. The reflectively experienceable part of one's stream of consciousness is, on the one hand, consciousness of subjective processes as imminent in the stream itself, and on the other, consciousness of other objects as transcending the stream. Consciousness is an intentional predelineating of processes in which objects will be intended, as the same or different within an all-inclusive objective context, i.e., the world. A pure phenomenology should describe not only particular intended objects, but also the intended world as intended.

Consciousness may be viewed as lying between two poles, the subject and the object. On the side of the subject lies the subjective attitude with its various qualitative forms such as believing, doubting, considering or willing and its modes of apprehension, such as presentation, representation, or symbolism. On the side of the object lies the object as well as its "essence" of ideal character. Midway between the two lies the datum of content, such as images or sensory experience.

The relation of the subject to the object is essentially one of sensing the intending, and implies that the object is approached or addressed, rather than constituted by knowledge. Thus the physical object cannot be presented except in partial aspects or in perspective, so that there is a large element of uncertainty and error in perception; but what is presented is, in fact, a part of the object.

In *Ideen* and later works, Husserl applied the epithet "transcendental" to consciousness as it is aside from its (valid and necessary) self-apperception, as in a world. Simultaneously, he restricted the term "psychic" to subjectivity in its personalized status as worldly, animal and human subjectivity. This contrast between transcendental subjectivity and worldly being is fundamental to the concept of pure phenomenology. Thus, Husserl defined pure phenomenology as the *eidetic science of transcendental subjectivity*. This was contrasted with psychology defined as the empirical science of actual subjectivity in the world. Thus, two antitheses are involved: eidetic versus factual and transcendental versus psychic.

For the subject matter of phenomenology is consciousness; in it all objects of consciousness assume the character of being objects of consciousness.

Because the difference between phenomenological psychology and transcendental phenomenology depends on a difference in attitude toward "the same" subject matter, their contents are widely analogous.

In this presentation, an endeavor will be made to scan this "widely analogous content" without strictly adhering to the subtle distinction between phenomenologic psychology and transcendental phenomenology. This is partly because the endeavor here is not toward constructing a philosophically discrete system but rather to understand the mind as a phenomenon. If toward this my own basic training in psychology and biological sciences prove handy, I should not hesitate to lean upon it merely for reasons of methodological purity or finesse.

RELATIONSHIP BETWEEN THE PHENOMENAL AND THE MATERIAL

This relationship has been considered at three different levels:

(1)   The mind-brain relationship,
(2)   The mind-body relationship, and
(3)   The relationship between the mental and the material.

The last subsumes the first and the second and hence has been preferred by philosophers as the issue of basic concern. The first especially baffles the neuroscientist when he becomes aware of the big gap between the brain and the mind.

Some of the philosophers have raised a query, "Have we here a parallelism, an epiphenomenalism, a monistic identity, an emergent phenomenon or what?" Let us be reminded of the words of Edel: "If we remain completely ('philosophically') parsimonious, there is no need for indifferentiating theory interpretations where the same scientific evidence is appealed to by the different ones." For example, the most that an identity theory can claim over a parallelistic theory is a greater protection against the reintroduction of metaphysical dualism of substance. Yet, an identity theory might find itself beset with

a double-aspect metholodology that would be a handicap in
meeting irrationalist claims for direct inner knowledge in the
science of the human spirit.

The mind-matter problem and even the mind-body problem afford the philosopher certain comforts which we miss in
the mind-brain problem. For example, one can be sure that
oneself has a mind, and that others surely have bodies and in
this dual certainty dissolve the mind-body problem. But when
we turn to the mind-brain problem there is little prospect of
dissolving it by translating mind questions into brain questions, the way that mind questions can be translated into body
questions. One knows that one has a mind, but one doesn't
know one's own brain.

"Should I try to think of my mental life as the electrochemical processes which the physiologists have discovered in
the brain calls?" one may ask with Sprague. The implication
in this question is that "mind" is an energy system. But does
an energy-scheme explain the mind?

I perceive the moon in the sky. Let us trace the energy-
scheme. The radiation from the moon passes into the eye, a
little image of light is focused on the retina, the ensuing photo-
chemical action in the retina sends out trains of action—
potentials along the optic nerve and radiation to the brain
which produce further electrical disturbances in the visual cortex. But how does seeing take place? "That is where," says
Sherrington, "the energy-scheme forsakes us. It tells us
nothing of any setting." Mind, if it were energy, would be
measurable quantitatively. "For quantitative measurement of
the mental, we resort to the energy-scheme. But the validity
of that resort is questionable. The search in that scheme for
a scale of equivalence between energy and mental experience
arrives at none. The two seem incommensurable. Further there
are great obstacles to quantitative comparison of one species
of physical fact with another: thus, between quantitative esti-
mation of brightness eperienced from a light and the loudness
experienced from a sound. But all these as physical stimuli are
quantitatively measurable in common terms and are compara-
ble with one another . . . No attributes of 'energy' seem findable
in the process of mind. The absence hampers explanation of
the tie between cerebral and mental."

Professor Feizl defends the view that phenomenal facts are identical with certain events which occur in brains. He derives this view from consideration of a cognitive network in which both phenomenal facts and corresponding brain events must find a logical location. It turns out that the location of both is the same. "Mr. Feizl realizes," comments Kohler, "that we do not generally identify facts unless thay have the same characteristics but I doubt whether he convinces his readers that such an identity as to content has been made plausible in the present case. Quite apart from such questions, his view . . . implies a form of emergence. For he does not claim that all physical and chemical events are identical with some phenomenal facts."

The phenomenal world is not coextensive with the "mental". Psychology investigates certain supraphenomenal "mental" facts also. The phenomenal facts, in themselves, do not constitute a functionally complete material. There is coherence among the phenomenal experiences of an individual which transcends the experiences themselves. One such transcendent experience is *memory* which makes temporally separated stages of the phenomenal flux coherent in spite of interruptions. And memory, once again, is a relatively permanent stage obtained very probably by converting the mental into the physical and presenting it in the latter form. Memory, again, is by no means a rare fact in physical nature. Is the phenomenal coextensive with the physical? Feelings, values, and motivations are definite aspects of the phenomenal, but one wonders if they are at all aspects of the physical. Feeling is a very unwelcome visitor in rationalistic circles. "The kernel of the scientific outlook," wrote Lord Russell, "is the refusal to regard our desires, tastes, and interests on affording the key to the understanding of the world." Mention your feelings to your scientific friends, and you will be met with a cold stare and the acid enquiry: "My dear Sir, what have your feelings to do with the matter?" I see a flower. It appears beautiful to me. Is this beauty there in the flower, or have I imposed it on it? My rationalist friends refuse to be concerned with this question; but for one like me: "Beauty is God's handwriting, and a Wayside Sacrament."

Whether it is some God's handwriting or not, it is surely

an experience, beyond the ken of my rational self and certainly within the gamut of my phenomenal world.

Leave alone the affective and the connotative, even at the cognitive level, the phenomenal and the physical cannot be expected to correspond. My phenomenal world is contingent upon my sense organs which are at best keyholes into reality (whatever that be). Out of a very wide array of energy waves, my retina is sensitive to only the familiar spectral range. Am I, then, aware only of a fractional aspect of reality? There is wide interspecies variability in respect to the structure of eyes. So the world as seen by me is different from the world as seen by a dog. Which of them is real? If this pertains not only to vision, but also to all our sense modalities, then isn't our phenomenal world "a world unreal as shell-hard sea?"

But the major impasse in our ability to reconcile the phenomenal with the physical is yet another one. Our "present epistemology refused to attribute *any* phenomenal characteristics to *any* fact in nature—whatever these characteristics be. It seems to follow that, in this respect, not a single part of the phenomenal world fits the premises on which the system of natural sciences rests." Are we prepared to cast a second look on these premises?

CONSCIOUSNESS

Macneile Dixon in his *Gifford Lectures* asked: "Could you tell me that consciousness, the eye with which the universe beholds itself, and knows itself divine, is simply a thing among other things to be placed alongside the river or the stone? I shall not be easily persuaded—you strain my credulity, gentlemen. You are of the opinion that the arrival of the audience in nature's theatre was an irrelevant accident . . . It would be for me too apropos and brilliant an accident."

Man is a puny object in the world, as trifling as a flower or a cloud. Yet, by a curious paradox, in its comprehension this insignificant object goes beyond and includes the whole world within which he lives. "Man is at once contained within, and himself contains the world in his thought." Nature, "the lonely, with her sightless eyes"—what value or significance, without man or other similarly endowed beings, has her existence at all?

Yet, cautions Abelson, ". . . nor can the grounds of human superiority be found in introspective consciousness. For how can an introspectionist prove to a behaviorist that he (the introspectionist), unlike machines and behaviorists, feels pain precious images, and lives an essentially private life? To prove something to others, one must appeal to publicly verifiable evidence. It is, therefore, self-contradictory to claim to prove that one has states of awareness which can only be observed by oneself."

Consciousness is the meeting point of the objective and subjective, but available to inspection only by reflections. How much of it has been fathomed has depended upon how far one has been prepared to reflect. In the *Mandukopanisad* four states of consciousness have been described—*jagrit* (awake), *swapna* (dreaming), *susupti* (deep sleep), and *turiya* (nondual consciousness). In the *Taittiriyopanisad*, five layers of consciousness are conceived: *anna-mayakosa* (physical consciousness), *prana-mayakosa* (vital consciousness), *mano-mayakosa* (psychic consciousness), *vijnanamayakosa* (intuitive consciousness), and *ananda-mayakosa* (beautitudinous consciousness). However, one of the most elaborate treatments of consciousness in Indian psychology is to be found in the eighth century Pali treatise *Abhidhammatthasangha* written by Anuruddha, a Buddhist monk. Herein the author describes not only consciousness (*citta*) but also its classes, conscious concomitants (*cetiska*), cognitive processes (*vithi*), process-free consciousness (*vithi mutta*), etc. It recognizes fifty-two different modalities of consciousness of which seven are described as "universal" in the sense that they invariably occur whenever any process of consciousness arises, and these are impression phases (both contact and impact): feeling (*vedana*), perception (*sanna*), volition (*sankhara*), one-pointedness (*ekaggrata*), the psychic life (*jivitindriya*) and attention (*manasikara*). Besides these six conscious states described as "scattered" or "particular" are recognized to occur optionally. They are enquiry (*vitakka*), investigation (*vicara*), decision (*adhimokkha*), effort (*viriya*), interest (*piti*), and intention (*chanda*).

All conscious process (and the book describes 89 types of

these processes) are classified under fourteen functions. The most significant distinctive contribution of this treatise is the concept of *bhavanga*.

Cittakhana, or the "moment of consciousness", is proposed as the ultimate unit of measurement—the duration of which is estimated to be between a billionth and two billionths part of the time taken to wink an eye. Each such moment has three aspects: genetic, static and cessant.

Bhavanga is "the indispensable condition of our being subjectively regarded as continuous". When an object is presented to any sense-faculty, the still passive condition of *bhavanga* is disturbed and set into vibration and immediately thereafter the stream is arrested. These three operations constitute the preparatory stage of a perceptual process. The subsequent stage starts with the operation of "apprehension" or "adverting" (*avajjana*): a conscious course is already on the scene. "This is followed by the uprising of a sensation appropriate to the sense-door through which the object is presented. The sense-impression thus attains preliminary clarity in the next operation described as recipient (*sampoticchana*), and is further determined in the subsequent 'investigating' operation (*santirama*). The second stage comes to a close with the full determination of the characteristics of the presentational object, which operation is styled as determination (*vothapana*). Each of these foregoing operations is said to consume one moment of consciousness." With the determining operation we pass on to the third stage, wherein seven "moments" occur in quick succession, enabling a full recognition of the object or appreciation. In this final stage, the object thus completely grasped is registered and identified by "retention" (*tadarammana*) consuming two moments. Altogether, in a process thus, there are seventeen moments of consciousness. After the seventeenth moment, consciousness again lapses into passivity: the *bhavanga* is regained.

I have not come across a more "ultramicroscopic" treatment of consciousness anywhere. This also brings home to us the possibilities of the introspectionist approach which modern psychology seems to have discarded by and large.

However, without going into minute detail about whose

empirical validity would cause the scientific community to raise its brows, I would like to restrict the scope of the present enquiry to the more familiar "macroscopic" levels of consciousness.

Ordinary Consciousness

Our ordinary awake consciousness is merely a personal construct. The fallacy that we commit is that we consider it to be the world, and believe that it represents the "objective" reality perfectly. It is hardly realized that personal consciousness is outward-oriented and specially designed for action that ensures biological survival. For achieving this objective three types of operations seem to be necessary: manipulation of discrete objects, sensitivity to faces which may pose a threat, and separation of oneself from others. And personal consciousness especially subserves these three functions.

A multilevel process of filtration of sensory stimuli occurs to ensure sorting out of the survival-related ones, to which attention is particularly directed. From the filtered input we are able to construct a stable consciousness.

Our sense organs are the first filters. Our eyes, for example, respond to a tiny portion—between 400 and 700 billionths of a meter of the entire elctromagnetic energy spectrum. We cannot possibly experience the world as it fully exists—we would be overwhelmed. We are restricted by our physical evolution to only a few sensory dimensions. If we do not possess a "sense" for a given energy system, we do not experience its existence.

The nervous system is the next filter that reduces the sensory input further. Letvin, Taturna, Moculloch and Pitts, in their experiements on a frog's eye, showed that only four types of potentials could be tapped from the optic nerve in response to a large variety of objects to which it was exposed; from this study of "what the frog's eye tells the frog's brain", the authors concluded that the four types of potential were clearly related to biological survival of the animal.

Spinelli and Pribram have shown that the motor output system of the brain (efference) influences the input (afference), i.e. the brain "selects its input". Jerome Bruner has emphasized that we develop stereotyped systems, or categories, for sorting out input. These categories are much more limited than the input. Once these categories are established, we begin to experience them, for it is they that are evoked in response to stimuli. This further waters down our experience of the external world.

Habitation or adaptation is another psychological process that tunes our recurrences of stimulations from the world, external as well as internal. Need for survival necessitates an analytic position toward the world involving dichotomizing self and nonself—the former to be protected from or enabled to thrive upon the latter. Analysis leads to linearity. By linearity is meant consciousness of events enduring in time, in sequence of causes and effects. "Such linearity is essential in the development of an organized culture; for learning from past experience and for planning in the future."

Language, which is an objective correlate of our subjective experience, especially epitomizes this mode of linearity. It allows us to dissect, discriminate and divide the external environment into consistent segments which can be actively manipulated; to record experiences cumulatively, and to transmit them across space and time. However, language provides us with *ready-made categories* that help shape individual consciousness. One is also compelled to ignore experiences that are excluded by the common category system of the language one speaks. Eskimos, for example, have scores of words for various forms of snow. We are unable to imagine them, for we have no corresponding categories in our language.

The nature of ordinary individual consciousness is, thus, a much evolved construct subserving biological survival, but essentially filtering inputs to exclude stimuli that are irrelevant for this purpose.

The Subconscious

Ordinary consciousness is not merely outgoing and reflective; it seems to have another dimension too—the dimension of depth. The deeper or *nether consciousness* has been called the subconscious or even the unconscious in psychoanalytic parlance. It should really be called inconscious ". . . for it is not altogether devoid of consciousness, but is conscious in its own way—the conscious is involved or lost within itself or it lies buried. It comprises these movements and impulsions, inclinations and dispositions that have no rational *basii*—they are not acquired or developed by the individual in his normal course of life experience; they are ingrained, lie imbedded in man's nature and are native to his original biological and physical make up."

Primarily, it is ontogenetic expression of phylogenetic aspirations, hopes, fears, desires and hungers that constitutes the rudimental and aboriginal consciousness. It is a veritable field of force that lies at the root of surface dynamisms.

Transcendental Consiousness

The stable consciousness constructed from multilevel filtration of sensory stimulation that serves our day-to-day survival purposes is the empirical consiousness. It is but one special type of consciousness, "whilst all about it, parted from it by the *filmiest* of screens, there lie potential forms of consciousness entirely different" (William James). Intuitive consciousness is one such form, for example.

On introspection, consciousness appears to be a dynamic principle, quickly succeeding one stage of fluctuation after another, and yet strongly bound and limited to the self-same principle of individuality and egohood which calls them all its own. The unchanging and the changing aspects of consciousness form a mysterious coalition. In the view of Hindu philosophers, it is neither the unchanging nor the changing alone which is the basis of experience. It is the coalition of both which forms the basis of experience within which the distinction of the subject and the object can be made. The unchanging consciousness which exists as nonactive *cit satta* is like the presupposition of the changing states of consciousness as well as of feelings of ego and personality.

In its transcendental aspect this unchanging consciousness exists as *kutastha* and *kevala*—self-same and nonactive— for activity implies noneternity and limitation which is found only in a state of experience where one object stands in relation of opposition to the other (Saksena).

This transcendental consciousness is considered free from the sense of personality and experience in Indian philosophy —both monistic and dualistic. Here all opposites are overcome

and all successions are embraced in successionless consciousness (S. Radhakrishnan). This Hindu view of transcendental
consciousness differs from that of Western philosophers, for,
according to the latter, the absolute and the relative are in
a way interdependent on one another. The absolute is as inconceivable without the world as the world without the absolute.
This is not so in Hindu thought, where the absolute is absolutely absolute, so that, while the world would not exist without it, it would exist in its own right. The transcendental
consciousness is the very ground and the presupposition of all
the changing names and forms of its *samsara prapanca*.

This nature of the transcendental consciousness is not to
be realized by logic and intellect for it is not a concept but a
suprarational reality of being. It transcends rational reality
of being. It transcends our finite thought. It is for that reason
not a mere abstraction, for it is experiencible. Logic and intellect are only parts of man's being and not his whole being.
Although an intellectual grasp of the transcendental consciousness is possible, it is but the first step towards the
realization. The realization of absolute consciousness is a
unique experience for it implies the freedom of consciousness
from the polarities of knowledge, and of all kinds of psychic
mutations. In the Western dualism of mind and matter, the
significance of transcendental consciousness is missed and
there is a tendency to confuse mind itself with transcendental
consciousness. In Hindu philosophy, both the material and the
mental have alike the same material basis, the two only differing in their subtlety—*suksamta*.

AESTHETIC MYSTICS AND EXTRASENSORY PERCEPTION (ESP)

Schopenhauer was of the opinion that: "We may regard the
phenomenal world, or nature, and music as two different expressions of the same thing." According to Sir Thomas Browne,
"Whatever is harmonically disposed, delights in harmony."
"Through rhythm, we are in the closest, most vital and intimate relationship with the entire cosmos," says Dixon. If
rhythm appears to be the dialect of the soul, imagery too has
an occult and arresting power. In the words of Emerson, "You

can speak truth uncontradicted in verse, you cannot in prose."
Beauty stretches the human sensibility to its utmost limit.

> Beauty: the vision whereunto
>   In joy, with pantings, from afar,
> Through sound and odour, form and hue,
>   And mind and clay, and worm and star—
> Now touching goal, now backward hurled—
>   Toils the indomitable world.
>
> —Watson

The toiling sensibility, in its efforts to clasp beauty within
its fold, stretches itself to its utmost limits and then, as if it
surrenders, does it experience a delightful wonderment, an
experience of sublimity. It is then that "we feel we are greater
than we know". The mind's hurrying motions are checked and
in such a moment of absorption, ". . .we awake to an amazed
and speculative wonder, and hear the overtones of existence"
(Dixon).

Mystic experience, in Ouspensky's terminology: "intensi-
fied feeling and abstract knowing", is another paranormal
realm of consciousness. Ouspensky describes his own experiments with mystic consciousness. During these experiments,
he found himself "in a world entirely new and entirely unknown
to me, which had nothing in common with the world in which
we live, still less with the world which we assume to be the con-
tinuation of our world in the direction of the unknown . . .The
unknown is unlike anything that we can suppose about it . . .
First of all, everything is unified, everything is linked together,
everything is explained by something else and in its turn explains another thing. There is nothing separate, that is,
nothing that can be named or described *separately*. In order
to describe the first impressions, the first sensations, it is
necessary to describe all at once. The new world with which
one comes into contact has no sides, so that it is impossible
to describe first one side and then the other. All of it is visible
at once at every point: but how in fact to describe anything
in these conditions—that question I could not answer—here
I saw the objective and subjective could change places. The
one could become the other . . .This strange world . . .resem-

bled . . . a world of *very complicated mathematical relations*." Ouspensky describes a series of mystical experiments and says: "In any case my experiments established for me with indisputable clearness the possibility of coming into contact with the *real* world that lies behind the wavering mirage of the visible world."

Psi, in the words of Rhine, "is an integral part of the universal system". The well-controlled experiments on ESP in animals suggest that "psi is an acquisition of the animal organism that even predates the (conscious) sensory specialization". Thus the psi capacity has a prehuman origin. The relationship of ESP scoring to attitudes, school grades, I.Q., extroversion and the like show that a natural function of the personality is involved. The absence of any association with neuroses, psychoses or personality maladjustments indicates that the psi capacity is a part of the healthy endowment of man. Even at this stage, the experimental result of the psi studies present phenomena that *require* the rejection of the conception of man as a wholly physical system.

Sri Aurobindo has postulated an evolutionary process of the ascent of the mind. At the lowest rung is the insentient, "inconscient physical individualization, a creation, not of beings out of objects. There are formed existences with their own qualities, properties, power of being, character of being; but naturally the plan in them and organization of them have to be worked out mechanically without any participation, initiation or conscious awareness in the individual object which emerges as the first dumb result of the action and creation of the cosmic consciousness."

In animal life there is the beginning of participation, initiation and awareness. There is a slowly emerging consciousness on the surface which puts forth the form, no longer of an object out of an individual being. This "imperfectly conscious individual although it participates, senses, feels, yet only works out what the force does in it without any clear intelligence or observation of what is being done, it seems to have no other choice or will than that which is imposed on it by its formed nature." In scientific parlance, tropism, reflex, and instinct belong to this level.

In the human mind there is the first appearance of "an

observing intelligence that regards what is being done and of a will and choice that have become conscious; but the consciousness is still limited and superficial: the knowledge also is limited and imperfect; it is a partial intelligence, a half understanding, a groping, and empirical in great part or, if rational, then rational by construction, theories, formulas. There is not yet a luminous seeing which knows things by a direct grasp and arranges them with a spontaneous precision according to seeing, according to the scheme of their inner truth; although there is a certain element of instinct and intuition and insight . . . the normal character of human intelligence is an enquiring reason or reflective thought . . ."

This, according to Sri Aurobindo, is "not the utmost of which consciousness is capable, not its last evolution and highest summit. A greater and more intimate intuition must be possible which could enter into the hearts of things." Here, it may be noted that a conscious force is considered an entity *sui generis* which enters and illuminates beings to a lesser or greater degree. This is the cosmic consciousness force. By ascent of the evolutionary scale, man can get into "luminous identity" with it when he gets a "clear control of his life or at least a harmony with his universe". And, "It is only a free and entire intuitive consciousness which would be able to see and to grasp things by direct contact and penetrating vision or a spontaneous truth sense born of an undying unity of identity and arrange an action of Nature according to the truth of Nature." This is a real participation by the individual in the working of the universal consciousness—force

"Mind is established here on the basis of Ignorance," says Sri Aurobindo, "seeking for knowledge and growing into knowledge: so supermind must be established here on a basis of knowledge growing into its own greater Light. But this cannot be so long as the spiritual-mental being has not risen fully to supermind and brought lower its powers into terrestrial existence." The gulf between mind and supermind has to be bridged; and this can be done by a *triple transformation*:

(1) *Psychic change*: The conversion of our whole present nature with a soul-instrumentation;

(2) *Spiritual change*: The descent of a higher Light, Knowl-

edge, Force, Bliss, Purity into the whole being into the lowest recesses of the life and body, even into the darkness of the subconscience; and

(3) *Supramental transmutations*: The crowning movement, the ascent into the supermind and the transforming descent of the supramental consciousness into our entire being and nature.

Sri Aurobindo postulates a number of transitional states between the mind and the supermind. These he terms as *spiritual* mind and *overmind*. The transition to supermind through these intermediary states is "a passage from Nature as we know it into Supernature". In other words, it is the passage from the phenomenal to the noumenal and for this "roads of ascent and descent have to be created where there is now a void and silence".

CONCLUSION

We have presented a somewhat unorthodox discussion of the phenomenology of the mind. If no conclusions have been drawn, it is because our knowledge of mental phenomena is so scanty that valid conclusions are difficult to be drawn. However, I have attempted to permit phenomena from whatever quarter they arrive to enter into the body of this discussion. Open-mindedness is the first prerequisite for comprehensive treatment, and prejudice the foremost assassin of rational thinking. It is unfortunate that even science has its prejudices. It slams its doors upon several lively human controversies. To take an example, memory has been considered to rest on several physical mechanisms—neocortical neuronal circuits, palecortical reverberations, RNA, etc. However, in spite of evidence from reincarnation cases, science has been reluctant to admit the possibility of some extraphysical basis of memory.

Scientists, when dealing with the mind, tend to be held down by the brain. "The part of the picture of the brain which may always be missing," said Ayer, "is, of course, the part which deals with the mind, the part which ought to explain how a particular pattern of nerve-impulses can produce an idea; or the other way round, how a thought can decide which nerve cells are to come into action . . . Since the mind has no position in space—it is by definition not the sort of thing that can have position in space—it does not literally make sense to talk of physical signals reaching it."

Alita Kesa Kamblin enunciated the theory that the development of the phenomenal world was like the unwrapping of a ball of thread dropped in space. According to him, there was little distinction between the physical and the psychical; they were but different manifestations of the same process. This view emphasizes the wholeness of experience, the subject we and the objective presentation occurring in a unified way. Paradoxically, the same author described some five hundred states of consciousness.

Science and philosophy are under the "necessity to seek new concepts for the interpretation of reality to redraw their antiquated map of the human mind, and cast their kingdom old into another mold".

The Psychology of Consciousness:
An Empirical Study

The empirical study of a phenomenon such as consciousness implies the ability to define that phenomenon, at least in part. One productive approach to the definition of consciousness is essentially reductionistic. If we can determine the critical components of consciousness, we may then proceed to an examination of the physiological and psychological structure of those components. An understanding of the aggregate phenomenon of consciousness thus hinges on an appreciation of its substructure.

The history of psychology since the era of Weber and Fechner may be construed as just such an attempt. Psychophysics has its roots in the attempted quantification of the relationship between the physical characteristics of external sensory stimuli and the subjective perceptual experience of those stimuli. In analogous fashion early (and somehwat naive) studies of learning were motivated by the notion that species exhibiting associative modification of behavior must be in some sense conscious. At any rate, experimental psychologists soon produced a compilation of phenomena that were, in one way or another, ultimately related to the phenomenon of consiousness. We believe it is worthwhile to consider such a compilation from the viewpoint of recent research in experimental psychology. While considering each component of the list, it is important to ask two questions. Is this particular component of psychological experience necessary to the phenomenon of consciousness? Is it sufficient for the manifestation of consciousness?

SENSORY-PERCEPTUAL MECHANISMS

It is apparent that the presence of sensory mechanisms in a given species is no guarantee of the presence of consciousness in individuals of that species. Unicellular organisms exhibit robust orienting responses to biologically significant stimuli, yet few psychologists would impute to them the qualities of consciousness. Thus it seems unlikely that the mere presence of sensory mechanisms is sufficient for a demonstration of consciousness.

It might be argued, however, that the presentation of the order information processing, rather than isomorphic representation of the physical stimulus, is sufficient for a demonstration of consciousness. However, such perceptual mechanisms abound in the invertebrates. The octopus is capable of a very high level of visual and tactile discrimination, yet we typically do not assume the presence of consciousness in this species. In the vertebrates, a host of similar examples can be given. The frog retina is designed for the detection of a specific complex stimulus configuration, the moving concave spot or "bug". Many avian species have the ability to perceive rather small visual differences in size and coloration between their eggs and those of the nest parasite cuckoo. Even so, we do not consider the reaction of these species to "sign stimuli" to indicate the presence of conscious behavior. Thus even rather sophisticated perceptual mechanisms are not sufficient for the demonstration of consciousness.

But are sensory-perceptual mechanisms necessary concomitants of consciousness? Here the waters are more murky. Was Helen Keller conscious before she developed a mode of communication with the outside world? All the evidence we have to decide the question is the subsequent testimony of a highly communicative Helen Keller, a testimony that may have been badly colored by her subsequent communicative experience. Still, there is the indication of a true consciousness, although rudimentary, in the young Helen Keller, even though that consciousness was in auditory and visual isolation from the world.

The sensory deprivation experiments of D. O. Hebb and others have shown that conscious experience can be maintained in the virtual absence of sensory input. However, there are peculiar hallucinatory intrusions on that consciousness, as the period of deprivation increases. In fact, it has been suggested that total sensory deprivation is not possible, since the central nervous system may synthesize its own intrinsic stimulation in the absence of external stimuli. Nevertheless, with this caveat in mind, it appears that external stimuli are not essential to conscious experience.

THE MEMORY FUNCTION

Another object of intense study by psychologists has been the memory function. Is memory sufficient to produce the subjective experience of consciousness? The history of Pavlovian conditioning indicates that this is highly unlikely. Memory, defined in terms of the retention of conditioned responses, has been demonstrated in a wide variety of vertebrate and invertebrate species not typically considered capable of consciousness.

Perhaps, then, memory is a necessary rather than sufficient component of consciousness. However, there is a large literature on the human neuropathology of memory. Damage to the hippocampal area in humans results in an apparent deficit in the ability to consolidate material from short term memory into long term memory. Chronic alcoholism and/or severe vitamin B deficiency results in damage to the medio dorsal nucleus of the thalamus and mammillary bodies. This damage appears to be instrumental in the production of Korsakoff's syndrone, a condition characterized by severe deficit in long term memory. Finally, electroconvulsive shock therapy can essentially obliterate short term memories. However, in all of those conditions, in spite of considerable mnemonic deficit, the subjects continue to exhibit verbal behavior generally considered indicative of conscious experience. Consequently, on the basis of available evidence, it is difficult to maintain that memory is a necessary component of consciousness.

LEARNING

Is the capacity for learning sufficient for a demonstration of conscious awareness? Here the answer is unequivocally no. The phenomenon of incidental learning indicates that a great deal can be learned about stimuli to which a subject pays no conscious attention! Is learning perhaps a necesssary characteristic of consciousness? Once again, the answer is clearly no. Subjects are typically most conscious and attentive in the learning situation *before* any significant degree of learning has taken place. In fact, as learning progresses and the learned response becomes rote, typically subjects become less and less aware of the learned responses that they generate. Conscious awareness may actually interfere with the production of learned responses. Eyelid conditioning is typically more robust when the subject is unaware that the eye blink response is being conditioned. Similarly, the Zen archer achieves more accurate performance by effectively limiting his awareness of the target. It appears that learning and consciousness may be easily disassociated.

ATTENTION

Is attention sufficient for the state of consciousness to exist? Clearly, the answer here is no. It is quite possible to be highly attentive and yet unconscious. For instance, one may become completely absorbed in a book yet maintain no consciousness of the external environment, the self doing the reading, or even the act of reading itself. Another example is the occasional considerable attention to the environment exhibited by sleepwalkers while in an "unconscious" state. Yet, one may argue that there is *at least* consciousness *of* the material being read or otherwise experienced. However, is this "consciousness of" any different from the act of attention itself? Organisms emit robust orienting responses of the appropriate sensory receptors in the direction of novel sensory stimuli. Is this attentive response qualitatively different from that of the human subject absorbed in his reading material? Clearly the attention span of the human may often be much longer than that of the infrahuman subject. But quantitative differences do not imply qualitative differences. There is no compelling reason to assume that the nature of attentive behavior in humans is any different in principle from that of attentive behavior in other organisms. Thus it seems reasonable to assume that attention is sufficient for "consciousness of". However, attention does *not* imply consciousness of the act of "consciousness of"; that is, what we may call self consciousness. If the attentive process *did* imply self consciousness, we would be in the peculiar situation of imputing self consciousness to any organism capable of emitting an orienting response, e.g., the lowly amoeba.

We may then ask whether attention is a necessary component of consciousness. We have seen that this is roughly equivalent to inquiring whether "consciousness of" is a necessary component of self consciousness. But self consciousness is itself the reflexive construction "consciousness of the act of consciousness of" or, in the terms of Bertrand Russell, a meta-"consciousness of". As Russell elegantly showed, one cannot assume the equality of statements and meta-statements. Therefore meta-"consciousness of" is not equivalent to "consciousness of" or attention. However, since self consciousness, as defined, is the consciousness of "consciousness of", it would appear that consciousness of (that is, attention) is a necessary component of the reflexive function of self consciousness. Could it be any other way? Could there be self *without* consciousness of? This is another way of asking what is the self that we are meta-conscious of? In many psychologists' views the self represents the epigenetic interaction of the human genetic matrix with the sum total of individual human experiences. It is very difficult to see how the self could develop at all without at least some "consciousness of" (or attending to the formative environment) experiences that are implicit in its formation. Of course, Freudian psychology is grounded on the formative power of *unconscious* experience.

However, it would be an incredibly extreme position to say that the development of the self is entirely dependent on events that the individual is not conscious of in childhood or adulthood. Furthermore, we all have traumatic childhood memories of events that certainly appear critical in our development. Consequently, we may safely assume that "consciousness of" or attention *is* a necessary component of self consciousness. We should not assume, however, that the self is an isomorphic representation of consciousness of, since it may reflect at least in part the influence of unconscious processes. Consciousness of self, then, is our conscious model of "conscious of", since it is impossible by definition to be conscious of that which we are *not* conscious of. In summary, "consciousness of" may be considered a modeling function of the world; self consciousness, then, is a mdoeling function of the modeling function itself.

A final question in this regard is whether we can ever separate the predicate of consciousness from consciousness, i.e. can a pure, objectless consciousness of self exist? Such consciousness would constitute consciousness *not* of anything or consciousness of nothing. But if there is nothing in consciousness, how can there be consciousness at all (assuming consciousness is a thing)? A possible resolution of this difficulty is simply to assume that objectless consciousness is yet another modeling function; in this case, a modeling function of unconsciousness. once again, this modeling function is not identical with unconsciousness, but rather a representation of it.

LANGUAGE

Is linguistic ability sufficient for a demonstration of consciousness? Apparently not. Verbal output is common in many instances when the subject is unconscious: talking in one's sleep, talking to one's self while engaged in an engrossing activity etc. Thus, the mere presence of language is no guarantee of conscious mental process.

Is language, then, a necessary concomitant of conscious experience? In two primate species, chimpanzees and gorillas, rudimentary linguistic ability has been demonstrated. The work of such people as the Garners and Premack has demonstrated a capacity for abstract symbolic manipulation in these species. Interestingly, as Gallup and others have shown, both of these species also exhibit behavior indicating some level of self consciousness. Gallup, for instance, has shown that a chimpanzee can recognize himself in a mirror. Gallup gives the chimps extensive experience with mirrors. Then the chimps are anesthetized, and their brows are painted with red food coloring. The next exposure to the mirror causes the chimps to exhibit vigorous rubbing motions in the the vicinity of the red stripe. Rhesus monkeys and all other nonpongid species are unable to make this identification of mirror image and body. These results imply that the chimpanzee is capable of at least a rudimentary self-concept. Similar, although more anecdotal, data has been presented for the gorilla. Orangutans are capable of self-recognition but have not been tested for linguistic capacity. It may be, then, that linguistic ability is highly correlated with consciousness. The symbolic mediational nature of language may be essential for the high order modeling function that we refer to as self consciousness. Clearly, other large brained species, such as the cetaceans, should be assayed for linguistic function and self consciousness. At the same time we must be careful of our own biases, as Griffin has pointed out, in assessing the symbolic capacity of other species. We must avoid assuming that our inability to decode a particular hypothetical communication system means that that system is ineffective or inconsequential.

If language is a necessary component of consciousness, the study of the physiological mechanisms of language may shed considerable light on the nature of consciousness. We know from the study of patients with traumatic cerebral damage that a critical language center resides in Wernicke's area in the left temporal lobe. Destruction of this area eliminates essentially all language function in adult humans. Recent work by Teyler and Mechelse indicates that auditory evoked potentials recorded over the left temporal lobe may encode semantic information. For instance, Teyler presents a tape recording of the word "rock" to a subject, while simultaneously recording auditory evoked potentials over the right and left hemispheres. There are two conditions in the experiment. In the first condition the subject is instructed to conceptualize the world as a noun; in the second condition the same subject conceptualizes the word as a verb. There are no differences in the auditory evoked potentials recorded over the right nonspeech temporal lobe. Robust differences, however, were observed in the wave forms recorded over the left temporal lobe. Thus, meaning of the stimulus alters the nature of the neural response under conditions where the physical parameters of the auditory stimuli presented are identical. The extraordinary thing about this study is that it appears to provide a method for the study of the neural correlates of subjective conscious experiences. The subject in the study is instructed to alter his "consciousness of" the stimulus word from noun to verb. The investigator records the change in the evoked potential as an index of that change in "consciousness of". More importantly, however, that change in "consciousness of" could not have been effected without a consciousness of consciousness of, that is, a self, capable of changing the response to the physical stimulus on the basis of its intended meaning. Thus we have not only a neural correlate of some perceptual-attentional process (consciousness of), but evidence for consciousness of that process, that is, self consciousness.

For some years it has been known that patients having undergone corpus callosectomy have cerebral hemispheres that are capable of isolated information processing. That is, it is possible for one hemisphere to "know" something that the other hemisphere doesn't know. Even in such patients, little divergence is seen in the "personalities" of the two hemispheres under ordinary conditions, since they continued to receive approximately the same sensory information because of bilateral representation of the various sensory systems. Furthermore, since only the left hemisphere typically has speech function, the right hemisphere cannot "tell us" very well what it knows that the other hemisphere doesn't. Recently, however, Gazzaniga has reported an atypical case in which both hemispheres have speech function. In this case considerable divergence between the hemispheres has been noted in terms of aspirations, personality characteristics etc. Thus, it seems at least theoretically possible that separate selves can inhabit the cerebral hemispheres. The minimum anatomical requirement for such a separate self appears to be one hemisphere. However, further localization of the self may indeed be possible, considering the reports of multiple personalities with upwards of thirty separate component selves. Of course, these multiple personalities may only exist sequentially or perhaps as parallel overlays, rather than in thirty separate cerebral locations!

In addition to reductionistic approaches to the definition of consciousness, we should consider more holistic approaches. One such approach is the epiphenomenal view. In this view consciousness is a kind of accidental byproduct of the brain, a kind of *deus ex machina*. One might of course wonder why, in an evolutionary vein, such an "accident" should be ubiquitous in the human population.

At any rate, it has been somewhat naively suggested that consciousness is simply an emergent property dependent on some minimal complexity of neural circuitry. By this view, artificial intelligence could be achieved merely by a brute force increase in circuit density of electronic computers. However, most experts in the field believe that intelligence is essentially a software problem, ultimately soluble perhaps, in terms of multiple parallel information processing networks.

How can we know whether an artificial intelligence is truly conscious? The only possible test is the Turing test. Equip two rooms with teletype communication. Place the putative artificial intelligence in one room and a human in the other. Select a panel of experts and have them present a series of questions via teletype to the two contestants. If the panel is unable to distinguish the contestants on the basis of their replies, we must assume the computer to be as self conscious as the other contestant. Any other test of self consciousness would be hopelessly anthropomorphic. Of course, the Turing test begs the question because it still doesn't define the criteria for human self-consciousness. Would a machine capable of passing the Turing test shed any light on the nature of consciousness? Clearly its circuits would be more accessible than those of a human! Considering the requisite flexibility for passing the Turing test, such a machine might prove to be a fairly good general model of consciousness (actually a model of a model of a model!). Of course, it would not be very reasonable to assume anything about the wiring (neural or electronic) of one system based upon an examination of the wiring of the other. But it might turn out that the higher level programing or modeling of the two systems would be quite similar. Perhaps the best use of a self conscious artificial intelligence would be to set it directly to work on the problem we are considering—the nature of self consciousness itself!

Another set of holistic approaches should be briefly considered. Duralistic notions such as psychophysical parallelism and interactionism assume that consciousness must be of a completely different nature than the physical brain. Such approaches seem to fail because of the difficulty of providing an interface between material brain and immaterial brain and immaterial self. How does one convert an immaterial volition into the movement of one's arm? Thus, it appears that the self and the physiology must be essentially coincident. Perhaps they are related in somewhat the way that higher level programing languages like Fortran are related to lower level machine language instructions. But, of course, both types of language are equally material. It is simply not necessary to know machine language in order to write programs in Fortran. Similarly, perhaps we are not typically aware of the machine language of self consciousness.[1] This can easily lead to the assumption that the higher level "language of consciousness" must be something totally removed from the machine level language of physiology. The project, then, of today's student of consciousness is to determine language of consciousness and how it is translated from the higher level code that is accessible to our awareness.

THE MANIPULATION OF CONSCIOUSNESS

Another approach to the investigation of the nature of consciousness entails the examination of procedures that affect the texture of consciousness. A catalogue of procedures that in some way alter subjective experience may shed light on that experience.

An early method of consciousness manipulation was accidentally discovered by Stratton in 1900. Stratton devised a mirror system which had the effect of projecting an image of his body at right angles to the vertical. The only visual feedback about his body that Stratton could receive was distorted in the above fashion. After some days of wearing this device Stratton experienced the momentary illusion of "being" in the 90° image, rather than in his actual body. Furthermore, he had the odd sensation of seeing his body from a vantage point at right angles to the usual orientation. It was as if his "center of consciousness" had been spatially displaced. Similarly, Jaynes reports that a patient who had suffered traumatic brain damage experienced a translocation of his "center of consciousness" to a corner of his hospital room. From that vantage point he was able to observe his own body. After some weeks the sensation vanished. Both of these observations seem to indicate the disruption of sensory feedback about body position in space, induced artifically or traumatically, may result in a relocation of the apparent center of consciousness from the head to some arbitrary location.

Observations such as those cited should be considered in the light of cultural context. Placement of consciousness in the head may well represent the historic bias which mechanistically required some "higher" function for that mysterious organ, the human brain. The Homeric Greeks, in contradistinction, placed the seat of mentation in the heart or lungs. But Renaissance physiology provided appropriate functions for these organs. Thus it was up to post-Renaissance phrenology to assign the elements of consciousness to the final black box of nineteenth century physiology.

At any rate the assignment of a resting place for the self right behind the eyes seems to be somewhat arbitrary. If the self is really a model of the attentional function, there would seem to be no logical necessity to assigning it a specific physical locus. That is, the physiological mechanisms that underlie self consciousness indubitably reside in the central nervous system. But the subjective sensation we call center of consciousness may well have considerably more degrees of freedom in its apparent location. Such considerations may help to explain "out of body" phenomena, astral projection etc. These phenomena are often reported in conjunction with use of hallucinogenic drugs, or extreme states of food and/or sleep deprivation. Such conditions may produce a state of sensory feedback distortion not unlike that seen in Jaynes' reported case, or Stratton's experiment.[2]

Psychotropic drugs, in particular, may radically disrupt monoamine balance in the central nervous system. LSD, for instance, partially mimics the effects of the neurotransmitter Serotonin. Serotonin, in turn, appears to be intimately involved in the regulation of the organismic state of arousal. This regulation may be attained by raphe nucleus modulation of the reticular activating system, a neural network long known to play a role in the control of activational state. The effects of LSD might then be a least partially explained in terms of hyperactivation of this serotonergic circuit, leading to the peculiar distortions of conscious experience that have been so often described.

The catecholamines, norepinephrine and, more importantly, dopamine, represent another monoaminergic circuit that appears intimately associated with certain manifestations of conscious experience. Extreme depletion of dopamine in Parkinson's Disease leads to a variety of motoric disturbances, such as festination, retardation and perseveration. Sachs has described a corresponding cognitive symptomatology consisting of such phenomena as repetitive language, echolalia, aboulia, lack of volition, stereotype and barrenness of thought processes. According to Sachs, the cognitive landscape of Parkinson's Disease is the psychological equivalent of a black hole. When thought (or movement, for that matter) does occur, it tends to be highly perseverative.

The only exception (in patients not under L-Dopa treatment) to this pattern occurs under conditions of high stress. Thus, the Parkinsonian mother, confined to her wheelchair for 20 years, observes her daughter drowning. She leaps from the chair, swims out to her daughter, drags her to shore—and immediately collapses, unable to move (Sachs: *Awakenings*). Recently, it has been shown that a stressful situation (tail pinch in the rat) results in considerable dopaminergic activation. Perhaps activation of residual dopaminergic pools allowed the temporary release from Parkinsonin symptoms, necessary for the rescue described above.

The motoric disturbances of Parkinson's Disease may be

produced in an animal model of the disorder. Teitelbaum has shown that particular midbrain lesions produce Parkinson-like behavior in rats. Similarly, in rats with ventromedial hyphothalamic lesions, a deficit in response inhibitory function has been demonstrated by Singh. This preparation produces such profound perseveration that prelesion experience with high fixed rate schedules or quinine adulterated water can establish response sets that are maintained so well postoperatively as to preclude the generation of typical ventromedial deficits, such as reduced motivation to work for food reward on difficult schedules or finickiness with respect to taste. Since the ventromedial hypothalamus is in anatomical proximity to the catecholamine rich ventral bundle, it is quite likely that ventromedial hypothalamic lesions may significantly impair dopaminergic function. It is not surprising that such impairment results in a behavior reminiscent of Parkinson's Disease.

Singh et al. have compared the ventromedial syndrome in rats to obesity in humans. Obese humans show strong evidence of a response inhibitory deficit. In addition, obese humans exhibit strong functional fixation, constituting evidence for a kind of cognitive perseverative deficit. It is tempting to speculate that human obesity might well be associated with a functional impairment of dopaminergic function. Finally, Singh has recently extended the comparison to another instance of perseverative behavior in humans, chronic alcoholism. The chronic alcoholic exhibits any of the response inhibitory deficits observed in the obese. Recent evidence for altered catecholaminergic metabolism in alcoholics lends further credence to the notion that this form of perseverative behavior is also associated with altered dopaminergic function. Perhaps individuals with impaired dopaminergic function are "at risk" for a variety of perseverative dysfunctions. The perseverative dysfunction may be expressed in a variety of ways: obesity, alcoholism, perhaps even drug addiction. In addition to these observations it appears that chronically low levels of catecholamines are associated with extreme psychological depression (not uncommon in Parkinsonians, the obese, or alcoholics). Monoamine oxidase inhibitors and other mood elevating drugs enhance catecholamine function.

On the other side of the ledger, we must consider the cognitive consequences of hyperactive catecholaminergic function. The catecholamine theory of schizo-affective disorders proposes that schizophrenia and related disorders are engendered by ultra high levels of catecholamines in the central nervous system. One of the primary distinguishing characteristics of schizophrenia is the disordered thought process. Thoughts are fragmented; ideational chains are bizarre and contorted. In this case, rather than the perseveration of a central set, we see an apparent inability to develop any consistent cognitive set at all. Breaking out of stereotypic modes of thought or cognitive sets constitutes the creative act. It is suggestive that the incidence of schizophrenia is highest among creative individuals. The suggestion here is that an intermediate level of catecholamine function may be associated with an optimal level of creative thought: too little catecholaminergic function results in cognitive stereotype and flat or depressed affect; too much results in cognitive disorder and corresponding elevated affect. Thus, the appropriate treatment for the dysfunctions described here is to restore the optimal level of catecholamine activity: in patients with depressive or Parkinsonian symptomatology, treatment with catecholamine enhancers like L-Dopa is indicated; in patients with hyperactive catecholamine function, treatment with catecholamine reducing agents, like chlorpromazine, is indicated. Further support for these notions comes from the observation that too radical a lowering of catecholamine level in schizophrenic patients may cause the emission of Parkinsonian-like motoric behaviors. Likewise, chronic use of catecholamine enhancers like metamphetamine may result in an "amphetamine psychosis" not unlike paranoid schizophrenia.

Much of the preceding material may be interpreted in terms of Kaada's somatomotor inhibitory theory. Hierarchically organized levels of inhibitory control over motoric (and perhaps cognitive) response systems extend from a frontal cortex "executive" through limbic structures like the hippocampus, septum and amygdala to a final common path in the hypothalamic-midbrain area. "Higher" levels of control function represent more finely tuned inhibitory modulation of behavior. Ultimately this inhibitory modulation may be identified with the integrity of catecholaminergic neuronal circuitry.

In the absence of the frontal "executive", the lobotomized patient exhibits extreme perseverative tendencies. Similar observations of perseverative behavior have been made in animal subjects with lesions in the limbic regions mentioned above. It would be most interesting to observe the influence of catecholamine enhancers like L-Dopa on the behavior of frontal lobotomized human patients.

In addition to neurochemical manipulation of conscious experience, it appears that some aspects of consciousness may be altered by electrical stimulation of the brain. Thus the classical experiments of Penfield showed that it was possible to activate dormant memories by electrical stimulation of the temporal lobe. Past experiences of the subject could be superimposed on the operating room environment in a more or less hallucinatory fashion. But the subject was always conscious of "really" being in the operating room, rather than in some past event. Thus, this appears to be a manipulation of "consciousness of", rather than of the actual locus or nature of self consciousness.

More recently, a noninvasive technique with potential for the manipulation of various aspects of conscious function has appeared. This technique is called *biofeedback*. It involves the external monitoring of a wide variety of physiological signals produced by a subject and concomitant reinforcement of a specific pattern of signal output from that subject. Using this procedure it has been proved possible to teach subjects to manipulate such disparate functions as muscle tension, blood pressure, heart rate and galvanic skin resistance. Components of the EEG, such as the alpha waveform, may be enhanced or reduced. The alpha waveform, in particular, seems to be associated with a specific conscious state similar to the objectless consciousness previously discussed. Enhanced alpha production has also been observed during various forms of meditation. It appears that meditation and alpha conditioning may significantly differ only in the perceived locus of control. In biofeedback or alpha conditioning, an external monitor is always employed. In meditation the locus of control over components of consciousness appears to be entirely internal. The underlying phenomena, however, may be identical in both techniques. In both techniques it appears that conscious control over at least some aspects of consciousness may be attained.

At any rate, the work described above implies that psychological states may have a very important role in the determination of physiological function. There is no reason to assume that this relationship is only present during biofeedback training or meditation. A growing body of evidence supports the notion that psychological factors are contributing factors in pathological disease states. The relationship between chronic psychological stress and cardiovascular disorders is well known. More recently it has been suggested that cancer is more prevalent among depressed patients than the normal population. In contrast, cancer is infrequent in the schizophrenic population. The implication is that mood and ultimately catecholaminergic function may in part determine immunological competence and concomitant susceptibility to cancer. Further support for this notion comes from occasional reports of the placebo cure. Under some circumstances merely the belief in the efficacy of a pharmacologically inactive drug may lead to the remission of a disease state. Perhaps faith healing may be explained in similar terms. Such phenomena suggest the possible extension of "consciousness of" from the external environment to any possible internal physiological function. With awareness of the function may come the possibility of control. At least, that seems to be the case with respect to the biofeedback technique.

A word of caution with respect to various modes of consciousness manipulating techniques is necessary. Mere sleep deprivation and/or dietary imbalance may result in considerable changes in neurotransmitter function in the human brain. Aserties have used such techniques as starvation, sleep deprivation and flagellation to induce hallucinatory states of consciousness. Some American religious cults appear to be practicing such methods on a mass basis in order to produce "religious experiences". Conveniently for the cult leaders, such techniques appear to increase the suggestibility of the cult members. The Guyana incident underlines the possible consequences of extreme suggestibility. Thus, certain methods of consciousness manipulation, in unscrupulous hands, can be deadly.

THE EVOLUTION OF CONSCIOUSNESS

Another question we must ask in our investigation of consciousness is what is consciousness for? Why did consciousness evolve? In terms of evolution, the ubiquitous presence of a character in a population implies very strong selection pressure for that character. This in turn implies that selection operated very strongly in favor of consciousness in our species.

What was the nature of that selection pressure? Recently Jaynes has hypothesized that consciousness developed in historic time. Jaynes sees pre-Homeric man as a species with extreme cerebral lateralization. We may ask, in turn, why the brain of homo sapiens should be so strongly lateralized. It has been suggested that the compartmentalization of speech function into the left hemisphere and nonverbal function into the right hemisphere made for more efficient parcelation of the cognitive work load. However, it must be noted that cerebral lateralization is not unique to homo sapiens; song birds also exhibit strong lateralization. Thus lateralization may be characteristic of species exhibiting elaborate patterns of vocalization. The vocal cords are a midline structure. An efficient method of reducing ambiguity (and inefficiency) in cerebral control of complex vocalization would entail restriction of vocal control mechanisms to one hemisphere only. Thus only one hemisphere is in control of the vocal cords at any point in time. (It has been suggested that one cause of stuttering in humans may be incomplete lateralization of speech function.)

At any rate, an immediate problem with cerebral lateralization is how does the right hemisphere communicate with the left hemisphere, if all speech mechanisms reside in the left hemisphere? How is information transferred from hemisphere to hemisphere? Jaynes' solution (and one that would seem difficult to apply to song birds!) is that the right hemisphere "speaks" to the left hemisphere through auditory-visual hallucinations. All the religious and oracular experiences of prehistoric man, then, represent externalized instructions from the right hemisphere. Consciousness, on the other hand, represents the internalization of the "god". Now the entity that instructs and advises the left hemisphere is the internalized self.

But why should there have been such selection for this internalized deity? Considerations of efficiency, once again, seem uppermost. Clearly an individual in constant communion with his right hemisphere would reach critical decisions more rapidly and efficiently than an individual dependent on intermittent oracular communications from the externalized right hemisphere. The former individual, then, might be expected to have a considerable advantage in fitness over the latter individual. Jaynes' model treats the schizophrenic as a recidivist example of preconscious homo sapiens. The oft-experienced "controlling voices" then represent the externalized right hemisphere in the schizophrenic symptomatology.

A somewhat different rationale has recently been presented for the evolution of consciousness by the anthropologist Richard Leakey. Leakey feels that consciousness supplied early man with the capacity for empathy. That is, if one knows that a particular action will injure one's self, one can infer that the same action will cause injury to another self should that action be performed on the body of that other self. Thus the rudiments of a kind of "Golden Rule" are provided by the mechanism of self consciousness. Do not do unto others what you would not have done unto you. Any number of activities requiring concerted effort are thus made more practical and less dangerous by such a mechanism. For instance, hunting may be organized in such a way as to minimize danger to any individual hunter. Society itself, then, has its origins in the appearance of consciousness. Clearly, integrated social action provides an immense survival advantage to the members of any group exhibiting it, and, by implication, consciousness.

Will consciousness evolve any further? One might argue compellingly that it must evolve if we are to survive as a species in the nuclear age. Teilhard de Chardin suggested that the next step in the evolution of consciousness will be a kind of social union of consciousness. An individual organism cannot commit suicide on the basis of instructions from an isolated organ to that effect. The human body politic, on the other hand, could well destroy itself as the result of the actions of some renagade organ-nation with nuclear capability. A more unified human consciousness might suffice to prevent destruction of the social organism through the action of some pathological national issue.

NOTES

1.   When we gain conscious control of some autonomic mechanism through biofeedback techniques, that may be equivalent to writing a compiler for that specific physiological function. That puts us in touch, at least temporarily, with the machine language of physiology.

2.   Another possibility is that extreme emotional stress, particularly in childhood, may result in two or more "selves" inhabiting the same locus, i.e., the multiple personality.

The Evolution of the Mind: Projections into the Future

UNDERSTANDING THE HUMAN MIND

The mind may be viewed in a number of ways. From a physical scientist's point of view, the primary conception of it is as an *interface* between the public world described by the physical sciences and the private world of personal experience and individuality. On the other hand, one may take the extreme point of view that the public world of the physical sciences is the only world, individuality and the mind being an *aspect* of matter. A more subtle view would be that in every action of the mind we see not the mind but a sequences of subtle causations, each one dealing with a finer level of action, but entirely describable by laws of physico-chemical systems. The mind as the seat of volition is then seen as the *limit* of this sequence. On the other hand, the physicist is not averse to seeing the world as a realization of an abstract thought system, formalized as an algebra and an associated rule of correspondence. In this view, which echoes the metaphysics of the *Rigveda* and *Sankhya*, the mind is just one *stage* of the embodied self, the stage before the sense organs. Like *Panchali* of the *Mahabharata*, the mind too unites with the five senses in turn.

A unifying quality that runs through these varied conceptions of the mind is that of a *relationship* which begins as an action and a reaction, or in the idiom of physics, as an *interaction* governed by the laws and entirely subject to them. If the mind were to remain at this stage of interaction, its movements are entailed, a reaction to the action of external causes on it together with the natural random movements of its own somewhat-like Brownian motion. Such primitive stage of the relationship exhibits the mind in its primitive state, the level of *vrttis* (of random movements) and of *karma vipaka* (manifestation of the past dynamical activity). But *evolution* is growth beyond interaction and points to an active principle that transcends a mere dynamic interaction. A conventional dynamical system with well defined degrees of freedom and laws of interaction is at best a channel for "flow through" of information which presents itself in newer forms in the course of time; and often the information is degraded and partially lost. But if the system transcends dynamics in that the element of self-referral is involved, the system may grow. In the context of self-organizing physical systems one talks of dissipative structures which have been considered seriously as models of life processes. When consciousness and creativity enter, the system may be viewed as manifesting creative intelligence. We shall see below the extent to which self-referral is an important characterization of the creative cognizing evolving mind and how this is expressed practically in the symbol of the guru.

Indian metaphysicists distinguish several stages of mind: *manas*, *buddha*, *ahamkara* to speak of three categories, which are merged in the contemporary usage of the word "mind". So while we can talk of *mano nasa* (dissolution of *manas*), we would hardly speak of the same situation as "having lost his/her mind". Since traditional metaphysics can be more adequately presented by several other participants, in this paper I shall talk of the mind in its contemporary connotation.

VARIETIES OF SECULAR EXPERIENCE

Physics is the science of measurement, the study of existence and change and also the science of imagination. In its humble form, it concerns itself with justifying what is already seen and known: its Sanskrit name *bhuta vijnana* literally translates itself into "science of what has happened". When we look at the evolution of physics during the past few centuries, we see the world picture of the physicist grow from the understanding of isolated phenomena to a global perspective of the entire physical universe as a connected whole. And in this inclusive vision of the universe as a dynamic whole is a new perception of the world, a new concept of existence:

Akhanda mandalakaram
Vyaptam yena caracaram
(permeating the static and the dynamic as an undivided whole)

Once the laws of motion of "small" objects (often referred to as "particles") were suitably visualized by Galileo and Newton, strides towards a global conception were rapidly made. The observations of Tycho Brahe on the motion of celestial objects were codified into Kepler's three laws of motion. Newton showed that these were the consequences of the gravitational force on the planets by the sun. Newton further related this to the dynamics of tides and of falling bodies. This was only a step to the dynamical view of all the quantities and qualities around us. The kinetic theory of gases and of liquids, the dynamics of rigid bodies, the study of elasticity in terms of a collection of numerous particles coupled together by interparticle forces, of acoustics and hydrodynamics; all these brought the physical world around us under the sway of dynamics. Viscosity and elasticity were not additional to dynamics, but aspects of it. With the study of wave phenomena and the understanding of laws of optics, it was a natural development to see optics as a wave phenomenon and wave motion to be a property of space; space endowed with this quality was called "aether".

These remarkable developments were made possible once the various categories of dynamical entities were distinguished and related. Galileo could barely distinguish between momentum and energy; but Newton's monumental work could not have proceeded without a clear distinction between these. In the nascent stages of thermodynamics we see the same circumstance in the difficulty to distinguish between heat and temperature. Perhaps in this is contained a lesson for the study of the mind. We must, as much as possible, distinguish different categories and their structural relationships so that a systematic theory can emerge.

Two other streams of ideas were yet to come into classical physics. The first stream related to thermodynamics and the second to electromagnetism. The phenomena of heat and heat flow, and the mechanical effect of heat and production of heat by motion were known for some time. The work of Rumford and Joule showed that heat was a kind of energy with a strict proportionality with mechanical energy; the principle of conservation of energy with the inclusion of heat energy became the First Law of Thermodynamics. But in the study of heat there is a new quality, the preferred heat flow from a hotter body to a colder body. The reverse can take place, but we have to exert ourselves to do it. Once the idea of a level of heat, called temperature, is established, this preferred direction of flow can be encompassed in terms of a new type of law. We demand (or "confess"?) that no conceivable process can exist which transfers heat from a lower temperature to a higher temperature without changes in the surroundings. This is the Second Law of Thermodynamics. If this principle is applied to "heat engines", which are devices for converting heat energy into mechanical energy, one is led to Carnot's remarkable result: there is a maximum efficiency of conversion of heat energy between any two temperatures. This efficiency can be used as a measure of absolute temperature. Temperature is a "state variable"; that is, it is a quality of matter which depends only on its (present) state. It is very much like kinetic energy, or any other dynamical attribute. But the quantity of heat is not such a quantity; it depends on the history. But it can be shown that heat energy changes in a quantity called "entropy" which is a "state variable". When more general thermodynamic changes involving pressures, volumes, chemical composition and species are involved, new state variables (usually called "thermodynamic potentials") get into the description. The Second Law of Thermodynamics states that entropy must increase (or, at least, stay constant) in all natural processes.

Does thermodynamics imply new qualities to be added to dynamics? Or can they be understood within the framework of dynamics itself?

The kinetic theory of gases gave the first indication of the possibility of constructing a "statistical mechanics" in which heat energy was related to disordered motion of the particles and entropy to be a quantitative extensive measure of disorder. The question naturally arises: How can a reversible dynamical theory sustain a thermodynamics in which entropy always increases? Where does the "arrow of time" originate? How could disorder increase? The questions was first answered by Boltzmann, who "proved" a theorem showing how the impossible happens. Many improvements have been made on this "proof", but essentially they all imply that entropy is negative information; and that loss of correlations leads to rise in entropy and, in turn, the arrow of time. It is as if one were to paraphrase Nagarjuna and say "ignorance is decay".

This possibility of correlations and their destruction implies, in turn, the practical need for dealing with the world around us as if it were broken into disconnected pieces with no subtle correlations between them. Every time we see the world around us, we fragment it into "island universes" and act surprised when correlations are seen between these fragments. Descriptions of such island universes are always "contractions" of the dynamics of the whole system and tend to introduce an arrow of time and increase of entropy.

In a fragmented universe, the fragment need not be entirely isolated. It may have intereactions with the surroundings so that dynamic quantities like energy and momentum can flow through the system. Such systems are referred to as "open" systems in thermodynamics, in contrast to "closed" systems, which are isolated fragments. The increase of entropy characteristic of a closed system need not obtain for an open system. Sufficiently far from equilibrium, an open system may create a new order, as long as the flows continue. Such systems, called dissipative systems by Prigogine, have been taken as conceptual models for living systems. New orders come into being as the unfolding of natural laws in the context of an open system. Life begets itself in the physical universe.

The development of electromagnetism brought new models into physical theory. The law of attraction between unlike charges and repulsion between like charges with an inverse square law of force introduced the electrostatic field as a mathematical convenience. But when changing electric charges and electric fields come in we deal with electric currents and their magnetic effects. There is a reciprocity in the interaction. A moving charge is influenced by a magnetic field and a moving charge creates a magnetic field. Permanent magnets produced magnetic fields which behaved like the magnetic fields produced by a solenoid of wires carrying electric current. Furthermore, a changing magnetic field produces electric potentials and fields. The laws of Coulomb on electrostatics, of Ampere on magnetic effects of currents, and of Faraday on the electric effect on a changing magnetic flux were all "source-laws", how one physical system acted as the source of another force field. But at this level the fields could be thought of as mathematical conveniences, as surrogates for the distance dependencies on the sources. But Maxwell saw that the laws of electromagnetism were not consistent without magnetic effects of time-varying electric fields (the so-called "displacement currents"); and, that, when these were also included, the laws of electromagnetism took on a highly symmetric form.

The equations describing this system are now known as Maxwell's equations and constitute the bases of our understanding of electromagnetism and light; and they are essentially unchanged even today. One of the most startling conclusions was the possibility of "sourceless" electromagnetism, the "free" electromagnetic waves in empty space. With Hertz's experimental verification of these waves traveling with the speed of light, the possibility of self-sustaining, self-governing, self-perpetuating oscillations of electric and magnetic fields becomes a reality. The field ceased to be a mathematical fiction and became a genuine dynamic entity. It could carry energy and momentum and be able to sustain its own characteristic excitations. But what is a field? It was space considered as the theater for various potentialities: if it was an electric field then electric forces acted upon particles in that region of space, while a gravitational field meant that particles in that region of space experienced gravitational forces. Space itself, in its role as a field, has become a dynamical variable.

The electromagnetic field theory, in its turn, caused the two modern revolutions in physics and altered our entire conception of nature. The combination of dynamics of ordinary bodies in interaction with the electromagnetic field could not be consistent for observers in moving frames; yet every effort to detect absolute motion ended in failure. It was found by Einstein and by Poincare that our "common sense ideas" about space and time had to be altered. These alterations involved a profound restructuring of physics, which is called the theory of relativity.

The impact of this new perspective on space, time and dynamical evolution is felt in almost all aspects of our understanding of physical processes. Time, in which configurations unfold, and space, which was the canvas against which these configurations were seen, are now seen to be distinct yet subtly interconnected. Duration and extension flow into each other, although their intrinsic character is maintained. One consequence of this is that simultaneity is no longer absolute; two equally competent people may disagree on simultaneity of two spatially separated events.

Another aspect of relativity is the dethronement of mass. In Newtonian physics, mass was the measure of matter. We were all told in school never to confuse mass with weight. Mass was the primary quality of physical objects, the inertia, the *tamasic* component of *bhutas*; and it was invariable. Energy, and momentum, the *rajasic* components, were superimpositions and variable. For each frame of observation, for every closed system, both these types of quantities were conserved, i.e. the sum total of the mass was invariable, the sum total of energy was invariable and the sum total of the momentum values was invariable. In addition, mass had an aspect as a "coupling constant" in that it determined the strength of the gravitational interaction. Relativity theory changed all that. Mass was no longer the dynamic inertia; the total energy, including mass energy, usurped that place. Mass was no longer conserved, but we now had an energy conservation law that included as special cases the conservation of mass in some reactions. But, effectively, mass was demoted to the role of a frame and movement-dependent quantity. And with the relativity theory of gravitation, the theory of general relativity, mass lost out the role of coupling to gravitation (which appears in the form of curvature of space-time itself), to a frame-dependent quantity called the stress-tensor.

In relativity theory, there is still a reminder of the old principle of conservation of matter (not mass) in the form of baryon conservation: the number of protons plus neutrons (plus some other such particles which are all called "baryons" or heavy particles minus the number of antiprotons and antineutrons) is invariable. There are also, possibly, two such laws of lepton (light particles, including electrons and neutrons) conservation. (It is still not considered possible to convert a cup of water into pure energy!)

With simultaneity and inertia as state-dependent dynamical variables, with duration no longer independent of the observer, we stumble in our linguistic modes because that is still "based" on (or stuck to) prerelativity physics. This unwillingness of language to follow where insight leads appears again and again in the course of evolution of the mind.

MAGIC, MYTH OR SCIENCE

If relativity theory forced us to revise our notions of space and time and how their values changed for different observer perspectives, quantum theory demands that we change our concept of what system is. Classical (prequantum) physics dealt mostly with particles and finitely extended bodies, but at times with fields. One such case is the electromagnetic field of Maxwell, which is sustained in "empty" space, in *akasa*. Thermodynamics deals with all systems; so why not with this field, too? If we now asked the question: What is the nature, quality and magnitude of the excitation of the electromagnetic field in empty space kept at a definite temperature?, it should be possible to answer the question precisely, using thermodynamics and the laws of Maxwell. And, if someone wanted to study the question experimentally, or even watch a fireplace on a winter's day, the predictions and observations should agree. But they did not. Theory not only gave correct answers, but also absurd answers. It said the vacuum has infinite heat capacity, that it could not be heated to a finite temperature. Since this was patently absurd, something had to be modified: Planck showed that the modification was in the dynamical nature of the electromagnetic field, that it was "grainy" in a peculiar manner, that it consisted of "quanta". In the hands of Einstein and Bose the hypothesis was developed into identi-fication of the photon or "light quantum" as the particles of lights. In the hands of Bohr, quantum ideas gave clues to the structure and functioning of the atom and the physical basis of chemistry. The work of Heisenberg and of Schrodinger de-veloped into what became quantum theory in its modern form as a transformation theory, as the realization of a noncommu-tative algebra of operations. Idea is reborn as matter; inertia, movement, interaction are all stage sets in the presentation of an abstract play. Mathematics of transformations was seen as the language of quantum dynamics and quantum descrip-tion. Dirac called the objects which displayed the transforma-tion the "career space", as the space of "State vectors". It is the terminology used today. Making a body move is a linear transformation in this space: all dynamics is transformation.

But what is superposition? If we had an atom in an excited state that wanted to deexcite to the ground state plus a pho-ton, is it not absurd to think of a superposition of such states? Chastity and honesty cannot be less than total; it is not so for excitation of the atom? Quantum theory says no; and, in that, contains the profound restructuring of our concept of reality.

Later in this paper I present some considerations to con-clude that in course of evolution of the mind, the quantum superposition principle becomes the clue to the functioning modality of perception: that is the right brain's language as much as it is the language of myth and poetry and of sub-atomic physics.

Light particles can be obviously created and destroyed: could we not expect this of other particles as well? Yukawa gave a theory of nuclear forces based on creation and destruc-tion of electron and neutron to construct a theory of radioactivity. We now believe that all matter is such that it could be created and destroyed and that many reactions are best understood in terms of such processes. Matter is characterized not by permanence but by change. But, then, what is the substratum of all dynamics?

It is the field, the potentialities of space-time seen as the carrier of noncommutative algebra of dynamical operations built up from creations and destructions:

Idatu mizi vamkunni prapancam samstham
Valatu mizi vamikum vahniyal bhasmamaki
Karumana palatevam kattiyatma swarupam
Sisuta visadamakkum vashuve satyamavu

(Create a configuration with the left eye, destroy it by the right: by such play is the true dynamic of the world demonstrated in a manner understood even by an infant.)

The unfolding of potentialities in the field is the technique of world-building and thus must we see the field as the primary dynamical body:

Idam sariram kaunteya
Ksetramityabhidhiyate
Ksetra kasetrajnayor jnanam
Yattad jnanam matam mama

(Know that the field is the body, O Arjuna! My view is that knowledge of field and of field theory is true knowledge.)

When dynamics is a realization of the noncommutative algebra of transformations, matter and mind stuff are no longer sharply divided. That is a strange answer to the old mind-matter dichotomy. Strange it may be: but strangely apt. The world is not different from me.

Atmaupamyena sarvarta
Samam pasyati yorjuna
Sukham va yadi duhkham
Sa yogi paramo matah

(Seeing himself in everything and everywhere equally O Arjuna! Irrespective of sorrow or glee, such a one is the unifier.)

Vistabhyam idam sarvam
Ekamsena sthito jagat

(All this [world] is only an aspect of self.)

What has all this to do with evolution of the mind?

PERCEPTION OF THE MIND

We are all physicists whether we admit it or not. We see the world as orderly, in that much of the dynamics is taken for granted. Any scientifically studied fragment of the universe obeys prescribed and simple laws; cause precedes effect, effect follows cause—effortlessly but inexorably. Yet the world around us is full of disorder. Anticipated events often do not occur. Unexpected events do occur. We are surprised. We become frustrated. None of this is possible in a world without order; nor can they take place in a world which is in total order.

This perception of an orderly world full of disorder is the birth of the theory-building aspect of the mind. The mind dwells in a parochial world with limited powers of extrapolation, retrodiction and prediction. Disorder of a fragment of the universe is seen against the background of order and the mind strives to eliminate the disorder without removing the fragmentation of the universe. It is a characteristic of this modality that the "unseen" (*adrsta*) is seen as the agent of the surprise.

We may see the mind as a parallel world with its own cosmology and cause-effect sequences. This parallel world has many points of contact and reference to the public physical world. We may even take this to mean that the public world is a consensus of these private worlds, a compromise solution to the diversity and partial agreement of the many private worlds. It is, then, reasonable to expect that one or more highly ordered minds can change the world for the better. The Buddhist understanding of the *bodhisattva*, the Christian notion of the savior, and the hypothesis of a one-per-cent population of the world in meditation altering the world and eliminating suffering (the "Maharishi effect") all echo this point of view.

May I digress at this point to say that suffering (at least human suffering, as distinct from physical pain) is of the mind; and intrinsic to it as it is the incompatibility of the parallel world of the individual mind with the (public) world. Stated in different words, suffering is the mismatch between natural order and the mind's desire: suffering is a misunderstanding. True knowledge is, therefore, referred to as "*bhava roga vaidyam*", medicine for the illness stemming from phenomena. Removal of suffering should, therefore, be characteristic of knowledge and enlightenment. Man is born to enjoy. Evolution of the mind should then lead to enjoyment in the world. We shall return to this point later in the paper.

In this modality of functioning the mind encounters a world of partial causation, in that it is aware of other minds and each mind has limited autonomy. We can anticipate things only subject to no other mind interfering. Concepts like luck, misfortune and providence arise in this context.

It is only one step from this position to ascribe all failures of causation to other minds, including the seen and the unseen. Natural forces, insofar as they upset our anticipation, are ascribed mind. "The wind bloweth where it listeth." Not only in pantheism and folklore, but also in our spontaneous reactions on being caught in a traffic jam, confronted with recalcitrant machinery, or becoming the victim of air traffic delays, do we find instances of such ascription of the mind to "natural" agents. Like multiple humans, these forces, too, are sometimes in conflict (shades of the Greek pantheon).

An effort to eliminate these "conflicts of interest" is the ascription of a Deity, a single Deity Who in Her/His infinite wisdom and knowledge guides all the seen and unseen forces. All the human mind can do is to act and anticipate in accordance with the divine will: "*Deo Volente.*" Causation is restored, but anticipation is permitted only insofar as one tunes oneself to the divine will. For this reassertion of causation there cannot be multiple divine wills. So says the Lord of the Israelites: "I am a jealous God: Ye shall have no gods except me."

As soon as the world is seen as designed by God, endless

questions come up regarding justice and fair play, suffering, sin and redemption. These questions have been asked and answered many times. It would not be appropriate for me to delve into theology here, but I must point out that the most satisfactory answers ask us not to apply human logic and reason to divine action. In other words, the ultimate is the ultimate because it is not subject to ordinary law. So it is said:

Sarvagamanamacaram pratham parikalpayet
Acara prabhavo dharmo dharmasya prabhuracyutah

In a somewhat more positive vein, as a cosmological theory, it is said:

Rsaya pitaro devah
Sarva bhutani dhatavah
Jangamajangamam cedam
Jagannarayanodbhavam

(Seers, ancestors, gods, verily all the elements and basic entities moving and nonmoving originate in Lord Narayana.)

But, then, it goes on to say:

Yogo jnanam tatha sankhyam
Vidya silpadi karma ca
Vedasasatrani vijnanam
Etat sarvam janardanat

(Knowledge of veda [ontology and metaphysics], sankhya [mathematical theory], literature, sculpture, and other crafts, and the science, all of them are from the Benevolent One.)

Thus, knowledge, too, is an aspect of the Supreme One.

THE DIVINE PEACOCK

Let us return to the discussion of the laws of nature. What is this "nature" of which we search the laws? How shall we know it? This question is akin to the question, "What is the mind?" and not essentially different from questions like, "What is the electromagnetic field?" or "What is life?"

In the case of the electromagnetic field there is now general consensus that it is something that obeys the electromagnetic field equations. It is a "realization" of the laws; and to the extent it is a faithful realization, we may identify the laws with electormagnetism itself. Self-replication, reproductive invariance, thermodynamic openness are all characteristic of living systems. Could we not possibly identify life with matter functioning in this modality? More generally, could we not take "nature" to be the totality of laws of nature? If so, nature becomes the embodiment of natural law: "Word becoming flesh," as St. John would say.

Natural law and nature then become coextensive with God, and everything is sacred, though they remain themselves. God is in everything and every process:

Ahamatma gudakesa
Sarva bhutasaya sthitah
Ahamadim ca madhyam ca
Bhutanamanta eva ca

(O Arjuna, I am the essence of all entities and reside in every entity, at their beginning, middle and end.)

This vision of the cosmos as God, and the individual mind as an aspect of it, is the *visva rupa* vouchsafed to Arjuna and to Yasoda. In this cosmic awareness all conflicts cease and supreme peace reigns. Arjuna says:

Pasyami devams tava deva dehe
Sarvams tatha bhuta visesasamghan
Brahmanam isam kamalasanastham
Rsims ca sarvan uragams ca divyan

(In you I see all the gods and the varied hosts of beings as well, the Creator himself on the lotus throne and all the sages and serpents.)

But the view of cosmos as an aspect of the absolute is euphoria at best and escape at worst, unless it enables us to function with increased, total awareness in the world. The marvel is not in having the cosmic vision, but enabling that vision to permeate and enliven here and now. Moses, after seeing the burning bush; Elijah, after being fed the burning coal; the three apostles, after the transfiguration; Akrura on the way to Kamsa's palace in the company of Krishna and Balarama; Paul, after the episode on Damascus Road: these are the paradigms.

There is a beautiful Kannada hymn, which begins "*jagadodharana adisidalu yashoda...*" (Yashoda played with the World Redeemer as if He were a boy, called Him her son...). This is the miracle of living after attainment of the vision of the cosmos as the absolute itself, being in full tune with all the natural laws to live like an ordinary person.

Ethics and aesthetics at this stage become cosmic ecology, a flowing with the tide, a coconspirator in the celestial harmony. All happenings are the unfolding of a harmonious order, a realization of the potentialities. One's own action is now assured, courageous, sucessful and without attachment. Neither sorrow nor elation touches him.

Duhkhesu anudvigna manah
Sukhesu vigata sprhah
Vitaraga bhaya krodha
Sthitibhih munirucyate

(Unaffected by sorrow or well-being, beyond the reach of hesitation, attachment, fear or anger remains the nonspeaking [wise] person.)

If you are in harmony with the laws of nature, what you wish is what is to be and all your desires are automatically fulfilled. You go beyond the tyranny of time and the agony of attachment.

Other words are used by wise people of other backgrounds. Krishnamurthi urges us to live in the total present with no past, no future. The past does not impose a constraint, nor does the future provide an aim. Each moment is complete unto itself. If you can perceive totally each moment, Krishnamurthi says, then only do you perceive. Otherwise, you are a "second-hand person". Do not form concepts, do not wish, do not crave. Be like the lilies of the valley, the birds of the field, with no thoughts for the morrow. Don Juan tells us through Castaneda that a warrior lives every moment as if it were his last; and if the warrior makes a habit of appearing at the appointed time at the appointed space, his enemies will pin him down. One must erase personal history. So creativity and spontaneity demand the breaking out of molds and patterns.

So the evolution of the mind towards a greater understanding of the laws of nature enables it to see nature and the individual mind itself to be in a harmonious unfolding of potentialities. The EST people put it crudely, but effectively, by declaring, "You are a damned machine; realizing that you are a machine is enlightenment"—a rather contemporary answer to the ancient question:

Sthitaprajnasya ka bhasa
Samadistasya kesava?

(Who is said to be established in knowledge, who is in samadhi?)

The plants do it, the birds and bees do it—why not we?

LIFE

The present-day understanding of life, at least in its simplest form, is an open thermodynamic system with flows in and out of physical and chemical entities. Energy of food or sunlight is converted and degraded to perform the acts of maintenance, growth, reproduction and maintaining reproductive invariance. The information carrying components of the living systems (possibly the DNA molecules, or their assemblies) carry enough additional information to activate food processing and digesting systems to enable them to reproduce and distribute the information carrying components. (In this context they are like research scientists who manage to arrange the world so that they reproduce themselves!)

In an open thermodynamic system, far from equilibrium, it is possible for a new order to generate spontaneously.

Using notions of noncovalent bonds in biochemistry, we can conceive of this order being biospecific and reproductive-invariant. Those that are unsuited for reproduction and survival can be weeded out by nonpurposive natural laws. The system could develop complexity and potentialities of multiple functions. We could then conceive of life as a "dissipative" self-reproducing, self-sustaining process. Life may be viewed as a special mode of functioning of "dead" matter. We are not complelled to look at life this way, but we may!

As systems become more complex, many flows enter into the functioning of the organism; and while this vast complex increases the ability of the organism to "move to the top of the class", its survival is threatened unless the external conditions can be maintained within rather narrow ranges. Consider, for example, the temperature ranges in which an organism can survive. To extend the range in which it could function, the organism should develop automatic adjustment of its metabolism or call into play internal mechanisms calculated to restore homeostasis. The higher animals all seem to have chosen combinations of both of these solutions to continue functioning.

Homeostasis is a characteristic of the "higher" organism, a mark of evolution. Note that both the dissipative structure and the mechanism of homeostasis are accomplished in full accord with laws of physics and chemistry. The second law of thermodynamics still holds valid for the system, but it is the strategy to make use of the openness of the system to "sail the natural laws" towards continued survival.

When we come to higher organisms, it is tempting to identify an element of volition in the strategy adopted. According to the principles of mechanics, a particle travels so as to make the "action" minimum. Animals seems to choose; biologists tell us that it is instinct, or genetic code, or conditioned reflex. Perhaps we ought not to accept the biologists' world-view unquestioningly—I do not consider myself competent to say whether dogs or dolphins have minds of their own. But they, like us, seem to make choices; perhaps they have minds.

However it may be, we could say that homeostasis is a characterization of an evolved organism and the mind is a possible byproduct: that mind emerges once homeostasis assures automatic adjustment to the physiochemical environment, and expresses itself in terms of freedom of choice, exercise of options. Evolution emerges as freedom in the context of natural law.

The mind that emerges thus is admittedly a prototype and not given to elaborate theory-building and contemplation. But it already has the ability to sustain a rudimentary world-view, a crude cosmology. The first step in the growth towards a contemplative mind is already taken.

To the extent we are an open thermodynamic system, we, too, are a dissipative system with flows, with mechanisms of homeostasis and limited options. Sociology and anthropology are special branches of ecology.

MIND IN EVOLUTION

Let us now come to the central question: Evolution of the Mind. The mind mirrors the living system in being itself an open system, which is self-regulating. It grows and absorbs and limits, thus permitting flow-through: not of matter, but of relationships and information. Instead of the word becoming flesh, word substitutes for flesh. Matter is the realization of laws of nature; the body complex is the realization of the mind. The openness of the mind allows flow-through and in such a circumstance a new order may be generated. Near equilibrium, the second law of thermodynamics says that order must decrease; but in open systems, far from equilibrium, dissipative structures can set in. In contrast to a standard computer through which information flows passively, the mind is far from equilibrium. A new order of the laws of nature suggests itself to the mind. The mind gains knowledge and insight.

What does the mind do when the external signals are not satisfactory? It could adopt the strategy of living organisms to hostile surroundings. The unevolved mind is at the mercy of the external world, but as it evolves more, it is at least able to modulate its functioning. The mind tends to escape the unpleasant and seek the pleasant. The mind seeking pleasure is at the state of evolution corresponding to a coldblooded animal—not a *sthita prajna*, not in homeostasis of the mind!

The efficiency of homeostasis is measured by the degree to which undisturbed functioning is possible even with significant external disturbances. It is very much like assessing the degree to which a hi-fi system is shielded: a good hi-fi system is sensitive to the proper signals, but is unaffected by external noise signals.

A practice aimed at accelerated evolution of the mind should, along the way, exhibit this relaxed wakefulness, this sensitivity and stability. Transcendental meditation has emphasized this relaxed wakefulness and the technique arranges for an effortless transcendence into the undisturbed state of awareness. Patanjali in his yoga sutra defines yoga as *citta vritti nirodha* (quieting the random movements of the mind). The most graphic description I have come across of this state is the description of the meditation of Dakshinamurthi:

Kar kondumindatoru kondal pole
Kallolamillatezu mazi pole
Kattilpeda dipavumenna pole
Nispandanay prananadakiveccum

(Like a cloud unblemished by darkness, like a sea unruffled by wavelets, like a long flame undisturbed by breeze, thus did he keep his vital forces beyond vibrations.)

Separated by time and space from Patanjali and Dakshinamurthi, Don Juan tells Castaneda that one must stop the internal dialogue to become a true warrior.

What is so meritorious about quieting the mind? Why not simply drop out? Or go to sleep? There is a definite thing to be gained, namely evolution of the mind. It is as if, faced with a hostile environment, a living organism asked itself, why achieve homeostasis, why not quit and quietly die? But if it did that, it would not evolve and possibly its mind would not emerge. The mind appears from life when life develops homeostasis. What happens when the mind develops the quiet state of alertness?

It is natural to assume that we achieve transcendence, and establishment in the transcendent state represents a definite evolutionary advance. Options not available at early stages of mind functioning now become available; just as options not available to the simplest organisms manifest in higher organisms with the onset of the mind. These new options are called *siddhis* in traditional literature. *Siddhis* are not violations of natural law, but efficient use of them. The total order of the cosmos is now beginning to become available. Harmony and knowledge yield to effortless and graceful action. In an era in which technology has provided us with electronic computers, lasers, super-conductivity and tomographs, *siddhis* coming from mastery over natural laws should appear only natural!

Just as the mind was to the living organism in a higher state of its evolution, does not the mind evolve into a higher entity? Many wise teachers have answered in the affirmative, though their vocabularies differ. And anyone who has been creative knows that the wellsprings of creativity come from something beyond the mind as we normally understand it.

Isvara Pranidhanam Va

A word of caution is necessary at this stage of the discussion. My aim has been to project the evolution of the mind into the future and not examine the pathways in a scholarly or critical manner. I have "played it cool" with regard to methods and even avoided the question whether many paths lead to the same goals. My own limited experience urges me to state that there are definitely distinct methods by which evolution can be enhanced. Perhaps others with more authority ought to comment on this.

But if I were to look back at Patanjali, one sees him saying *isvara pranidhanam va*: alternately, by surrender to the Lord. The path of devotion is apparently as efficacious as, or more than, the path of exercises. We may note here that byproducts of surrender to the deity are acceptance of the world order as divine and actions without attachment. One view of this is expressed by Abraham on Mount Moriah and Paul in his Epistle to the Galatians. Echoing these sentiments is the stanza from *mukanda mala:*

Nastha dharme na vasunicaye naiva kamopabhoge
Yadyal bhavyam bhavatu bhagavan purva karmanurupam
Tat tat prarthyam mama behumatam janma janmantarepi
Tvat padambhoruha yugagala niscala bhaktirasthu

(I have no commitment to duty, nor to the enjoyment of action and its fruits; let destiny unfold in whatever way it is to do so. My only prayer is that through the myriad happenings my devotion be to Your lotus feet.)

In this path you do not practice stilling the mind; it is an accomplishment along the way (like a Master's Degree along the way to completing a doctoral program!) It is then the business of the Lord to make sure that all goes well, if that is what goes well.

Earlier I talked about word-becoming-flesh. But what word? The spoken, linear prose-order, grammatical word is very powerful and when it becomes flesh we get houses and cities and taxes and bridges and computers and cars and mortgages. In sensitive hands, it may even yield ecology and compassion. But there is a limit to which it can climb. Like a propeller plane, which needs aerodynamic lift, the civilized linear word can rise only so high, since it needs a civilized paradigm to rise. But there is another kind of word that is not linear, not grammatical, not related to the concensus public cosmology. This is the word that is the secret word, but a word of power. It appeared as split tongues of flame to Elijah, as the burning bush to Moses, as the dove at the River Jordan and was written on the tongue of Kalidasa. It was the word about which Kalidasa wrote in the opening stanza of the *Raghu Vamsa:*

Vagarthaviva samprktau
Vagartha prati pattaye
Jagatah pitarau vande
Parvati paramesvarau

(May word and meaning abide together and assist each other to bring out significance just as *Lord Siva* and *Devi Parvati*, the progenitors of the world: to Whom adoration.)

People who know about neuroanatomy say that the brain

has a left and a right half and they function in different ways. The left brain is civilized and linear-orderly, logical and articulate; the right brain in inventive and nonlinear, inarticulate and illogical. While both halves of the brain function, some actions and activities are more left- or right-brain oriented. The words of the right brain are mute with their poetic symbol, the *pranava*, the *aum*, the sound of the essence that blew over the dark waters at the beginning of creation.

I do not know whether it is wise to localize modalities of function in either half of the brain, or whether the two halves of the brain have the functional identification as stated above. But I do see the distinction between these modalities. In the rest of this paper I use the "right" and "left" brain to identify the two modalities.

Anyone blessed with the touch of the divine either in creativity or supreme excellence in performance ("inner tennis") knows the unspoken sacred secret word. It is the subtle vibration in the quiet of the self that is the impulse of creativity. The *veda* says: *yasmin deva adhivisve nesedu* (in whom reside all the gods with their powers).

HATCHING FROM THE EGG

In everyday life we are prisoners of our culture and paradigms. Newton suggested that light is corpuscular, but others said that it is undulatory. People did experiments to decide between them and decided unanimously in terms of waves. Yet several decades later Planck and Einstein reestablished the corpuscular nature of matter. What then happens to the court that decided against corpuscular theory and the evidence assembled? When the possibility of control of automatic metabolic functions was well known, scientists paid no attention; yet once it adopted the scientific paradigm, it was a "hot" research area. In politics and international relations strange things occur showing how even wise men are in bondage.

Can we do without words? Or should we try to use words in such a manner as to survive their tyranny? Perhaps, if we listen to the words and see what they really say and use them as pointers to the actual experience, we could escape being imprisoned by them. But most of all, we should listen to the unspoken word and let the "right brain" decide whether the articulations of the "left brain" make sense.

The gentle art of nurturing creativity in the theoretical sciences and word-mode arts is to use the fragile connections that support the flow of the spontaneous from one side to the other. Any time the word-mode takes ascendance, the flow of nectar ceases. The creative writer has to go about like a hen about to lay an egg until the fully developed idea is ready to emerge. Attempts to bring it out earlier invariably fail. On the other hand, the irresponsible right brain does not keep the ideas in indefinite abeyance: and if the clerk (left brain) is not ready, the idea simply disappears. It may appear again, but then, it may not appear again.

A more satisfactory state would be one in which this relationship is more streamlined. The left brain should be directed by the right brain, however irresponsible it may seem at first sight. The pathways between these two must be strengthened and developed. A refinement and restructuring of neurophysiology should result as a sign of the evolution. Neurophysiological correlates should be measurably changed for the better. Such neurophysiological changes could induce, in turn, somatic and genetic changes that may become noticeable. Societal and interpersonal interactions would change and change for more orderliness, more *santi: antariksam santi* (let orderliness be the ambience). The individual evolution leads to species evolution and general uplift of society.

THE ENCHANTED WORLD

We spoke of correlations as a concomitant of the evolved state of mind. In physics, correlations are most important, when physical phenomena transcend the limitations of space or, more generally, there is any fragmentation. While classical physics makes the choices of conventional language, where a thing either is or is not, quantum mechanics may or may not make such a distinciton. In cases in which it does not make such a distinction we have the superposition of two possibilities. The superposition of two states is not an ignorance as to which of the two states it is; in fact, it is neither! It is a new state, a new situation altogether. Admission of such a large category of states creates a separate reality, one for which we have no word-description, but only the abstract mathematical description. Whether this comes about because classical physics is a presupposition of conventional language or the other way around, I do not know. But it appears that many scientists are persuaded to say that quantum mechanics is a theory that cannot be comprehended fully! Measurement which is vital to physics, if formulated in conventional word-language, makes bizarre statements about measurements and measurability in quantum physics. Rather than abandon the language, we abandon comprehension. A veritable bed of procrustes, indeed!

It seems to me that it is not only possible to perceive quantum superpositions directly, but we make such perceptions often. What is difficult is not the perception, but a discourse on the perception. We cannot carry on an explanation in word-language either to someone or to oneself in the internal dialogue. So, like the actors in an incident of the television serials "I Dream of Jeanie" or "Bewitched", we enter into a conspiracy to firmly deny that which cannot be verbalized.

The direct quantum mechanical perception involves the cognition of a coherence array, of which only a one-dimensional projection can be verbalized or displayed in classical measurements. Yet the array has a movement and a wholeness which is lacking in the projections, which is not only abridgement of the information but fragmentation of the system and, therefore, untrue. The language of coherent superpositions is the language of dream and poetry, of the twilight zone. Despite the fact that quantum theory is taken as the basis for understanding the structure of matter, we say we do not comprehend it. We do comprehend, but we feel embarrassed when we attempt to verbalize. It is like telling the content, ambience and import of a dream to someone who shakes his head and says, "Oh, yes, of course, I see what you mean," but you know that you are not communicating.

I strongly suspect that the superposition language of quantum mechanics comprehended as a whole is the language of the "right brain". If this were so, much of the miscommunication between left and right could be understood as a translation problem. Also, if this were indeed the case, we would have a marked increase in the mode of total perception in which superpositions are natural. As the neural pathways are developed and strengthened, as the neurophysiology is refined, not only would there be physiological correlates that can be observed, but the modality of perception, itself, should change. Dreaming and awakening, poetry and prose will no longer be strangers.

It has been the tradition that as the evolution of the mind advances, the witnessing mode of awareness would come to be established; and a sure sign of this onset is the ability to witness sleep and dream. Witnessing the dream is quite different from recalling the dream, in that you are aware of the dream mode of functioning (rather than squeezing incidents from it into a waking mode functioning), and as such represents an interpretation. Happenings take on a new softness, a gentle harmony, which is as different from the usual modes of happenings as ballet or *bharatanatyam* is to playing leap frog.

One way of referring to the quantum superposition principle is as "long range order". There is no more fragmentation and no more separation. The future and the past are no longer distant either; they become continuous with the present. Space and time become intertwined and not only in the mathematics of relativity—melody and rhythm may be seen as aspects of the same. Time is now duration without succession, development without discreteness. Time and space are no longer agents of fragmentation. One is able to transcend time and space in the same sense as in watching a play or a beloved music peformance; one is at all times and all places, yet there is no blindness; instead we find the full richness of unfolding. The *vedic* role of "every adult a priest" invokes and sustains the movement of the elements, and of Melchizadek, who is without ancestry and geneology in this timeless existence, or what Eliade calls existence in the "sacred time" as opposed to the "profane time" of ordinary existence. In myth, too, time is unfragmented and succession is not. Yet evolution and unfolding takes place.

Witnessing a state of awareness is myth and reality. Time takes on a magical quality. Everything is as it is, and yet everything is changed. Dynamics is transformation and what is transformed is the self. Superposition is modality and all is play. Becoming and being merge and time is transcended. Being-becoming is bliss beyond boundaries: it is *ananda*. This evolutionary stage is the result of deliberate and discriminating practice, the result of search for the holy grail, the wellsprings of knowledge: *anndeti abhyasat*.

SELF-REFERRAL: THE SYMBOL OF INFINITY

Evolution of mind, then, leads not only to increased abilities but to transcendence. The stuff of the living organism is the stuff of the chemical thermodynamics of open systems. But from that level it evolves and comes to have a mind of its own. When the mind emerges, options have already emerged in the domain of laws of matter. When the mind is treated as a developing open system, it, too, has a level of structure, but the flow in and out of the system is now not matter and its attributes, but natural laws themselves. The knowledge of the relative is the stuff of which the structure is the mind. What emerges when the mind develops to the point of a new level of awareness? World order is the flow in and out. The faculty of the evolved supermind is creation and dissolution of worlds.

What is the emergent reality? In this state of awareness, universes are created and destroyed, *pralaya* and *sristi* are nothing unusual. What is the stuff of this functioning? It must be knowledge and the functioning entity must be the embodiment of knowledge itself. This level of functioning is the traditional notion of the *guru*, the remover of darkness (*guru*), in whom are united all the insights and modalities. The *guru* is the ultimate in that causality; time and space are transcended. The long range order introduced by the quantum mechanical perspective finds its fulfillment in the total transcendence of all events and all causation. So it is said:

Virastha sarvasandeham
Ekikrtya sudarsanam
Rahasyam yo darsayati
Bhajami gurumisvaram

(Removing all doubts, welding together the beautiful vision and thus enabling the vision of secret knowledge: to that principle of knowledge my adoration!)

and

Jagrati yatra bhaghavan guru cakravarti
Visva sthiti pralaya nataka nityasaksi

(Functions there the principle of knowledge as the maintainer of natural order, eternal witness to the drama of maintenance and dissolution of worlds),

and finally,

Guruh brahma guruh visnu
Guruh devo maheswarah
Guruh saksat parabrahma
Tasmai sri guruve namah

(The principle of knowledge is the Creator, the Maintainer, the Destroyer. It is the Absolute verity. To Such my adoration.)

That is the evolution of mind.

The Science and Knowing
of Higher Consciousness

What I would like to do here is to raise three questions and make some brief remarks about them. These remarks are intended for discussion and are not meant to be definite conclusions or assertions.

How does higher consciousness relate to reality?

There are two different senses in which the idea of higher consciousness is understood, with different implications for the practice and theory of evolution of consciousness. One sense is that a spiritually advanced person (which is more or less synonymous with a person with a higher consciousness) is aware of an order of reality which is *other* than the one an ordinary person is aware of. (Whether this order is within a person or outside him is a further differentiation—dividing, in general, the Hindu tradition from the Christian.) The other sense of higher consciousness, in contrast to the first one, is more inclusive. It is not another reality that a spriritually advanced person is aware of, but the *same* reality is perceived by him much more clearly than by an ordinary person. It is possible to reconcile these two views in theory and by scriptural authority; but in practice they have been held by quite different schools. Both of these have been highly developed and practiced in India, but the latter view seems to have departed from India with Buddhism nearly a millennium ago.

This issue is more than merely academic. Ramakrishna, for example, may be polite to a Zen master who might make one of his delightful, and pregnant, remarks like "Trees are trees, and mountains are mountains," but he is likely to find it puzzling to find this statement regarded as a mark of spiritual vision of high order. I think it is more than a matter of mere temperament. Most of the Indian tradition (excepting Buddhism), both theoretically and practically, is less interested in what is here and now and much more interested in what is there and then—in some realm "beyond the beyond", as I once heard a Swami remark. (Hindu temples surely are the only places of worship in the whole world where one may be justified in concluding that spirituality is indifferent to cleanliness, if not actually opposed to it.)

This fundamental difference between the two meanings of higher consciousness, which is classically exemplified by the opposition between Buddhism and Brahmanism, is represented in contemporary times by Krishnamurti's revolt against Theosophy. One of them has a tendency to get more and more austere, inward and nontheistic, and the other one tends to become more and more extravagant, outward and polytheistic —filled with endless gods, angels or saints. There have been many bold attempts at integrating these two tendencies in the past—Tibetan Vajrayan Buddhism is an example—but the synthesis needs people of great being to contain these contradictions in creative tension, and usually goes one way or another in the absence of such people. As far as I am aware, there have been only two major contemporary systematic attempts at such integration, namely by Sri Aurobindo and by Gurdjieff. This cannot be said of Raman or Krishnamurti— to take only two examples of men of great being and vision.

Is THERE EVOLUTION OF CONSCIOUSNESS?

The most important objection raised by the traditionalists to Sri Aurobindo, Gurdjieff, Teilhard de Chardin and others, is that the whole idea of evolution is *psychologistic* and that from the point of view of orthodox metaphysics, such as Shankara's Vedanta, there can be no *evolution* of consciousness. What is at issue is the whole relationship between time and eternity (in the sense of a dimension which is independent of time, and not in the sense of being everlasting), and between becoming (maya) and being (Brahman). This is related with one of the classical objections to *Sankhya* as well: namely the relationship between prakriti and purusha. In modern terms, the question is directly germane to any intercourse between physics (including psychology) and metaphysics and also to discussions about means and ends.

It is occasionally said in traditional literature, and has been forcefully stressed by Krishnamurti in contemporary times, that there is no path to truth. There is no method, technique or way by which one can come to truth. The reason is simply that all methods and ways operate in time whereas truth (or being or Consciousness) is timeless. Perhaps this is what the Protestant Christians mean by saying that salvation is not by *work* but only by grace.

From the perspective of someone whose consciousness is situated in the absolute, all movement along the way or even the very idea of a why is illusory. Thus, only a deluded consciousness can think of following a path. Nevertheless, from this side of the great veil, the human situation in these circumstances appears quite hopeless. A totally radical detachment of being from becoming inevitably leads, in the hands of intellectuals, to a thorough devaluation of the whole world of space and time (Samsara). In the case of the sage himself, whose perspective is of being because his whole being is in fact merged with it, such a danger is not so manifest. It appears that for him the usual intellectual contradictions do not hold, including the one between being and becoming, and he acts as he must according to the whole. But for a theoretical mind, metaphysical thought without the corresponding organic transformation and vision is bound to yield puerile speculations.

CAN SCIENCE LEAD TO TRUTH

A part of the consideration here is the same as in the previous section. Since science is a product of the movement of thought which operates only in time, how can it lead to Truth which is timeless? This question, however, applies equally to rituals, arts and science.

There are some specific considerations with respect to science. I have tried to point out elsewhere (see specifically my articles in *Dalhousie Review* 1975-76 and in *Manthan* 1978) that modern science proceeds with several philosophical presuppositions about the nature of man, reality and knowledge. I shall mention only one of these presuppositions here, namely, the assumed separation between being and knowing. What sort of a person a scientist is is irrelevant to the kind of knowledge he produces. Thus, his knowledge—of anything whatever—remains inevitably external. One consequence of this is a denial of interiority not only in the so-called inanimate objects but even in human beings (as is the case in scientific behavioristic psychology). Another consequence is the urge to control and manipulate what one investigates and from which one is separated by assumption.

Now, it seems to me that there is something quite absurd about investigating "higher" consciousness with an attitude and methodology of controlling it. If it is really higher, how can it let itself be controlled by the lower consciousness? Surely, the question is not how we can appropriate higher consciousness for our ends—however sane they are, like averting a nuclear holocaust—but more how we can be appropriated by higher consciousness for its ends. That is why there is so much emphasis in mystical literature on surrender of the ego.

It has been stressed from ancient times that the knowing involved in approaching being is of a very different kind from that involved in subject-object knowing. It is the transformational knowing which is needed in which knowing and being are intimately connected. According to Parmenides, as well as Plotinus, being and knowing are the same. This point is very much emphasized in the Upanishads where it is said that a knower of Brahman becomes Brahman (*Brahmanvid Brahmaiva bhavati*).

The question, however, remains: What, if any, is the relationship between science and the perception of higher consciousness?

Order and Openness

The concept of *order* and the concept of *openness* have become poles around which an increasingly passionate debate seems to have gathered. The debate which has till now involved philosophers, educators, and scientists, has currently broadened into an argument over the definition of that most fundamental of human attributes, *consciousness*, and a concern for how best to preserve and enhance it.

The purpose of this paper is not to force a choice in favor of one side or another but to evaluate the issues involved historically and to suggest a humanistic technique for resolving the conflict equitably.

The concept of order, which not too long ago was considered a marvelous heuristic device for the interpretation of man and nature,[1] is now the object of considerable intellectual abuse. "Order" is considered to be a closed concept that is rigid, coercive, artificial, and static. Accordingly, to use the concept of order as a guide to human life and action is said to be dehumanizing. The concept of "openness", by contrast, is admired as a more flexible, free, natural, and dynamic guide to the understanding of man and the shaping of our environment. Humanizing man and the world is understood, therefore, to follow from any process which increases the degree of openness available.

The biological theory of evolution is frequently used to validate the elements of this comparison and to demonstrate the advantages of openness over order.[2] Evolution implies change, and the conclusion is intuitively obvious that those processes which are open to change are favored over those systems whose closed characteristics make adaptive change difficult or impossible. But the theory of evolution, even as Darwin left it, is not intuitively obvious. It seems sensible, therefore, to suggest that any analogies drawn from it be drawn carefully. Moreover, it is especially necessary when making these analogies to distinguish between the process of change and the phenomena which are changed. It is through an examination of this distinction that the effort to reconcile advocates of the concepts of order and openness will be made.

The theory of evolution is intellectually breathtaking not just because of its universality but because of its epistemological uniqueness. The evolutionary theory seeks to explain phenomena systemically and dynamically, to explain changing phenomena entirely on the basis of internal considerations. Evolution shows how the interactions between things taking place over time account for the creation of new things. As a philosophical construct, it is almost tautological. When all is said and done, for instance, the explanation of life offered by the theory of evolution is as self-contained, self-justifying, and self-sustaining as a work of art.

Now to explain something without reference to something else, for Western philosophy at least, is almost impossible. Typically, the Western explanations of anything are offered in terms of logical deductions drawn from some general concept which is assumed to be known already and to have an *a priori* existence independent of the object being explained. To have defied that convention was a real source of Darwin's originality and a major cause of the misunderstandings his work suffered. But the theory of evolution makes no appeals to outside causes or forces. After Darwin, the goal was to explain the origin and development of life in its many forms strictly according to the interaction of material forces. It is an heroic goal and one which must be kept in mind by anyone seeking to use the theory of evolution as a model in the debate over the concepts of order and openness and their impact on our understanding of the problem of consciousness.

The one academic discipline at hand which shares the epistemological demands of the theory of evolution is history. To be sure, in the contemporary intellectual world, history occupies a very humble position. Technically it is defined as the arrangement of specific factual data into a chronological sequence that "tells a story".[3] Unlike the physical and social sciences, history offers no laws and formulates no generalizations. In fact, because history proclaims the inviolate individuality of each human personality, professional historians insist that no such thing as an historical order is possible. As most of its practitioners describe it, history is the most open process imaginable. Nevertheless, history is not as antiintellectual as its critics maintain, for while it may deny itself the pleasure of a system it does not rest on a profound philosophical proposition. History ultimately claims that man can understand himself by learning the story of his own development. Combined with the biological theory of evolution, history promises to show how thinking matter, on the basis of its own experiences, came to think.[4]

History, then, is a process. As such it is dynamic and open-ended. But a process requires something to process, something to move through time and change in indeterminable ways. In the case of history that which grows and changes is human consciousness.[5] Consciousness is to a large extent the product and the property of human communities. Consciousness begins in self-awareness and develops through the effort we must make to understand the self we see reflected in the eyes and actions of others. Consciousness is the byproduct of relationships—it develops through human interaction. Thus each self is developed, made more aware and deeper, by its contact with others which it similarly stimulates and molds. To produce these effects, a medium of interaction—"culture"—is necessary.

Culture is the structure through which mutually developmental information is exchanged between individuals. But although culture is often the object of change, it is not itself a process, it is not open. Culture, on the contrary, is a system of order men impose on themselves and their environments. By definition, it is closed. Culture is a more or less highly regularized structure organizing knowledge, communication, and behavior into a unique pattern which seeks to perpetuate itself.

To the advocates of openness, culture stands as the principal obstacle uprooting and corrupting man. From Rousseau to Roszack, culture in its anthropological sense has been seen as an artificial force narrowing and circumscribing human consciousness.[6] Culture, the advocates of openness tell us, frustrates the human potential by inhibiting the full, rounded, and expanding qualities of consciousness. By distinguishing between peoples, culture isolates them from one another; by focusing on man's mental and emotional drives, it restricts the range of those capacities; by imposing artificial and incomplete world-pictures, culture denies people access to the full range of natural and intellectual experience; and by limiting man's imaginative capacities, culture restricts evolutionary opportunities, risking the biological survival of the species by prohibiting the development of ever enlarging spiritual possibilities.

From the vantage point of this paper, however, the anti-cultural argument misrepresents the process of historical development by neglecting the significance of the individual steps which make up that process. To begin with, the anti-cultural argument fails to appreciate the profound intellectual contribution made by culture to the growth of consciousness. The key goal of consciousness is understanding—of the self, the world, and others—and culture is what makes understanding possible. Without culture, it is conceivable that things could be known but not that they could be understood, for understanding means the ability to place a fact within the context of an idea, to relate knowledge logically to a generalization.[7] Facts, even physical phenomena, are not in themselves meaningful. At best they are simply there. Meaning and understanding lie in the web of values and ideas in which the facts and phenomena are located, in the cultural structures inside our heads. That is as true in simple societies as in complex ones. According to the historian of religions, Mircea Eliade, archaic men were only capable of recognizing the existence of phenomena when they were able to place those phenomena contextually into their existent mythical structures.[8] For archaic men, in other words, nothing was real until it was mythic. Jean-Paul Sartre has reconfirmed this insight for contemporaries. In *Nausea* Sartre shows that when myth—the accepted set of cultural generalizations with which we usually live—loses its hold upon the minds of men we cannot see the world whole. Instead we see a plethora of parts, each isolated, each distinct, all meaninglessly there in a disordered equality that makes us sick with despair.[9] Thus cultures are the supreme intellectual accomplishments of men in groups. They are the mental constructs that organize life and give it meaning. But every culture is unique because the organizing structures cultures impose upon experience are the results of particular circumstances. The meanings and values people find in life, therefore, vary from group to group.

This is an important point and it needs to be made directly. Comparative analysis of people in different cultures finds repeatedly that while they can all find meaning in life they do not find the same meaning. Meaning is not universal, although the quest for it may be. The meaning of meaning must therefore be clarified. Meaning is the result of our capacity to place reality in an intellectual context. Meaning is not found "out there", in a platonic form or eternally given, but "in here", in the human consciousness. Meaning is a human creation. It is something we attribute to experience by imposing goals and purposes on events. Perhaps the best way to emphasize this point is to briefly recall the philosophical implications of contemporary physics. As Bohr, Heisenberg, Born, and the other theorists associated with Quantum Physics, developed twentieth century science they revolutionized its traditional assumptions. Earlier theorists, e.g. Ernst Mach, had described science as an exercise in which the realities of external nature were "mimetically reproduced in thought.[10] Science thus copies nature, which was thought to exist independently of the men who studied it.[11] But Bohr and his associates clearly demonstrated that the techniques used to study nature carried with them philosophical presuppositions which conditioned the picture of nature that emerged. Science, in J. Bronowski's phrase, does not contemplate the world but "tackles it."[12] Consequently it is absurd to suppose that we can ever find what exists naturally. Scientists create our understanding of experience generally, by fabricating "laws which organize data in logically coherent forms." Of course, the laws must be tested experimentally. But since the experiments are based on the epistemological assumptions of the laws they are designed to test, ultimate confirmation of the truthfulness of scientific laws inevitably lies in a constantly receding future.

In organizing life and making it meaningful, cultures play a role analogous to games. The individual component part of any sport—running, striking a ball, moving a carved object—are in themselves meaningless. Yet these same actions within the game structure become charged with meaning.[13] The marked-off playing surface, the rules of play, the time constraints—all combine to isolate the game experience and, by framing the action, to give it intense significance. Hemingway's analysis of the bull ring reveals the same characteristics most vividly. There is obviously, said Hemingway, no ultimate or final purpose in fighting bulls. Yet once the participants have entered the arena, a space so rigorously dimensioned that it is virtually holy, every gesture, every step is moral or immoral, beautiful or ugly, profound or trivial.[14] Extended to the whole of human experience, culture becomes the game everybody plays. It alone can give order and meaning to our lives.

The implications of this argument are clear and still, in the later twentieth century, frightening. Man stands alone; he must account for himself and to himself. Yet, if thought through, there is much in this position which is life-enhancing. To be sure, in the past man's existential predicament was the cause of great despair. According to the slightly older and more individualistic approach to the problem of consciousness associated with Freud, Heiddegger and Sartre, consciousness arose from man's awareness of his inevitable death. Psychotic or inauthentic man reacted against that awareness, constructing cultural mechanisms designed to conceal or overcome the reality of death.[15] At first these self-deceiving mechanisms could be simple because of the limited experience of the peoples who embraced them. But new experiences tended to undermine the acceptability of early mythopoetic structures, thus reviving man's dreadful realization of the temporary quality of his life. Successive efforts to overcome this condition led to increasingly complex cultural structures, each of which contributed to the further development of consciousness. In the eighteenth and nineteenth centuries, modern Western science challenged tradition by attempting to explain life strictly according to existential phenomena. Consciousness, it would seem, had achieved a breadth of knowledge and a rigor of understanding adequate to the needs of our existential predicament. However, the form of modern science used as a substitute for the traditional explanations of man and his place in the world was not without its unattractive characteristics.

The theory of evolution as Darwin and Huxley propounded it, for instance, was a brutal and mechanistic conception which reduced life to a meaningless struggle determined completely by physical forces in which there was no room for freedom, beauty, or spirituality. In a sense, this effort to explain consciousness on its own terms was self-defeating, since the explanation rendered the phenomena of consciousness meaningless. Contemporary science, however, paints a very different picture of the world. The place man can create for himself in this new world is much more attractive, characterized as it is by the attributes of freedom, creativity, and beauty. This is a world, as Sir James Jeans said, fit for men to live in.[16]

According to the contemporary scientific view of existence, reality is made up ultimately of extremely small elements, which may be either wavelike or particulate, whose interactions are too complex to be specified exactly. Consequently, whatever happens in this world can only be described in terms of probability statements. This limitation on scientific knowledge once distressed humanists who, at the same time, of course, were denouncing the older scientific world view for its mechanical determinism. But we cannot have it both ways. If the world is determined rigidly by mechanical forces, we can know it completely but at the cost of our humanity. If we want to preserve some area in which the concept of humanity remains meaningful, we must give up any expectation of knowing the world completely. Science has chosen the second path. Humanists should welcome the opportunity to explore its significance.

Applied to the problem of life and the theory of evolution, contemporary science suggests that life originated "accidentally". Life, that is, resulted from the chance interaction of basic elements. The odds against such an event occurring are very large but not prohibitive, especially in an infinite universe. Thus, no mechanical process determined the necessity of life. In the words of Jacques Monod, life did not have to be but it has a "right" to be.[17] "Freedom", at least in a restricted sense, is therefore present at the very origins of life. But that is not all. In the contemporary scientific view, life is characterized not just by its physical and mechanical elements as it was in Darwin's day. Instead life is now seen to be characterized by its particular structure, by the arrangement of its physical components. Now structure is not a physical phenomenon; it is a concept—and an esthetic concept at that. Life is therefore characterized by its elemental beauty and its essential freedom, attributes which must be fundamental to any humanistic view. But life is not "open". As a structure life is a system of order: it is "negative entropy".[18]

It may be possible to translate some of these scientific themes into historical terms. Here, of course, the structural systems to be studied are the cultures men have built. The origin of these cultures is best understood in very specific terms whenever any actual historical research is involved.[19] But, for our purposes, we can define them as systems of organization produced out of a complex of human and environmental factors moving unpredictably in a manner similar to the "Brownian Motion". Apparently men build cultures as they invent games or scientific theories, by a more or less spontaneous creative act which arranges the existing real world phenomena into an acceptable shape. What soon becomes critical, from a highly general perspective, is that the culture produced will be, as Durkheim found by studying the Australian aborigines, an extended image of the social and physical environment in which people live.[20] The test of its acceptability is that the shape incorporates all known phenomena into a functional system which will enable its creators to understand themselves, live in one another's company, and exploit the world successfully. The exciting part is that the arrangement, once made, takes on special attributes. It is not seen as a human creation but as an eternal given: culture becomes cosmology in the minds of the people who possess it. Cultural space is privileged space, just as game theory suggests, and the rules of the culture direct and justify the lives of the people living in it.

Cultural orders thus take the world as it is perceived and treat that perception as if it were an eternal and unchangeable truth. They seek to preserve the world as it is known and understood. They seek, moreover, to keep the world in that same fixed circumstance, so that succeeding generations will be able to live as the founding generations did. Fortunately that is an unattainable goal in most cases. Culture wars against the second law, but the effort is almost always doomed to eventual failure. Too many external forces, both natural and human, work against cultural efforts to freeze time. Moreover, few cultures are ever so effectively adapted to their environments or so powerful in their efforts to dominate the minds of their children that they can prevent all change from taking place. Eventually the small variations which occur can add up to produce significant departures from the original cultural type at which the society aimed. Finally, contemporary ecological theory suggests that even when a culture is highly fitted to the environmental niche it occupies, the mere operations of its adaptive behaviors will gradually transform the environment until it is quite different from the one to which the cultural organism had initially been adapted. Thus the process of change will continue despite the fact that the medium through which it works, culture, is designed to prevent changes from taking place.

Culture is the set of relationships governing man's behavior in the world. The culture and its environment must, therefore, be symbiotically related, and by attributing a transcendent value to the culture that balance is maintained indefinitely. But not permanently. Eventually the symbiosis breaks down. When that happens a condition prevails that historians call an "era of transition". To describe the "open" situation which results from an era of transition Durkheim coined the term "anomie".[21] If the advocates of openness were right in extolling the values of this condition, transition eras should appear in history as highly admirable states in which great creativity occurred. Using examples from Western history, such as the Hellenistic era, the Renaissance, or the scientific revolution, that appears to be the case—to historians. But Huizinga pointed out that to the contemporaries of these mighty eras the present rarely seemed creative and progressive.[22] On the contrary, to people doomed to live in what the Chinese sage called "interesting times" the present more often seems characterized by decay. Most people, it seems, do not experience change positively, or even neutrally. Most see change negatively, as the decline and death of the world they know and love and at best its displacement by some new cultural configuration which is perceived as markedly inferior.

According to the psychologist Erich Fromm, most people find the trauma of living in an era of transition overwhelming. Instead of welcoming the openness available in anomic states where anything quite literally goes, they seek to "escape from freedom" by creating new systems of order.[23] They may, to be sure, attack old systems but not because the old systems are oppressive. On the contrary, in transition eras old systems are attacked because they are weak, because they cannot control the environments in which people live. Attacks on the older systems of order are designed as a kind of cultural housecleaning which removes obstacles to the creation, not of more open systems but of systems capable of ordering the world effectively.

To the Swiss historian Jacob Burckhardt the proponents of these new systems were "terrible simplifiers". They sought to substitute for the confused plurality of their own day an ideal system based on some elementary principle which would resolve all the problems facing them in real life. Often their efforts are very bloody. But periodically the "terrible simplifiers" will hit upon some device which turns out to be so effective that it will not only resolve their own psychological difficulties but the anomic conditions of their time as well. They will, in other words, find a suitable substitute for the old culture and lay a foundation upon which the new culture can be based. Perhaps the clearest example of this process can be found in the scientific revolution of the seventeenth century. As

Koestler pointed out, those who made that revolution were "sleepwalkers": they knew neither where they were going nor how to get there.[24] They functioned like human equivalents of the particles in Brownian Motion. But by ruthlessly reducing all existence to matter in motion treated mathematically these sleepwalkers laid a base so strong that the whole of modern culture and the Industrial Revolution could be built upon it. They resolved the moral and social chaos of the transition era by restoring order on a new foundation.

To many people the loss of traditional values, especially the spiritual values, associated with the seventeenth century scientific revolution constitutes an immeasurable loss to civilization. The efforts of the proponents of openness, insofar as they are aimed at disrupting the classical scientific order, can be seen as efforts to retrieve these lost values. But as the brief discussion of the second scientific revolution mentioned above suggested, science has already transformed itself into a discipline which now has a much more receptive attitude towards the essential spiritual values—mind, freedom, and beauty. To oppose classical modern science, therefore, is to oppose a ghost long since exorcised by science itself. To oppose contemporary science, on the other hand, is to run the risk of opposing a set of ideas whose very essence is the expression of human consciousness raised to its highest form.

Studying the steps by which the second scientific revolution took place is instructive. Scientists did not start out to overthrow the classical scientific world view. Instead, men like Planck, Einstein, and Bohr remained loyal disciples of the Galilean and Newtonian world view. In the beginning of this century their goal was simply to complete that world view and, perhaps, correct a few anomalies which recent research had discovered in it.[25] Their goal, as they frequently expressed it, was to carry out the more exact measurements of the scientific world machine sketched in the seventeenth century. But as they made the measurements more exact they realized that certain of the fundamental assumptions of science were unattainable. Einstein, for example, showed that no absolute frame of reference from which to view the universe was attainable.[26] But the work of Bohr was much more radical. With his disciples Bohr showed that the very basis of classical nature, the physical world itself, was a much more problematical reality than scientists had previously realized. Through his analysis of the act of experiment, Bohr realized that the physical world, at least as we know it, was not the crudely material phenomenon classical science had supposed. The world as we know it is the world as our explorations of it make it appear.[27] The scientific observer observes his own mind when he observes the world. The fundamental stuff of the world is therefore "mind stuff".[28] All this sounds very revolutionary, and it is. But the critical point to remember in tracing the events by which this revolution took place is that all these discoveries, radical as they are, took place because scientists remained fiercely loyal to the essentials of the scientific order, the method of science as it had been conventionally defined. The most fundamental discoveries took place when excruciatingly exact experiments were unable to measure either the drift or to determine the constitution of the fundamental particles. These failures required scientists to rethink the meaning of experiment and with it the basic assumptions of science. Moreover, the most radical conclusions resulted when scientists refused, despite their newly won appreciation of its limitations, to abandon the method of experimentation. The Copenhagen interpretation of Quantum Physics produced a new definition of science and nature because it insisted on strictly observing the requirements of the scientific method despite the recognition that the scientific method and the philosophical presuppositions it made were both inherently limited.

Evolutionary progress took place, then, not because a closed order—the system of classical science—was rejected in favor of a more open one but because a refined order was able to sharpen scientific wits to the point that they were able to produce a new order which was even more profound. Contemporary science does not overthrow or ever displace classical science; it broadens and deepens classical science. Contemporary science makes classical science a special case, a system for viewing part of nature that is true only in this limited sense. Now it seems possible that an extended analysis of this situation might well produce a model by which to greatly improve our understanding of cultural change. There is no room to do that in this paper, but a few words on the subject would be appropriate.

If the foregoing summary is correct, the second scientific revolution took place because the implications of classical science, worked out in full detail, revealed themselves to be inadequate. New Ideas needed to be generated. The remarkable thing about the process, however, is that it is continuous —radically new ideas develop through the use of conventional methods and assumptions. Even when the conventional methods fail and the conventional goals are revealed as unattainable the conventional scientific rigor is retained—the men at Copenhagen, for instance, remained ardent advocates of Machian positivism long after they had abandoned Mach's effort to mimetically replicate reality in thought. It seems highly unlikely that the progress made during those years could ever have been made without the original scientific method, assumptions, and goals. At least we know that the Quantum Theory, as it now stands in all its refined glory and specificity, was never produced elsewhere without having been worked through the legacy of modern scientific thought. Clearly, therefore, it seems reasonable to suppose that the experience of classical science was essential to the revolutionary development of contemporary science. The process of growth resulting from the maturation of classical science was a prerequisite to the invention of twentieth century science.

CONCLUSION

Order and openness are, therefore, not mutually exclusive factors in the world of historical development. If openness be taken as the ultimate aim of a human consciousness made deeper and broader, then it is a goal which can only be achieved through the step-by-step succession of ordering systems, each one of which contributes to the process by which the ultimate goal is attained. Evolution teaches us that nothing exists whole and automatically, like Venus. Consciousness, too, must grow and develop. Its growth may be a process, but its process passes through stages, which are systems of order. In fact, according to Ernst Casirer, order precedes consciousness, cosmology precedes introspection, we organize our knowledge of the outside world before we use that knowledge to understand ourselves.[29] Yet evolution also teaches us that the conventional Western concepts of cause and effect are inadequate tools for understanding the organic relationships which exist in natural processes, where every effect becomes a cause and vice versa. Thus when we apply the patterned knowledge we have of the outside world to ourselves, we develop heightened tools with which to reexamine the knowledge we have of the outside world. And when we increase our knowledge of the outside world we learn more about ourselves. But without the pattern, nothing can be known: "The innocent eye," says Ernst Gombrich, "sees nothing."[30]

Now the pinnacle of scientific knowledge in the twentieth century combines evolutionary theory with Quantum Physics. In its fullest flowering only the esoteric langauge of mathematics can describe the results of that union, where cause and effect reflect back and forth on one another in a self-sustained and indeterminable process. Understanding the world in these terms strains the limits of our inherited consciousness. But we can apply that knowledge to our understanding of man through the epistemology of history. Seen in these terms, history is the process through which man made himself and the medium through which man can understand himself. Through history man sees himself imaged in the mirror of his own experience.[31] History offers us a humanistic definition of humanity and a mode of organizing that definition which is a process. This is a great advancement, one which the Western philosophers have been struggling to articulate for over two hundred years. It requires mental discipline, for it foreswears the aid and comfort of external forces invented for the sole purpose of explaining the previously inexplicable. History, like the theory of evolution, obliges us to make all explanations through the operation of internal causes. History, literally, makes man a work of art in his own eyes.[32]

Moreover, an historical explanation offers us an escape from the self-alienating consequences of traditional definitions of man. In a sense, defining man as the creature of God offers us some comfort—the comfort of knowing where we came from. But, as Feuerbach pointed out, that comfort is purchased at the expense of our own spiritual welfare in an ultimate sense, for when we attribute the creative power to God we despoil ourselves of our own most cherished capacities. History offers a more organic definition of man as the product of his own actions. Of course, man's powers are not equal to God's, but that is their greatest virtue. For if we are God's creatures, we must be judged by God's standards, standards which are by definition unattainable by men. We can be at home with an historical understanding of ourselves since it recognizes the limits of our capacities in the past: historically man is judged by human standards, since they are the only ones allowed in a positivistic sense. But those standards are still higher than the ones developed during Darwin's era, for man may have originated in matter in motion but through the growth of consciousness he has risen above the brute limits of material forces. Man, viewed historically, may be lower than the angels but he is higher than the molecules. And the developmental process goes on, for the understanding of what we are, gained by reflecting on the knowledge of how we got to be that way, becomes the stimulus for further growth. Cause and effect, mirroring back and forth on themselves internally in man's consciousness of his past, exchange roles in the most sublime evolutionary manner.

Through history, the order people see in the world becomes a human order. But if Durkheim is right, the order people see is their own world abstracted and universalized into a cosmos. Reality thereby becomes perfected, and perfected it becomes a challenge to further growth. The cosmological vision derived from experience becomes the idea at which future action must aim. Put in ecological terms, the system of order derived from the world becomes the stimulus for the gradual further transformation of the world. Order is man's way of adapting to a particular historical niche. By adapting to that niche he changes it, forcing himself to develop new systems of order, and each new system of order represents a growth of consciousness. Eventually consciousness must become universal, and history, despite its athletic denial of all but cultural causation, is the vehicle by which that development can take place. For the vision of history if the vision of humanity, of the whole past time, and that vision perfected into an order is global in its scope. If the human mind, as Hegel said, is the organ by which matter becomes conscious of itself, then it becomes the vehicle by which man and nature are defined, for what man says he is nature knows itself to be.

NOTES

1.   Paul G. Kuntz (ed.), *Concept of Order* (Seattle: University of Washington Press, 1968).

2.   Michael J. Grady and David E. Johnson, "The Brain, Evolution and the Purposes of Evolution," *Proceedings of the Fifth International Conference on Improving University Teaching* (London: 1979): 601ff.

3.   Roland N. Stromberg and Paul K. Conkin, *The Heritage and Challenge of History* (New York: Dodd, Mead and Co., 1971).

4.   Giambattista Vico, *The New Science* (Ithaca: Cornell University Press, 1968).

5.   Julian Jaynes, *The Origin of Consciousness in the Breakdown of the Bicameral Mind* (Boston: Houghton, Mifflin, 1976).

6.   Theodore Roszak, *The Making of a Counter Culture* (Garden City: Doubleday and Co., 1969).

7.   Carl G. Hempel, "The Function of General Laws in History," in Patrick Gardiner (ed.), *Theories of History* (Glencoe: The Free Press, 1959), pp. 344-356.

8.   Mircea Eliade, *Cosmos and History* (New York: Harper Torchbooks, 1954).

9.   Jean-Paul Sartre, *Nausea*, trans. L. Alexander (New York: New Directions, 1959).

10.   Ernst Mach, *Popular Scientific Lectures*, trans. T. O. McCormack (Chicago: The Open Court, 1910), p. 193.

11.   Erwin Schrodinger, *Nature and the Greeks* (Cambridge: Cambridge University Press, 1954), p. 94.

12.   J. Bronowski, *The Common Sense of Science* (London: Heineman, 1951), p. 104.

13.   Roger Callois, *Man, Play and Games*, trans. M. Barosh (New York: Free Press, 1961).

14.   Irving Howe, *A World More Attractive* (Freeport: Books for Libraries, 1970).

15.   Norman O. Brown, *Life Against Death* (New York: Random House, 1959).

16.   James Jeans, *Physics and Philosophy* (Ann Arbor: University of Michigan Press, 1965), p. 216.

17.   Jacques Monod, *Chance and Necessity*, trans. A. Wainhouse (New York: A. A. Knopf, 1971), p. 44.

18.   Erwin Schrodinger, *What Is Life?* (Cambridge: Cambridge University Press, 1967), p. 75.

19.   Rushton Coulborn, *The Origin of Civilized Society* (Princeton: Princeton University Press, 1959).

20.   Emile Durkheim, *The Elementary Forms of the Religious Life* (New York: Collier Books, 1961).

21.   Emile Durkheim, *On Suicide*, trans. J.A. Spaulding and G. Simpson (Glencoe: The Free Press, 1951).

22.   J. Huizinga, *The Waning of the Middle Ages* (Garden City: Anchor Books, 1954).

23.   Erich Fromm, *Escape from Freedom* (New York: Avon Books, 1965).

24.   Arthur Koestler, *The Sleepwalkers* (New York: Grosset and Dunlop, 1959).

25.   Barbara Lovett Cline, *Men Who Made a New Physics* (New York: New American Library, 1965).

26.   J. Bronowski, *The Ascent of Man* (Boston: Little Brown, 1973), p. 249.

27.   Werner Heisenberg, *Physics and Philosophy* (New York: Harper Torch Books, 1958), pp. 70, 75; Hermann Weyl, *The Open World* (New Haven: Yale University Press, 1932), p. 54; W. N. Sullivan, *Contemporary Mind* (London: Humphrey Toulmin, 1934), pp. 152, 632.

28.   Arthur Eddington, *The Nature of the Physical World* (Ann Arbor: University of Michigan Press, 1963), p. 276.

29.   Ernst Cassirer, *An Essay on Man: An Introduction to the Philosophy of Human Culture* (New Haven: Yale University Press, 1944), pp. 3-4.

30.   Quoted in Stanley Burnshaw, *The Seamless Webb: Language-Thinking; Creature-Knowledge; Art-Experience* (London: Allen Lane, 1970), p. 20.

31.   J. Huizinga, "A Definition of the Concept of History," in R. Klibansky and H.J. Patton (eds.), *Philosophy and History: Essays Presented to Ernst Cassirer* (New York: Harper Torch Books, 1963), pp. 1-10.

32.   José Ortega y Gassett, *History as a System*, trans. H. Weyl (New York: W.W. Norton, 1942), pp. 203, 217, 231.

Consciousness and the Idea of Progress

Let me speak mostly about the transformation of the idea of progress in our day. Here was one of the sweeping conceptual ideas that seized hold of Western man's imagination, especially from the sixteenth century Renaissance and the seventeenth century scientific awakening onwards. For close to five hundred years the idea prevailed that man could "extend his empire" over nature, as Bacon wrote; that he could improve his lot on earth—the human condition, in Malraux's phrase—and expect his situation and that of his children and their children to be constantly improving. Man could himself move toward infinite perfectibility, as writers like Condoreet liked to believe. Through the nineteenth century, and as the twentieth century dawned, the belief still predominated. Democratic institutions, self-government, constitutions, national independence had spread in the West. True, the colonial world remained under the firm hands of Western conquerors who had extended their sway in some early modern centuries—the "age of Vasco da Gama" (Panikkar). But that too could be resolved one day. The European tutelage would end, the *mission civilisatrice* would have accomplished his purpose, and the white man's burden laid down. The triumphs of science were breathtaking as were the advances in the technology, communication, public health, education, literacy, material wealth and human well-being. Why should the twentieth century not be the greatest century of all, with all humankind on the threshold of advancing achievement and greatness?

But at some point in the twentieth century the idea of progress began to falter. History recorded in this century two cataclysmic world wars, a global depression, cruel dictatorships, revolutions that lost their pristine liberating impulse and turned into brutal repression, human enslavement, organized attempts at genocide for a time, the ruins of an industrial society throughout most of Europe, a peace that in 1945 led quickly to a cold war and then to hot wars in South-East Asia. True, the two world wars so weakened the older imperial powers that they could no longer rule the colonial world and a great outburst of national movements led to independence for close to a hundred new nations, large and small. The problems of their peoples—economic, social, political—did not cease with independence, nor did independence and self-government lead to genuine participatory democracy, but at least they were free to govern themselves and make their own mistakes.

And what of science? Science had moved forward along with its partner technology to harness new sources of energy, to tap the secrets of the microcosm and the macrocosm, of the atom and of the galaxies. At the same time it had unleashed hitherto unprecedented forces of destruction with a potential even for global annihilation. The advances of modern medicine, with penicillin, sulfa drugs, the victory over poliomyelitis, were tremendous. But new types of illnesses and ailments of a mental and psychological nature accompanied the strains and stresses of modern life and modernization; psychiatry and psychoanalysis were hard put to it to cope with neuroses on a wholesale scale—the *angst* of the modern age. Technology and industry meanwhile were discovered to be exhausting the natural resources of the earth, a mere planet with limited resources indeed of soil, minerals, even oxygen. The smokestacks of Pittsburgh, Manchester and Delhi, once thought to be the symbols of progress, were now seen as symbols of pollution.

People began questioning the great secular faith of modern times, faith in the idea of progress. They asked whether some new kind of relationship between man and nature—a partnership, a harmony perhaps, long known in other *Weltanschauung*—was not preferable to the Baconian, indeed Faustian, human "conquest" of nature. Young people, especially, began questioning the premises of modern society—a society capable of nuclear self-destruction, environmental pollution, an unrestrained armaments race in which one spoke not of the older balance of power but of a balance of terror and in which one calculated human casualties in "mega-deaths"—some asked whether the virtues of industriousness, education, hard work were as admirable as their parents said those virtues were, or whether these admirable traits did not lead to the monotony, tensions, pressures, and anxieties of contemporary life. Some young people turned to drugs, while others to new religions. Some became freaked out on allegedly mind-expanding drugs and became useless to everyone, including themselves. Others turned to new religions, fundamentalist and revivalist Christian sects, or to Eastern religions that sometimes took on a strange character when transplanted on Western shores, and often submerged the original emancipatory impulse in mindless authoritarian forms.

Everywhere there was a groping, a questioning of the older certitudes, a repudiation of the notion of linear progress. Science had created the means for the vast improvement of the human lot but also the means for the destruction of humankind. The humanists—the students of history, literature, religion, philosophy—searched for answers. The social scientists had discovered they could serve as a guide. Thoughtful men and women did not lose faith in human rationality, although they were aware that irrational, nonrational, and subconscious impulses influenced the individual and social behavior more than one cared to admit. They knew that truth was often acquired not through incremental advances only but through sudden bursts of insight as poets and spiritual leaders had always known. They knew that the values of a rapidly changing society needed to be questioned, that the world they lived in was no longer a Western-dominated, white-dominated, indeed male-dominated world. But what new values were to take the place of the old?

The humanists were constrained to continue the great

dialogue over man's fate—the human condition—in the light of all past universal wisdom and in the light of present changes and challenges. They conceded that they had no easy answers to the three major relationships with which the humanistic disciplines, and the humanistic tradition, have always had to contend—man's relation to nature, man's relation to God, man's relation to his fellow man. It became increasingly clear as the twentieth century moved into its closing decades that these three relationships were more closely intertwined than ever before. Or perhaps with increasing wisdom and humility human beings were more conscious of the interrelationships than ever before. To find a synthesizing answer to this inter-relationship became the greatest challenge to scientists and humanists, to philosophers, and indeed to modern man.

The philosopher and scientist René Dubos said something of this in his recent *Phi Beta Kappa* speech. He first recalled Francis Bacon's words on *The Advancement of Learning*:

> The invention of the mariner's needle which give the direction is of no less benefit for navigation than the invention of the sails which give the motion.

Have we not, Dubos asked, given attention to the motion, and not the direction? If scientists and technologists, understandably, by the nature of their vocation, have concerned themselves with the motion—indeed the means—have the humanists been concerned with the ends? He described the most important task for contemporary thinkers as achieving the integration of the sciences and the humanities. I would only add that scientists, social scientists, and humanists, putting aside their specialized, overtly fragmented disciplines, and acting as wise and thoughtful, rational and sentient human beings, must set themselves the task of rethinking the goals of our society and of clarifying the human and social values of the world in which we live, and wish to bequeath to our children.

The Present Quantum Shift
in Consciousness and Society

A million lotuses swaying on one stem.
World after colored and ecstatic world.
Climbs towards some far unseen epiphany.
                              Sri Aurobindo, Savriti

The whole story of the ascension of consciousness is the
story of an 'unshuttering' and the passage from a linear and
contradictory consciousness to a global consciousness.
                    The Adventure of Consciousness 213

The purpose of this paper is to develop aspects of the
thesis expressed below by Haridas Chaudhuri:

The theory of evolution upholds an optimistic vision of the
future. It calls attention to the supreme reality of life as a
creative process. It stresses the truth that man's reality
cannot be separated from his historicity. It is through participation in history that he can evolve and manifest the
unsuspected glories of his inner being. Integral nondualism
holds that the nontemporal and the evolutionary are two inseparable aspects of Being...
    It follows from the above that man, who is a self-
conscious mode of expression of being, has also two inseparable aspects. On the one hand he has the formless and timeless depth dimension of his existence. He needs to realize this
in order to attain peace, wisdom, freedom and love in their
perfection. But, on the other hand, he has the historical
dimension of his being. He is born in a specific historical context and part of his ultimate goal of life lies in playing an
active role in the march of history. It is no doubt by diving
into the depths of his being that he can glimpse life's supreme

values. But it is by actively participating in the evolutionary movement of life that he can increasingly manifest higher values in society and human relations.[1]

A SYSTEMS APPROACH TO THE HISTORY OF SOCIETY

In the late 1920's, von Bertalanffy called for an "organismic biology" whose fundamental task would be the "discovery of the laws of biological systems at all levels of organization". In advocating this "new philosophy of nature", he rejected logical positivism with its epistemology determined by the ideas of atomism, physicalism, and reductionism. In place of the analytical procedure of classical science, with linear causality connecting two variables as the basic category, von Bertalanffy and other investigators developed a general systems theory. It stressed concepts such as "wholeness", isomorphism, steady-state maintenance, and goal-directedness. In his words: "If reality is a hierarchy of organized wholes, the image of man will be different from what it is in a world of physical particles as ultimate and only 'true' reality governed by chance events."

A simple definition of "system" is in order. It comprises a constitutive complex whose characteristics depend on the specific relations of its parts. Thus the atom is an organized structure or system of protons, electrons, and neutrons. Moreover, every atom as a system of energy reveals unique characteristics which cannot be reduced to the properties of its components. The universe can be conceived as a myriad of systems, ranging from the atom to, say, the metagalaxy, each with its own distinctive properties and relative autonomy, at the same time interacting with the particular environment (or superordinate system) in which it "nests". In other words, a two-way flow of energy/information continuously occurs.

In systems terminology, "feedback" is the means by which a system equilibrates with its environment. There are two types. Negative feedback processes correct deviations in the existing system-environment relation (for example, the thermostat on the wall is designed to maintain constant temperature in the room). In contrast, positive feedback amplifies deviations from the existing "norm" (as in the case of growth or, again, decline conditions in a system). In complex systems, such as human societies, both types of feedback coexist and interact. By means of these processes, we can better account for a system's capacity to (1) exercise some kind of environmental control, (2) persist in time, and (3) engage in periodic major systematic and environmental transformations, such as are associated with different levels of organizational complexity among human societies.

Our paper is particularly concerned with a dual question: how can we account for both continuity and discontinuity in socio-cultural systems? Specifically, why is twentieth century society apparently in the midst of a quantum shift, i.e. a "revolutionary" transformation in perceptions, structure, processes, and values? Let us attempt to relate this question to negative and positive feedback processes. Continuity results when deviation-correcting mechanisms operate so as to ensure that structure and function remain viable within the parameters of a given system. quantization occurs when deviation is amplified to the point where no deviation-correcting mechanism can prevent the rupturing of the basic systemic framework—in other words, where the latter can no longer contain and canalize the energies and thrust which have been generated. The overall result alters the relationship with its environment, creating new spatio-temporal, structural, and functional boundaries. In short, the system is transformed to a new level of internal organization and environmental integration.

The relation of species other than the human to their environment is determined primarily by Darwinian, genetically-coded mechanisms, so that the evolutionary process at subhominid level can be described as *adaptive* equilibration. This is because, while the overall evolutionary process is mutagenic and open-ended, and hence exhibits positive forms of feedback, mechanisms dominate in the maintenance of individual species and their members.

Conversely, organisms with sensory-cognitive circuits are at the stage of *manipulative* equilibration to the extent that they possess deviation-amplifying capabilities. It is by "man the toolmaker" that the equilibrating process shifts progressively from a reactively adaptive to an actively manipulative role. Hence our model recognizes the crucial function of technology and science in the development and transformation of socio-cultural systems from Paleolithic times to the present. In other words, science and technology—which we can designate *material technics* (t^m)—largely serve as positive feedback processes. Concomitantly, we recognize the role of societal institutions and moves to maintain continuity and persistence in any socio-cultural system. In this respect, therefore, *societal technics* (t^s) often function as negative feedback processes to maximize overall stability and societal invariance under technological and environmental transformations.

Understandably, individuals and societies alike tend to be *status quo* oriented, to be apprehensive of change, and to regard "stability" as the *summum bonum*. But if Heraclitus is right, change is the one invariant in nature and human affairs, and the evolutionary process attests to continuous mutation and quantization. When we look at biological systems, for example, we perceive that they are not stable so much as "ultrastable", that is, they possess variable norms with the capacity to adapt to environmental contingencies. (In systems language, they employ positive feedback mechanisms to settle into new steady-states coded by different norms when the thresholds of error-correction have been surpassed.) For example, living species renorm their steady-states through mutation and natural selection, while social systems renorm their economic, political, and cultural equilibria when confronted with external or internal threats and challenges. Translating this language into our immediate concerns, how shall our contemporary society renorm its structures and values to meet the challenge of a global environment in transformation?

Ultrastable systems can be distinguished according to their capacity to extrapolate from present to future states or conditions. Laszlo has distinguished three such classes of ultrastable systems. The first class has little or no capability for extrapolation; it includes biological species wherein mutations are given selective advantage under environmental stress. However, they are produced *reactively*, not in anticipation of impending environmental changes. The second variety of ultrastable systems has predictive capability: it can *anticipate* changing conditions as related to the limits of its existing stabilizing functions. Thus, socio-cultural systems can monitor their internal states as well as the external environment, and can mobilize forces to deal with the new conditions. If the conditions head towards the limits of their ability for self-correction, internal forces (such as reform or revolutionary movements) are activated, forcing the system towards transformation. The third variety of ultrastable systems has a still higher level of capability: it can extrapolate the possible transformations, as well as anticipate the dangers which make them necessary. Such systems are endowed with a specialized self-monitor which enables them to run through alternative scenarios, assess intrinsic desirabilities, and assign weightings. These are not "reactive" but "proactive" systems—*and only human beings appear to come into this category.* Applying his distinctions among ultrastable systems to studies about the future, Laszlo argues:

> The challenge before us is to bring the fruits of high-level human extrapolation into the domain of societal transformation. This means envisaging the future in positive terms, rather than conceiving it as a strategy to prevent or manage crises. Sociocultural systems, even if they anticipate dangers, are mainly reactive; human beings are proactive. The added human capability can pay off in the form of focusing goals and aspirations in meaningful terms, rather than merely reacting to perceived needs of adjusting the social structure. Crisis prevention and crisis management are sensible from the viewpoint of societies, but deficient from that of human behavior. Their principal motivation is fear and this may well be insufficient to bring about the value reorientations required for effective action. Since social transformation cannot be achieved without motivation for behavior change, good strategies *for society* are not enough. They must be joined with good strategies *for people*. . . In short, we must couple the reactive, crisis-prevention strategy for our social systems with a proactive, achievement-oriented strategy for human beings.[2]

Laszlo's argument is congruent with that of Sri Aurobindo, who contends that the individual must be regarded as "the key of the evolutionary movement. . .The movement of the collectivity is a largely subconsicous mass movement; it has to formulate and express itself through the individuals to become conscious; its general mass consciousness is always less evolved than the consciousness of its most developed individuals, and it progresses insofar as it accepts their impress or develops what they develop."[3]

From the foregoing it can be seen that while General System Theory can apply to all levels of systemic organization—physical, biological, and socio-cultural alike—we are concerned at this juncture with concentrating upon human systems, involving as they do a two-way exchange of energies between our species and our planetary environment (or ecosystem). Moreover, we intend to focus upon the man-environment nexus within an overall historical framework—because, to repeat Chaudhuri's words, man "is born in a specific historical context and part of his ultimate goal of life lies in playing an active role in the march of history".

HISTORICAL OVERVIEW OF SOCIETAL QUANTUM SHIFTS

Inasmuch as "manipulative equilibration" comprises an active rather than reactive adaptation to the environment (as in the case of other species), this means that human societies will reflect the extent to which material and societal technics are able to free their members of the constraints of their physical habitat and engage in activities which maximize the prospects of physical survival and, in addition, satisfy supra-survival needs and goals. For our purposes, we are looking at the man-environment nexus in terms of (a) "environmental *control* systems" and the inputs made thereto by technologies and societal institutions, and (b) the values and goals consciously held by individuals who form the collectivities in these sociocultural systems.

Mankind's model-making propensity displays itself in the construction of specific cultures, each of which possesses a "world-view" (*Weltanschauung*). This is a particular mode of cognition that characterizes an entire social system, being shared in common by most of its members. Another name for this mode of cognition is *paradigm*—a broadly accepted model of reality—that displays configurations or gestalt patterns by which the cultural system's members regulate their percep-

LEVELS OF ORGANIZATION

SOCIETAL LEVEL	PROPERTIES	EMERGENT QUALITIES				
		TECHNOLOGY	SCIENCE	TRANSPORTATION	COMMUNICATIONS	GOVERNMENT
S_5	BELOW +	Electrical-nuclear energy Automation Cybernetics	Einsteinian relativity Quantum mechanics Systems theory	Supra-surface inner space systems Outer space explorations Surface systems Sub-surface vehicles	Electronic transmission (simultaneity) throughout expleted space)	Ecumenocracy (Supra-national polities) Multi-level transaction Sovereignty invested in global mankind
S_4	BELOW +	Transformation of energy (steam) Machine technology Mass production	Greek miracle Scientific method Newtonian world-view	Maritime technology and navigation Thalassic and oceanic networks Highway networks Railroad technology	Mechanical transmission (printing) Alphabet	National state system Emergence of democracy Sovereignty of state (as primary actor)
S_3	BELOW +	Non-biological prime movers (wind, water) Metal tools Continuous rotary motion (wheel) Irrigation technics	Mathematics Astronomy	Sailboats Riverine transport Wheeled vehicles Intra- and inter-urban roads	Writing	Ancient bureaucratic empires Theocratic polities Sovereignty of god-kings
S_2	BELOW +	Animal energy Domestication of plants and animals Polished stone tools Spinning Pottery	Neolithic proto-science	Animal transport Paths, village routes Neolithic seafaring	Ideograms	Biological-territorial nexus Tribal level of organization and decision-making
S_1		Human energy Control of fire Stone and bone tools Partial rotary action		Human transport Sleds Dug-outs, canoes	Pictograms	Biological nexus (family, hunting band, clan)

tions and thus adjust themselves to their environments. The shared gestalts of a world-view are translated (or codified) into the symbolic cultural patterns of art, religion, law, language, etc. In effect, we tend to make things in the image of our gestalts. Hence, our world-view expresses itself in our culture.

Let us briefly recapitulate. The proactive, consciousness goal-oriented members of our species are the creators of new paradigms or models, and of the tools by which a given society implements such a model. In mankind's planetary existence, material and societal technics are employed either to stabilize an existing sociocultural system or, alternatively, to reformulate beliefs, values, and goals so as to transform the existing system. Periodically in history—and at an accelerating tempo —major transformations, or quantum shifts, have occurred. We can diagram these quanta in terms of a taxonomy of sociocultural stages, in effect, a generalized synopsis of the evolution of societies from stone-age times to the present (Table 1). We are being selective in order to demonstrate successive stages in the organization and complexity of human communities.

Viewed horizontally, each level schematically depicts transaction occurring among various environmental and societal factors. It is a geosocietal model inasmuch as we have broadly correlated levels of technological and government organization with stages and dimensions of environmental control. Viewed vertically, these stages of progressive overall environmental occupancy assume a geometrical sequence: point-line-plane-volume as mankind's control capabilities increase (within a global context). As the "Properties" column attests, this sequence also exemplifies a major principle in systems theory; each such level builds upon the properties and societal experience of the level(s) below and in turn contributes its own *emergent* attributes which take the form of new technologies and societal structures, accompanied by new apperceptions of the man-environment relationship. We can discern progressive development in complexity and heterogeneity (although in any one historical situation a different, or even contrary, experience may occur).

In summary, the table provides a grid showing both societal-environmental stabilization when viewed horizontally (process in planetary *space*-time) and societal-environmental quantization when examined vertically (process in planetary space-*time*). Mankind's overall experience has been to expand anthropogeographic perimeters concomitantly with its accelerative contraction of temporal sequences associated with new stages of environmental control, i.e., from S_1—the food-gathering level of environmental control—through S_2—the food-producing quantum—and sequentially to S_5—our current emerging level of geosocietal experience and organization. When we examine this schematic presentation, we can perceive in today's world the continued existence of some stone-age societies. However, the fact that they are vestigial (and often situated in geographical cul-de-sacs) attests that the center of gravity in societal evolution has long shifted to new levels of organization and complexity. As with stages of biological evolution, the "simplest" comes first.

1. Mythos as World-View

The first level of sociocultural organization comprises the greatest single segment of human time-space. It extends for 99 per cent of the three or more million years since *Homo*'s appearance, and over all areas of the earth that were then accessible to the species. This comprises the Paleolithic age/stage, where man is a hunter-fisherman equipped with a flint and bone technology marked by structural simplicity, durability, and conservatism. This technology developed slowly in the direction of progressive specialization and miniturization with the invention of microliths. But the capacity of our Paleolithic forebears to manage their environment was stringently constrained by the tool-making limitations inherent in flint and bone, the small amount of energy produced by human muscle power, and by the fluctuations in food supplies available in a hunting-fishing economy. Such societies had to spend much of their time and energies just to maintain the struggle for physical survival. What technological innovations did occur took place over a vast Paleolithic time-scale and within a societal organization that was in turn structurally simple, highly conservative in its societal technics and mores, and hence resistant to change. And because a food-gathering economy can sustain only a small population and show demographic densities, these societies had minimal contacts—and therefore minimal cross-fertilization of ideas—in comparison with those at more advanced societal stages.

However, in time men and women conceptualized a radically new relationship with their environment, and consequently created a societal transformation. Described as the "Neolithic Revolution", this major quantum occurs with the domestication of certain wild grasses and animals—and, so far as we know, independently in the Old and New Worlds—thereby augmenting the technology acquired at the lower, or Paleolithic, stage. No longer must all members of the species remain food-gatherers; a growing number become food-producers. This increased capability—which includes tapping new energy sources in the form of animal muscle power—permits men and women henceforth to "stay put", that is, to localize their environmental control and to become sedentary, which *inter alia* calls for village nodes of settlement and new domestic crafts (such as weaving and pottery). The village node helps create new societal attitudes and institutions. Whereas food-gathering peoples are linked primarily by ties of kinship, the man-environment nexus has now assumed a less "biological" in favor of greater "territorial" significance. However, at this stage of incipient agriculture, limited water sources in Southwest Asia, for example, set rigid limits upon societal development and the transformation of the landscape.

These two levels of societal organization were not only lithic (stone-age) in their technology but mythic in their shared world view. Magic and religion colored primitive man's outlook and interpenetrated material and societal technics alike. This mode of thinking should not be regarded as the antithesis of science. Both are modes of acquiring knowledge, "require the same sort of mental operations, and they differ not so much in kind as in the different types of phenomena to which they are applied".[4] In our empirical tradition, we approach nature in terms of the existence of things as determined by general laws. But the mythic approach views the world in dramatic terms: "a world of actions, of forces, of conflicting powers. Mythical perception is always impregnated with these emotional qualities . . . Here we cannot speak of 'things' as a dead or indifferent stuff."[5]

In effect, lithic man attached importance to both his physical and psychical states, and entertained no dualism between matter and spirit. Mythic thought is geared to the present tense, in the sense that reality is something conceived to be existing or occurring now, rather than as having occurred yesterday, or at the beginning of the world. Hence it can always be "tapped". While lithic man can functionally differentiate subjects or objects at one level of reality (a man is not a tree), man and tree alike embody a life-force which can be expressed as a single value: "It is." *Mythos* enables men and women to identify themselves with any or all aspects of the phenomenal world.

Within such a perspective, "cause" and "effect" are two ways of regarding a single action. Rites and symbols are viewed not as distinct from that which they signify or evoke, but as vital embodiments of those things. They are designed to tap the universal reservoir of power which enables the desired action to occur. *Mythos* represents a world order that is not temporally "progressing' but is ever-repeating. This is congruent with a type of sociocultural system in which negative feedback processes dominate, thereby maximizing its viability and continuity by means of societal conservation rather than material innovation. Thus, among the Neolithic peoples the rites relate to the annual recurrence of the growing and harvesting seasons, while the women generate life from generation to generation even as the Earth Mother is worshipped as a universal womb-tomb-womb generatrix, so that the supreme purpose and value of human life is to adhere to an order that maintains its telluric balance.

2. *Theos as World-Order*

The transplanting of agricultural innovations to the rich bottom lands of the Nile, Tigris-Euphrates, Indus and Ganges, and Huang-ho rivers resulted in a new quantum leap in societal organization and environmental integration. This transplantation yielded a hundredfold increase in food harvests, making possible what has been described as a "social surplus". This raised population numbers and densities unprecedentedly, and freed many persons to work in occupations and localities at some remove from the fields. Hence the rise of towns, accompanied by more complex governmental and administrative structures, hieratic elites, etc. In short, the "Urban Revolution" describes systemic quantization and environmental transformation. It is marked by the shifting of the sociopolitical center of gravity to the cities which henceforth control the "lower order" countryside with its villages. From an anthropogeographical standpoint, the technological capabilities of this environmental stage may be described as one-dimensional. They control the length of a river valley, but are still limited laterally to the river's immediate hinterland (where irrigated by canals and ditches).

These "hydraulic civilizations" eventually reach a plateau of stabilization because of inherent environmental constraints. By our standards, they are noteworthy for their longevity and conservatism, though they are also marked by important technological and other advances. These include the use of metals (in particular bronze), the calendar's invention, the advent of writing, and what has been described as "proto-science". And as these societies are theocratic world-states, territory is conceptualized as a sacred land belonging to rulers who are either divine or possess a mandate from Heaven.

What is the nature of *Theos*, which we might describe as the "celestial paradigm"? This view of reality begins with the emergence of cosmos out of chaos: such a concept is hardly surprising, considering the purpose of cosmogonies, but the process begins *ab initio* instead of building sequentially upon previous lithic constructs of reality. Whereas the mythic worldview was telluric and emphasized the paramountcy of the Magna Mater principle, the theocratic paradigm is celestial in orientation and stresses the primacy of the principle, not only in the cosmogenic creation myths but in the wielding of authority. The cosmos is viewed as an organic polity possessing sovereignty and power which in turn maintain cosmic order and harmony. The attributes of the cosmic "state" have been created by a supreme being (who is a male deity); subsequently, his powers may be wielded by other deities as well. The cosmos is hierarchically ordered, and since it is a divine state, its governmental and societal structure on earth assumes the form of a theocracy. Consequently, terrestrial kingship exists by divine fiat in order to embody and legitimize celestially-derived authority and power. In such societies, the exercise of this authority and power is absolute and unidirectional, that is, it is from "on high", and makes no provision for any other locus or exercise of authority and power. As with the *mythos* of the telluric paradigm and its embodiment in lithic societies, once again we are dealing with sociocultural systems in which negative feedback processes are dominant. More specifically, after hydraulic and other material technics have reorganized riverine society at a new and more complex level of organization, the resulting symbiosis with the environment is maintained by means of appropriate political, bureaucratic, and religious-sacerdotal technics.

3. *Logos as World-Order*

From the second millennium B.C. especially, we find a new pattern of environmental control beginning to take shape. Indo-European speaking peoples fan out over much of southern and western Eurasia, equipped with an iron technology. Through the development of maritime technics, the Mediterranean with its hinterland becomes the setting for a number of maritime states— Phoenician, Hellenic, Carthaginian, and Roman. Because of its maritime technology, accompanied by the opening up, in Roman times, of trans-Alpine Europe by means of a remarkable road and transportation network, this stage of societal organization comes to control the terrestrial environment on a broad scale—in short, in terms of two-dimensional "flat earth".

In the millennia following the era of classical societies, this two-dimensional control extended from maritime to oceanic and, finally, to continental environments. In the fifteenth century, for example, new types of vessels, equipped with navigational aids such as the compass and astrolabe, and armed with cannon, enabled Europeans to set out on globe-girdling voyages of exploration, followed by the imposition of overseas commercial and colonial empires. This geopolitical development went hand in hand with the emergence of the new nation-

state with its assumptions of independence and sovereignty—
a process that resulted in the maturation of the nation-state
system at the end of the Thirty Years War (a political model
described by Falk as "the logic of Westphalia").

In the 17th, 18th and 19th centuries, science and technology transformed mankind's relationship to its terrestrial
environment as well as its understanding of the nature of the
phenomenal world. The invention of the telescope permitted
the mapping of the heavens, while the microscope revealed new
insights into the structure of matter. Science was placed on
a "modern" basis by Galileo and his contemporaries, while a
succession of conceptual innovations culminated in the Newtonian synthesis with its unifying model of celestial mechanics. Technologically, the era of wind and wood gave way to that
of steam and iron, that is, the advent of the Industrial Revolution with its reliance upon new forms of energy, creation of new
forms of economic organization, and establishment of the
factory town. And with it also came the emergence of an inter-
continental capitalism by which raw resources from every
quarter of the globe were shipped to the factories of Manchester and other Western industrial center, to be manufactured
into new products and then shipped to consumers throughout
the world. A steam-and-steel rail technology opened up for
massive economic exploitation and settlement of the vast
continental hinterlands of the two Americas, Africa, Australia
and much of Asia. This process of two-dimensional expansion
and progressive environmental transformation culminated
around the end of the 19th century with the "conquest" of the
two poles by Peary and Amundsen. At this juncture, mankind
has run out of *terra incognita*, so that immigration laws begin
to be enacted to screen and restrict the movement of peoples.
Such restrictions are the harbinger of an uncomfortable awareness, that is to grow as our century proceeds, that the planet
is finite in its dimensions and resources alike.

"We are all Greeks," said Shelley, speaking of the cultural
heritage of the West—for it is upon Hellenic conceptual foundations that the edifice of the Western world-order was erected.
We might single out three terms in this Hellenic paradigm
because of their far-reaching cognitive and normative implications especially for the West: *logos, arete* and *metron.*[6] Ac-

cording to Gilbert Murray, *logos* is the "most characteristic word in the Greek Language" and "lies at the heart of philosophy, science, religion. Everything in the world has a *logos*, it says something, means something; God himself is saying something. If we listen carefully we can understand."[7] *Logos* is the instrument for finding out what is rational and true. Moreover, man is not only a reasoning creature but has a special worth, or virtue (*arete*). His nature finds fulfillment in certain ends, and to do so he must develop his *arete*, or inborn capacities, so far as he can. Because of this sense of human worth and its potentialities, "the Greeks believed in liberty, since only the free can fully realize their natures; and they were quite logical in doubting whether a slave can have *arete* in any real sense, since he is not free to be himself as he would wish to be."[8] The concept of *logos* as order and reason responsible for everything in the cosmos, and the special worth of man as a reasoning creature capable of understanding the cosmos and of making rational decisions, represent a view of reality—and body of values—altogether different from the theocratic, pyramidal paradigm encountered in the riverine societies (S^3 in our diagram).

The third term, *metron*, means "measure". (What we are about to suggest is said with deference to our Indian colleagues who are invited to improve or correct both our etymological and philosophical interpretations below.) According to our understanding, from the same Indo-European linguistic root came two words, the Sanskrit *maya* and the Greek *metron*. In the view of some scholars, they represent a conceptual bifurcation between Eastern and Western approaches to the nature of reality. The Eastern route has been described as *philousia*, the study of essential Being. In this approach, *maya* recognizes the significance of measurement in connection with understanding the phenomenal world, but underscores the Indian view that it is an illusion to suppose that the supraphenomenal world can be measured in terms of the physical senses since it is not subject to the constraints of time and space. Thus *philousia* concerns itself with being and pure continuity which defies categorization and measurement in phenomenal terms. In contrast, the Greeks involved themselves in *philosophia* which called for an emphasis upon factual knowledge of the phenomenal world—hence the central value of *metron* in order to measure and comprehend the world of the senses. When we combine *logos* and *metron*, we obtain a basic key to Greek, and subsequent Western thinking: reason should apply itself to a cosmos that is largely measurable; hence the emphasis upon logic, quantification, and the scientific method as we know it today.[9] This Hellenic approach "heralded the beginning of the great European adventure which, within the next two thousand years, was to transform the human species more radically than the previous two hundred thousand had done".[10] Moreover, the Greeks linked the concepts of *measurement* and *proportion* in order to avoid *hubris*. It was essential "to remember the rule of *Meden Agan*: Nothing too Much: and to avoid above all things *Hubris*, Insolence or Excess the deadly error to which all life is subject and which leads always to a fall".[11]

These concepts have far-reaching societal and normative implications. The S_4 paradigm gives a new status and worth to man *per se* in the scheme of things. He has evolved from a state of dependence to one of independence, possessing reason, dignity and freedom of choice and decision-making in his own right. In the sociopolitical sphere, the emphasis is upon the independence of the polity, which is absolute in its claims, and whose citizens possess innate political and legal rights held in common. Individualism applies in turn in the socioeconomic sphere: the farmers, artisans and merchants are their own masters.

The advent of Christianity modifies the classical paradigm significantly, and with it societal goals and values. We find the conceptual change in the opening lines of the Fourth Gospel: "In the beginning was the Word (*logos*), and the Word was with God, and the Word was God . . . And the Word became flesh and dwelt among us . . ." Here the concept of *logos* as reason and as a cosmic ordering principle remains invariant, but the creator of the universe is revealed to be a single, divine source. The paradigm continues to be anthropocentric but in a new sense: *logos* has incarnated—God is made man. And whereas the Greeks employed *logos* and *metron* to search for impersonal laws governing the cosmos and man himself as a microcosm, the Christian view of reality shifts perspective from an objective "It" to a subjective "Thou", i.e., from natural philosophy to revelation. To synthesize reason and revolution is the object of the medieval schoolmen. According to St. Thomas Aquinas, "Sacred doctrine makes use of human reason, not to prove faith but to make clear (*manifestare*) whatever else is set forth in this doctrine."[12]

In the Renaissance, the humanists consciously identify with the classical paradigm, though conditioned by the intervening medieval apperception of reality. Thus Pico della Mirandola has God place man "in the center of the world" and endowed with a new intrinsic worth (*arete*) in his own right. For its part, *metron* calls for determining the dimensions not only of man but of the macrocosm itself. Hence the impetus to explore the terrestrial environment—the Age of Discovery—and the invention of the telescope and microscope to explore and measure the largest and smallest phenomena alike.

Thus do *logos* and *metron* combine anew to lay the foundations for scientific enquiry in early modern times. In this enterprise, Galileo has been called the prime mover in the development summed up in the phrase *Science is Measurement.* ("He maketh all things by number, weight, and measure.") More than anyone else, Galileo altered man's concepts of the kind of knowledge that was to be sought. His conception of the world called for a search for mechanical principles. Brought to a triumphant synthesis by Newton, the mechanical paradigm employs *logos* to demonstrate the potency of *metron*. But it has nothing to say about those "secondary qualities" which Galileo could not measure, such as "sweetness" and "well-smelling" or, again, virtue (*arete*) and wisdom (*sophia*). Actually, Galileo and Newton had engaged in a restricted pursuit: they studied not the phenomenal world *sub species aeternitatis* as philosophers do, but rather the way in which we experience it. But because of the predictive success of this paradigm in accounting for the relatively few variables in celestial mechanics, eighteenth century physics and astronomy were fastened upon to provide a world-view. "Hence, no sooner was the conception of inert bodies passively following the dictates of blind forces seen to be applicable to the motion of mass-points, than it was immediately generalized into a world-philosophy."[13]

What was happening to man as once envisaged by Protagoras ("Man is the measure") and Pico della Mirandola? Three theories stripped him progressively of the unique place which Hellenism and Christianity had accorded him, both as the microcosmic *metron* and one set in the center of things. First, Copernicus' heliocentric theory had already robbed man's terrestrial home of its fixed centrality in the universe. Then, Darwin's evolutionary hypothesis divested man of his traditional heritage of having been created by a special act of divine grace. Finally, Freud's plumbing of man's unconscious mental processes seemed to shatter his cherished belief in his own *logos*, or power of reason. The nineteenth century created a paradigm that mechanized the world and conceived man as a stimulus-response machine: to be conditioned, controlled, and manipulated—by a science that purported to be objective and value-free, and by a society that embraced Social Darwinism with its justification for competition and conflict in the name of the survival of the fittest.

Two-valued orientations—Aristotle's logic with its principle of the excluded middle and the perspective of either/or—dominated man's thought processes and values alike. Just as sovereignty was compartmentalized into spatial containers of political property, so the values of nationalism and loyalty were conceived in absolute terms: "our country, right or wrong". The pronouncements from the pulpit were unqualifiedly two-valued: saved/damned; and from the judge's bench: innocent/guilty. Yet these either/or orientations but reflected how man from classical times had conceived his relationship with the rest of the world. He regarded himself as apart from it, and with his dualistic perception man looked upon nature as something to control and exploit by means of *logos* and *metron*. This anthropocentric view, and an accompanying tendency to limit *arete* or worth and dignity to his own species, proved a dangerous *hubris*. It led in turn to its own *nemesis*, whereby *logos* and *metron* eventually fashioned a mechanistic world-view in which man was stripped of his own *arete* and made over in the model of a simple push-pull mechanism (or, again, an equally simplistic stimulus-response organism). However, this paradigm with its absolute, two-valued orientations was in turn to be replaced by a new model—that of Planck and Einstein and their successors—one which would be relativistic in its orientations, multivalued in its logic, and holistic in its scope, so as to include man and his works as integral parts of a global ecology, and endowing all aspects of the universe with *arete.*

TOWARDS HOLOS: A GLOBAL CONSCIOUSNESS AND SOCIETY

Our overview of four seismic societal quantum shifts— food-gathering societies, early food-producing societies, archaic riverine civilizations, and classical-Western societies— is based upon research which disclosed that certain identifiable factors were present in each of these stages of societal transformation. We now list them:

1. *Technological/scientific innovations*—These included:
  (a) The initial invention of flint and bone tools at the food-gathering stage, thereby setting off *Homo* from all other species in environmental relationships;
  (b) Subsequent changes in tool-making and invention, marked by increasing specialization and efficiency;
  (c) Increases in the production and consumption of energy;
  (d) The systematic study of natural processes (which began as far back as stone-age societies).

2. *Increased environmental control capability*—This is the direct result of the application of technology and scientific methods to our terrestrial habitat—hence mankind's progressive ability to move on the planet's surface and to exploit its resources.

3. *Population growth*—Since our species survives as a direct consequence of the application of technology to available resources, an intimate relationship exists in turn between the effectiveness of that technology and the numbers of members of our species who can be supported on this planet.

4. *Societal complexification*—Each new societal stage witnessed an increased division of labor within the work force, a more complex institutional structure, changes in the acquisition and transmission of information in the decision-making

process, and in the size and functions of settlement nodes, from the village to the city.

5. *Shifts in world-view*—Every society is sustained by a particular view of reality, resulting form its environmental and historical experiences, and the opportunities afforded thereby to permit a change and development in both individual and collective consciousness—and this view suffuses and conditions all activities occurring in the different segments of its culture pattern. (As we have seen, lithic peoples were animistic; the peoples of riverine civilizations constructed theocratic societies; while the Greeks emphasized the paramountcy of human reason and developed institutions and values that gave a central place to the role and worth of the individual—a status which in turn underwent a significant change especially with the advent of industrialism in modern times.)

6. *Aesthetic indicators*—The prevailing societal view or paradigm in turn manifests appropriate and unique forms of aesthetic expression. Each new paradigm calls for the artist to make his particular statement about his perception of reality. (Hence the cave paintings among Paleolithic hunting societies; the geometric patterns of expression found in Neolithic pottery and weaving; the monumental architecture and statuary in riverine theocracies; and the emphasis upon the human dimension and form in Greek, and again in Renaissance, art.)

When we come to our own century, we find that *without exception these indicators of societal quantization are again present*. Consequently, we contend that, regarded s a cluster of interacting forces, they comprise *prima facie* evidence that we are in the midst of yet another seismic quantum in societal evolution. In effect, it is a shift from the level of political and economic competition and confrontation, national organization and nation-state perceptions and interests, towards a level of transnational perceptions, of progressive interdependence, and of global orientations and organization, accompanied by new values, goals, and priorities appropriate to this emerging stage of societal integration.[14] We have space only to describe cursorily the presence and behavior of each of our quantizing factors as applied to developments in the 20th century.[15]

1.   *Scientifically*, we have been witnessing revolutionary conceptual advances, notably Quantum Mechanics and the Relativity Theory. *Technologically*, equally revolutionary advances have occurred in transportation, in automation and cybernation, in information-gathering and communications, and in the creation of entire new industries—electronics, computers, aircraft, plastics. New prime movers have been acquired: nuclear sources of power, while tidal, thermal, and solar power is in the offing. A quantum increase in the production and consumption of energy has already occurred. (Whether this exponential growth can be maintained, however, raises serious questions relating to the "limits of growth" thesis.)

2.   That a quantum shift has occurred in our *environmental control capability* is attested by movement in a new, or third, dimension—hence the advent of the Space Age. It is marked by man's ascent into the atmosphere and beyond to outer space—including his landing on the moon and satellite photographing and measuring of the surfaces and atmospheres of our sister planets. Concurrently, we can now descend into the hydrosphere and the inner space of ocean beds and continental shelves. Movement in this third or vertical dimension is unique in human history, and its implications, including the usage and ownership of the resources thereby made available, raise political and juridical issues which have yet to be satisfactorily resolved—especially from the standpoint of the modalities of the nation-state system whose concepts of sovereignty and control were developed on the basis of two-dimensional "flat earth" and its surface waters.

3.   Previous sociocultural quantum shifts could be correlated with dramatic *increases in population*. But never has the increase been so sudden, dramatic, or pervasive as in our own century. In 1900 the world's population amounted to some 1,550 million; in 1976 it passed the 4,000 million mark, and the latest forecast states that by 2000 A.D. the figure will reach or exceed 6,000 million. On the basis of current growth trends, especially in the developing regions, that figure could double sometime during the 21st century.[16] Our contemporary "population explosion" calls for fundamental rethinking about the interaction of the variables of population, energy, and food, and

a new awareness of the impact of such interactions upon traditional national boundaries and policies.

4.   It is surely a truism to suggest that we live in the *most complex stage in history*. Random evidence of exponential growth might be cited: the number of learned journals which have been founded; manpower in the electrical engineering industries; the increase of cities and metropolitan conurbations and the services which they require; the proliferation of new nation-states and international organizations alike since World War I; and the advent of multinational corporations. We appear to have reached a new stage in the relationship of societal complexification to the amount of available resources. This relationship calls for intensive analysis (especially in the context of the Club of Rome's findings).

5.   Our century abounds in *aesthetic innovation* in architecture and all the other arts. From the Renaissance to the end of the 19th century, spatial perspective had constituted one of the most important facts in painting, and remained a constant element through all changes of style. The three-dimensional space of Renaissance painting was the space of Euclidean geometry and had "rooted itself so deeply in the human mind that no other form of perception could be imagined". But in modern physics, space is conceived of as relative to a moving point of reference, not as the absolute and static entity of the Newtonian system. Breaking with traditional perspective, the Cubists, for example, viewed objects relatively, that is from several points of view, with none of them possessing exclusive authority. Every point in time-space is a center. Such a presentation of objects "introduces a principle which is intimately bound up with modern life-simultaneity. It is a temporal coincidence that Einstein should have begun his famous work, *Elektrodynamik bewegter Korper*, in 1905, with a careful definition of simultaneity."[17]

6.   The traditional *Western world-view* was based upon the premises of a positivistic, empirically-oriented science, purportedly value free, but which actually accepted certain normative assumptions. One was the value of economic growth and political power *per se*; a second was the concept of the separation of man from nature and his "right" to exploit and

"conquer" his environment. Still another was the preeminence accorded individualism and independence in all spheres of human activity. As we are about to see, this paradigm is now being seriously questioned. Communications technology shrinks the planet progressively to a "global village", and this new apperception underscores a shift in turn from national independence to international interdependence. Similarly, the traditional separation of man from nature has been giving way to a new ecological perspective, while "growth" values with their emphasis upon quantitative, GNP-based criteria are being challenged by a "quality of life" ethos and ethic alike.

Any number of scenarios about the future are being developed these days; when examined, all represent variations on three forecasting themes. These are: (1) society is pretty much going to remain as it is now and, on balance, we shall probably be better off; (2) the present structure and values of our society will be retained but things are going to get a lot worse both quantitatively and qualitatively; and (3) society will have to be transformed both to resolve the global problems confronting humanity today—population pressures, diminishing nonrenewable resources, mounting environmental pollution, and dysfunctionalism and alienation within virtually every society —and to preserve the biosphere for future generations. These three alternatives have been described as the Expansionist World-View, the Malthusian World-View, and the Ecological World-View.

Given the perspective afforded by our preceding historical indicators of quantization, only one of these world-views becomes relevant—inasmuch as the Expansionist paradigm represents a linear extrapolation of existing societal structures and behavior, while in the last analysis the Malthusian model anticipates an entropic quantization or collapse of the first. Let us therefore look more closely at the Ecological World-View as one basis for a fundamental transformation of society

Its keynote is not optimism or pessimism—but innovation. More explicitly, it calls for quantitative prudence and restraint, coupled with qualitative expansion. It does not come down on the side of either societal "nurture" or physical "nature" but welcomes their combined contribution to the evolution of human consciousness. Such a concept is integral to a world-view that regards the universe as a unified system, all of whose parts are connected and interdependent. Logically, since man is an inseparable component of a vast ecosystem, it follows that he can never "conquer" his environment—he stands or falls with it because the universe itself is a manifestation of "integral nondualism".

This paradigm has a different sociopolitical and economic orientation from its counterparts. It is both conservative and socialist in the sense of seeking to "conserve" nature's balance and resources for future generations and, at the same time, maximizing the social allocation of current resources to meet fundamental needs on a global basis. (In this sense, it is allied with the findings and recommendations of the various United Nations conferences on the environment, population, food, the high seas, human settlement, and desertification.) And where the Expansionist paradigm tends to emphasize managerial centralization—in the interest of economies of scale—and the homogenization of culture across regional boundaries, the Ecological World-View advocates a mixture of centralization and decentralization, as well as encouraging cultural diversity (even as in nature itself we find the one and the many, uniformity and heterogeneity, coexisting and interacting). On this basis, the needs common to all mankind—basic standards of nutrition, health, shelter, education—must be met on a global scale, and the resources required to meet these needs call in turn for international management and allocation. At the same time, the *specific* uses to which these resources warrant devolution of the decision-making process to regional, national, and indeed local levels of society so as to take account of cultural and communal diversity and uniqueness. Whereas the Expansionist Word-View places its faith primarily in the managers and experts, this paradigm calls into play the views as well of the so-called ordinary people to redress technocratic values because "small is beautiful".

The Ecological World-View has its own strategy. Unlike the Malthusian model, it does not call for total zero growth, nor on the other hand does it countenance continued exponential growth. It recognizes the ills of arbitrary and sudden cutoffs, which must mean loss of the social and psychological momentum that has sustained Western societies over the past several centuries, and also the need of underdeveloped regions to continue to increase productivity and improve living standards. Growth, however, should be selective in order to strike a viable balance between consumption for today and conservation for tomorrow. Hopefully, population growth will begin to decrease in the decades ahead in the poorest countries (comprising what is now called the Fourth World) as living standards improve, while the industrially advanced regions should plan to have a smaller output of nonrecyclable goods but with a longer life expectancy, and larger output of services. The desired objective would be a multivariable steady state by the next century, one that recognized flexibility of approach and methods among the world's major regions.

There is involved here another kind of shift—from an emphasis upon material goods towards a new lifestyle, physically simpler but stressing new qualitative factors. One study of forces for societal transformation in the United States during the second half of this century tends "to confirm a view that the current situation facing this nation may be not temporary deviation from continuous, suprise-free development but rather a more fundamental challenge of unknown proportions, *a successful response to which will require changes in some of the central elements of the cultural value system underlying our society and a consequent transformation of structure and purpose of many of our institutions.*"[18]

A subsequent study stated that "an adequate image of mankind for the postindustrial future" would be characterized by conditions that could:

1.   Convey a *holistic sense* of perspective or understanding of life;

2.   Entail an *ecological ethic*, emphasizing the total community of life-in-nature and the oneness of the human race;

3.   Entail a *self-realization ethic*, placing the highest value on development of selfhood and declaring that an appropriate function of all social institutions is the fostering of human development;

4.   Be *multileveled, multifaceted, and integrative*, accommodating various culture and personality types;

5. Involve *balancing* and *coordination* of *satisfactions* along many dimensions rather than the maximizing of concerns along one narrowly defined dimension (e.g., economic);

6. Be *experimental, open-ended,* and *evolutionary.*[19]

Despite the "deep psychological resistance to both the new image and its implications", there are "increasingly evident signs of the imminent emergence" of this new image.

> *An interrelating set of fundamental dilemmas, growing apparently ever more pressing, seem to demand for their resolution a drastically changed image of man-on-earth.* We seem able to tolerate neither the ecological consequences of continued material growth nor the economic effects of a sudden stoppage. We fear the implications of greatly increased control of technological development and application, yet sense that such control is imperative. We recognize the fatal instability of economic nationalism and a growing gap between rich and poor nations, yet seem unable to turn the trend around. We seem unable to resolve the discrepancy between man's apparent need for meaningful work and the economic imperatives that cause much human labor to become superfluous or reduce it to make-work. A massive challenge is growing to the legitimacy of a business-government system wherein pursuit of economic ends results in such counteracting of other human ends. We face a cultural crisis of meaning—it is not clear who is at the helm, how the ship is steered, nor where is worth steering toward.[20]

A "serviceable image of man-on-earth" must not only reflect human interdependence but "provide him with meaning for his struggles, above and beyond that involved in learning to manipulate his physical environment. It must enable him to appreciate and deal with the peril which his unbridled Faustian powers of technology have brought upon him."[21]

As Sri Aurobindo emphasizes,

> "The evolution of mind working upon life has developed an organization of the activity of mind and use of matter which can no longer be supported by human capacity without an inner change. An accommodation of the egocentric human individuality, separative even in association, to a system of living which demands unity, perfect mutuality, harmony, is

imperative... the problem is fundamental and in making it
evolutionary, Nature-in-man is confronting herself with a
critical choice which must one day be solved in the true sense
if the race is to arrive or even to survive."[22]

Our awareness of the problem and its magnitude is growing, and hopefully it is not too late to make that correct choice:

"Just as one day a human being endowed with rational self-
consciousness evolved out of the matrix of animal consciousness and built his society, culture and civilization, so, too,
we have now come to a point of evolution when there are
signs and indications that a still higher level and power of
consciousness is likely to be manifested, laying the foundation of a new global society."[23]

Let us conclude with a metaphor to describe the journey
of this transitional and transformative century of ours. We
might liken it to a space capsule launched towards the future,
propelled by the concepts of Quantum Physics, Relativity, and
Kittyhawk. When our Century Spaceship is launched, it is
weighted down by traditional forces: conceptual, political,
economic, social, and ideological. However, as the capsule
begins to accelerate through the decades towards its goal—a
new societal environment—the "gravitational field" of the
future begins to exert a progressively stronger pull upon the
vehicle and its occupants. Such a field comprises: new conceptual gestalts, such as trans- and supranational political paradigms; new socioeconomic actualities; and, above all, awareness of the need to *plan* to meet the physical and social problems which, as the capsule's occupants gaze towards their
target, begin to loom increasingly large on the horizon.

As with any space capsule traveling between the earth and
another celestial body, we are never in a vacuum—space is not
a void but a plenum—so that as we move from one locus to another, the gravitational fields of both planets are affecting us.
But our space capsule finds that the gravitational field of the
locus from which it departed is applying less pull until a point
in the transit occurs where the capsule's movement towards
the new locus in time-space begins to accelerate.

In our metaphor we are suggesting that even as the earth's
gravitational pull is much greater than the moon's, so that a

NASA space vehicle has accomplished much more than half of its flight before the moon's gravitational field becomes dominant, so the weight of traditional forces—conceptual, political, economic, ideological—has dominated well into the second half of our century. But now it would appear that the forces of the beckoning future are quickening. And the next landing place for us Earthlings is looming up with its physical and other characteristics becoming increasingly clear. We must expect anxious moments before landing on our new plateau of societal organization. But remember, we are not on a "space shuttle"—there is no going back. The flight is unidirectional, and the success of our landing will depend upon the vision that illuminates our societal transit.

Slightly more than a century ago, such a vision was captured by a life-intoxicated poet from Brooklyn. Walt Whitman seized upon the opening of the Suez Canal to herald the coming of a new age that would encompass the West, the East, and the spaces enveloping the earth:

Passage to India!
Lo, soul, seest thou not God's purpose from the first?
The earth to be spann'd, connected by network,
The races, neighbors, to marry and be given in marriage,
The oceans to be cross'd, the distant brought near,
The lands to be welded together.
O vast Rondure, swimming in space,
Cover'd all over with visible power and beauty,
Alternate light and day and the teeming of spiritual Darkness,
Unspeakable high processions of sun and moon and countless
    stars above,
Below, the manifold grass and waters, animals, mountains, trees,
With inscrutable purpose, some hidden prophetic intention,
Now first it seems my thought begins to span thee.

Passage to more than India!
O secret of the earth and sky!
Of you O waters of the sea! O winding creeks and rivers!
Of you O woods and fields! of you strong mountains of my land:
Of you O prairies! of you gray rocks!
Of morning red! O clouds! O rain and snows!
O day and night, passage to you!
O sun and moon and all you stars! Sirius and Jupiter!
Passage to you!

NOTES

1. Haridas Chaudhuri, *Being, Evolution and Immortality: An Outline of Integral Philosophy* (Wheaton, Illinois: Quest Books, 1974), p. 33.

2. Ervin Laszlo, "Goals for Global Society," *Main Currents in Modern Thought*, Vol. 31, No. 5, May-June 1975: 141.

3. Sri Aurobindo, *The Life Divine*, II, p. 28.

4. Claude Levi-Strauss, *The Savage Mind* (Chicago: University of Chicago Press, 1970), p. 13.

5. Ernst Cassirer, *An Essay on Man, An Introduction to a Philosophy of Human Culture* (New Haven: Yale University Press, 1965), p. 76.

6. For a detailed exposition of the evolution of world-views from *Mythos* to *Logos*, see our "Societal Transformations from Paleolithic to Contemporary Times," *Philosophy Forum*, 1977, Vol. 25: 323-398.

7. Gilbert Murray, *Hellenism and the Modern World* (London: George Allen and Unwin, 1953), p. 28.

8. C.M. Bowra, *The Greek Experience* (London: Weidenfeld and Nicolson, 1958), p. 199.

9. Our interpretation appears to be compatible with Chaudhuri's views: "In the Vedantic-Buddhist spiritual tradition, dominant emphasis is upon the formless Being. Names and forms (*nama-rupa*) are unreal (*mithya*). Unreal because they are ever-changing, ephemeral, evanescent (*anitya*). In contrast to this denial of forms and names, it was given to the genius of ancient Greek philosophers like Plato and Aristotle to emphasize the reality of names and forms. According to Plato, particular things and things and beings are no doubt ever changing and perishing, but their essential forms (Ideas) are eternally real. They are the formative principles of things. Forms and ideas are indeed supremely real. Concepts and definitions are real insofar as they are the structural principles of things. Thus Plato's doctrine of ideas laid the groundwork for a different line of cultural development from the Oriental mystical tradition. In the fullness of time it gave rise to the approach of precise scientific formulation and logical formulation and logical articulation. It stressed the need for the organized way of doing things according to definite principles and ideologies. Science's emphasis upon mathematical formulation and well defined laws as the essence of things is the logical culmination of the Platonic doctrine of ideas. The gradual perfecting, in the West,

of social and political institutions has also been, in a large measure, due to the rationalistic regard for determinate forms as structural elements of reality.

"Integral nondualism reconciles the mystical truth of formless Being with the rationalistic theory of forms and ideas. It holds that it is wrong to identify reality exclusively with formless transcendence. Forms and ideas are no less real. Formless transcendence on the one hand, and eternal forms and ideas on the other, may be said to represent two equally real dimensions of Being. Realization of the formless transcendence is essential for attaining spiritual depth and universality of outlook, whereas realization of the reality and value of forms, ideas, determinate principles, etc., is essential for human progress in scientific, technological, social, economic and political spheres. The former is necessary for world peace and harmony. The latter is necessary for the gradual improvement of human institutions, and for continuous betterment of the conditions of living in this world." Haridas Chaudhuri, *Being, Evolution and Immortality: An Outline of Integral Philosophy*, pp. 31-32.

10.   Arthur Koestler, *The Lotus and the Robot* (New York: Macmillan, 1961), p. 283.

11.   Murray, op. cit., p. 25.

12.   Thomas Aquinas, *Summa Theologiae*, I, qu. I, art. 6, c.

13.   Charles Singer, *A Short History of Scientific Ideas to 1900* (Oxford: Clarendon Press, 1959), p. 420.

14.   We do not mean to imply that there is any predestined assurance that this level of societal organization will be attained. History is replete with "falls" from a more complex and sophisticated to a simpler level of equilibration with environment—the experience of the Roman Empire in the West being a notable example. For more on this sociopolitical challenge for our times, see our monograph, "A Systems Approach to the Political Organization of Space," *Social Science Information* (XIV-5), 1975: 8-40.

15.   For a more comprehensive account of these quantizing factors, see our monograph, "The Present Quantum in Societal Evolution: An Analysis of Historical Indicators," *Proceedings of the Fourth International Conference on the Unity of the Sciences*, Vol. II, November 1975: 1191-1219.

16.   The Population Reference Bureau, Washington, D.C., demographic estimates reported by Patrick Brogan, *The Times* (London), 7 April 1977, p. 9.

17.   S. Giedion, *Space, Time and Architecture* (Boston: Harvard University Press, 1962), pp. 431-432.

18.   *Forces for Societal Transformation in the United States, 1950-2000* (Menlo Park, California: Stanford Research Institute, SRI Project, 6747, September 1971), p. 114.

19.   *Changing Images Images of Man* (Menlo Park, California: Stanford Research Institute, Policy Research Report 4, May 1974), p. ix.

20.   Ibid., pp. 238-239.

21.   Loc. cit.

22.   Sri Aurobindo, *The Life Divine*, II, p. 28.

23.   Haridas Chaudhuri, *The Evolution of Integral Consciousness* (Wheaton, Illinois: Quest Books, 1977), p. 13.

Education and Transformation
of Human Consciousness:
A Future Possibility

I

In looking towards the future development of higher education
for the emergent and foreseeable needs of the individual and
society, a few major trends may be marked. There is considerable evidence, backed by empirical and general studies, that
higher education has to play a crucial role in facing the threats
and promises of the future with firmness and foresight. Such
a promise implies the emancipation of the individual from
multiple fears—nuclear, biological and psychological—and unfolding the possibility of his evolutionary growth leading to
the emergence of new designs of living and a harmonious world
society.

In a rapidly changing environment, if the West is disturbed by the pollution of environment and various kinds of
alienations—alienation from the self, from one's fellowmen,
from society, from nature, from what one does and, finally, God
or the mystery of being—the East is equally disturbed by
poverty and impoverished rural environment. Is poverty not
the greatest pollutor to the human environment? Poverty and
alienation are the two major factors which are making the
human race uncomfortable. In such a climate of opinion, the
question to which we have to address ourselves today is how
to evolve new technologies, new learning methodologies and
technical know-how and know-why to accelerate the pace of
development to improve our physical degraded environment
without dislocating the beauty of nature, and ensuring an

integrated development of man and social organism. We have to treat this planet as though it were a living organism, with all the love and care and understanding which any living organism deserves. This is a delicate balance which we have to strike thoughtfully. Indeed, this balance has to be between technology and transcendence, science and insight, and know-how and know-why.

In any analysis of the educational system of both the developed and developing societies, we cannot afford to overlook the divergent problems faced by them, depending upon their level of technological and economic growth. Intoxicated by the spell of trimphant technology and dialectical materialism, western man has acquired the power "to wreck the biosphere, and while wrecking it, to liquidate himself". By wiping out creatures of "extraordinary beauty and forests" he has rushed in where angels feared to tread, and in ignorance and arrogance has everywhere upset the ecological balance in a very alarming way. Out of step with nature, with self and with the laws of historical or evolutionary growth, man has gone out of focus.

Living under the shadow of multiple fears: nuclear, biological and psychological, modern man continues to be "haunted by realities he has refused and denied, the fury of unpurged images, flame upon flame". The decisive element in the predicament of modern man is that he has lost his glassy essence and is playing such fantastic tricks which make the angels weep. He has become a misfit in a world he has himself created. "Schizophrenia pursues him like wild furies." Basically, his choice is between two possibilities, turning into a robot or becoming a responsible actor in the evolutionary process. Simply: a victim or a hero? What is to be blamed for this state of affairs, if not academic specialization and fragmentation? In such a situation, can we think of evolving an integrated system of education which will facilitate the process of the modern man's recovery from the beastiality, boredom and anomies? Or is he beyond redemption?

Let us briefly look at the role of education in developing societies which has to be different from developed societies. These societies are engaged in determining their priorities and goals of development for eradicating illiteracy, poverty, ignorance and disease. Unlike the West, these societies have to use science and technical education to accelerate the pace of development for improving their impoverished rural environment and to fulfill the basic minimum needs of their population. At the same time, they have to guard themselves against all the onslaughts of ecological imbalances so that the aesthetic beauty of the human environment is not endangered. Consequently, the focus of education has to be on the total development of man because he is the object and subject of development. It must cover man's hopes, aspirations and welfare. The quality of life rather than mindless consumerism, growth with social justice rather than GNP should be the determining variables in the developmental programs. As Norbert Weiner has said: "We must make a human use of human beings. We need creativity, not to fulfill degree requirements, but to fulfill human lives."

Education is a multidimensional process and it must strive to actualize the maximum potentialities of the individual. It must build the fundamental bridge between the world of objective observation and intellectual abstraction and of what may be called the married world of immediate experience in which nothing can be separated. Alone, this process can provide a viable future to the entire human race which currently is harnassed on hearing the sirens of prophets of gloom and doom, the prospect of a planet in peril, neantization, when an idiot hour can destroy what it has taken centuries to build. It, therefore, represents a profound challenge to human creative and evolutionary growth and should be education's first, if not only, concern.

II

What does the contemporary education scene tell us? Glib generalizations about the educational crisis have become very common on the educational landscape. Let us not forget that the credibility of the educational system is everywhere threatened by a general irrelevance as well as a philosophy of meaninglessness. There is a mood of cynicism, helplessness, drift and even futility against the way it operates in the total system. A set of questions are being openly posed against the existing educational systems in the world. These are: What is this education for after all? What is ahead? Does it prepare us to face the challenges of the future with firmness and foresight? Who are we? What is the nature of human nature? How should we be related to the planet on which we live? How are we to live together satisfactorily? How are we to develop our individual potentialities? How are we to liberate our minds from fear and generate the spirit of fellow-feeling and sense of belonging to the community? How can education satisfy our biological and psychological needs and open our various layers of consciousness? How can it generate love, understanding and help us in transcending our empirical ego? These and many other interrelated questions are being debated on the public platforms, at educational conferences and seminars. To answer these questions would call for a fresh look at the total perspective of the educational system.

Looking in depth, in our eroded educational milieu, everything human has been reduced to the state of a robot and man has become a cosmic or evolutionary dropout. No wonder the lifestyle of the people tends to be casual and superficial. Human heritage and values are faced with a set of challenges. This loss of seriousness has adversely affected the quality of life at every level. As the young architect told the sage of Popthink, Marshal McLuhan, "You see, my generation does not have goals. We're not goal oriented. We just want to know what is going on. Not going on, but perhaps going out," the pursuit of the fleeting, fragmentary and untenable has resulted in a one-dimensional milieu where most of us are reduced to playing the role of part-man or, worse, non-man.

In such a climate of opinion, where the center cannot hold because there is no center, everything conspires towards a philosophy of meaninglessness, boredom, and absurdity. Nobody associates a life of values with the university system. The student community is faced with a set of fundamental questions about the meaning and aim of life, power and authority, love and sexuality in human relationships, the relevance of the family institution to the contemporary lifestyle, and the intelligent use of increased knowledge, and are looking for their satisfactory solutions. The need for the stability of their cultural heritage, and ethical and spiritual values for their sociopsychological adjustment, is greater than ever before.

III

There is a fair consensus among educational thinkers and practitioners that the body of knowledge taught currently in the institutions of higher learning is not effectively and efficiently organized to fulfill the emergent needs of the present and foreseeable future. What adds to our irony is that instead of unfolding the possibilities of individual evolutionary growth, it tends to create fragmentation of life. It does not acknowledge the fundamental fact that all life is unity, mutuality and harmony. The problems of life are neither disciplinary nor interdisciplinary, but they go beyond the kingdom of values, which a Buddha, Christ, Mohammad, Tagore, Kabir and Swami Vivekananda were able to actualize. The existing educational curriculum does not train our sensitivity, nor organize our emotions and insights and understanding, but only makes us an expert in the manipulation of material things. The curriculum can easily manipulate economic, technological and scientific approaches. But the questions concerning intuitive awareness, immediate experience and ethical values have been found to be beyond the grasp of fragmented disciplines of knowledge. How education can build bridges between art and science, between the objectively-observed facts and immediate experience, between morals and scientific appraisals for the recovery of sanity and personal growth and a more integrated contact with the whole self, is a problem of problems.

Indeed, the discipline-bound pedantic system closes our mind to the new areas of human awareness. It does not encourage convergent and holistic thinking, or creativity and innovative spirit required to find the appropriate approach to meet the threats and demands of the future. On the contrary, what we find is that Pavlovian techniques of stimulus-response are effectively applied in the teaching-learning process. These techniques find their latest expressions in behavioral objectives which tend to stifle individual creativity, initiative and flexibility. It is easy to apply these objectives to the quantitative areas of the smallest units of cognitive procedures but extremely different to deal with issues of holistic goals, with the problems of self-concept, human attitudes, feelings, beliefs, meaning and intelligence.

Another major implication of this highly specialized knowledge is that it has brought the human species to the verge of self-destruction and it has become now an open question as to whether or not man is going to be able to survive his own technological ingenuity. Say, for example, there are enough indications of a large-scale manipulation. Artificial insemination and test-tube babies are no longer mythical characters of Huxley's *Brave New World*. Once the DNA code is deciphered, "genetic material is sure to be used at will". Scientists are engaged in discovering the chemical composition and structural configuration of matter that is the physical enabling condition for bringing matter to life and for awakening a living organism to consciousness. If the worth of a society depends on the quality of the person it produces, "it would seem we are poised for the mass manufacture of faceless and fractured non-persons".

With the development of transplant surgery, "the problem of identity will take a new turn and man may even cease to exist". Supposing brains and hearts and even memory can be grafted or replaced; "the old embarrassing question: Who are You?" loses its *raison d'etre*. We shall have millions of manipulandum, not human beings. Already advertisements, drugs, propaganda and brainwashing have spread their nets far and wide and influence the minds of people in ways no ancient tyrant would have dreamed of.

IV

In such a computerized and atomized educational milieu, both the inputs and outputs of the educational system are bound to experience a total alienation from the academic and social environment. This is precisely what is happening. The psychoanalyst Erik Erikson suggests that the most deadly of all sins has been the mutilation of a child's spirit. The mutilation is visible everywhere—mutilation of the spontaneous joy in learning, pleasure in creating, and the sense of self. This mutilation could be partly located in the sheer absence of the significance of imaginative insight, intuitive awareness, the capacity for affection, love and understanding in the current educational curricula and content of courses.

Perhaps it is again due to the absence of these intangible areas that our student body remains unimaginative and insensitve, lacks coherence of mind and finds it difficult to develop in itself a moral and aesthetic awareness. We need both intellect and lively affection, both the capacity to analyze and the capacity to feel, if we are to find answers that have a lasting meaning. Thinking alone does not make a human being. Facts and logic are sacred but there are more things in heaven and earth than facts and logic. The capacity of the individual for inward experiencing, sense of belonging and sharpening of the will, attitude and a continuing flow of vitality, are equally important for an integrated growth of man and social organism. The inward life is a life of imagining and feeling and upon its health and vigor depend the quality of living convictions. If the enormity of imbalance and sickness is to be avoided, we must strike out for an integral creative humanism in the outer and the inner life to find their equal balance. Here is an insight from W.B. Yeats:

> God guards me from those thoughts men think
> In the mind alone;
> He that sings a lasting song
> Thinks in a marrow bone.

Implicit in this is the general assumption that the course content of all disciplines—humanities, social sciences, natural and physical sciences—are under the heavy dominance of three prophets: Darwin, Freud and Marx. These prophets take us through the portrait gallery of the animal, the machine, the nihilistic, the absurd and the collective self. But perhaps they reflect their inability and unwillingness to look forward to the emergence of a luminous self, a holistic value-system with ontological and metaphysical disciplines to guide our way "beyond the faded, fractured and frustrated specimens". Say, for example, we continue to teach that the human being is nothing but the result of a mindless, meaningless and purposeless process of evolution that mutation played upon by natural selection for a sufficient length of time; this accounts adequately for the differentiation of life into diverse species and for the success of some species in surviving and for the failure of others. But this process does not leave any scope of deliberate choice on the part of the human species and tends to promote an image of man based on ruthless competiton. Contrary to this assumption, there is another image of man revolving around the concept that the essence of being human is an awareness of a spiritual presence behind the phenomena, and it is as a soul, not as a psychosomatic organism, that a human being is in communion with this spiritual presence or is even identical with it in the experience of mystics. This image of man is based on self-realization and ecological ethics and needs to be structured in our educational curricula and content of courses.

Another major implication of the educational system is that it has encouraged increasingly sensate, manipulative and valueless aspects of culture. This results in the crucifixion of life's higher values. No wonder, as primarily it has been structured on the premises that man has only bodily, mental, and vital needs and he lives within the limits of his circumscribed individuality without any psychological or inner compulsions.

The paradox remains: while educational thinkers and practitioners have been talking at the top of their voices for many years about educational objectives in terms of individual evolutionary growth, development of a coherent picture of the universe and an integrated vision—a *samanavaya* of the different items of knowledge—at the operational level the system is tending towards the process of biological, psychological and sociological engineering.

Alarmed by these symptons and forces which are currently operating aimlessly yet compulsively, some of the dissidents, though perceptive thinkers, have begun to voice their loss of faith in the operational viability of the educational system. The debunkers of the schooling myths are: Ivan Illich, Paul Goodman, John Holt, Daniel Bell, Aldous Huxley, Arthur Koestler, Rabindranath Tagore and Sri Aurobindo. They are

firmly convinced that educational institutions instead of enlarging our areas of awareness and cleansing our doors of
perception have, in fact, polluted our consciousness. How to
liberate the individual consciousness from various kinds of
bondages and tyrannies to enable it to develop an integrated
personality, and learn to live in harmony with the nature, with
the self and with the laws of historical or evolutionary growth,
is the task which education has to address itself. Let us not
forget that man is an evolving creature and is more a promise
than an achievement.

If the existing components of pedagogical learnings are
not in tune with the evolutionary needs of the individual, it
would be sheer abdication of our responsibility to blame the
learning processes as such instead of identifying a set of new
indicators of an educational system for preserving, enhancing
and creating a new quality of life and psychologically healthy
environment.

This naturally tends to lead us to know what we want and
how to become it, for the person includes an appropriate environment and certain interlocking social, political, economic,
technological and cultural institutions. What are the possibilities and alternatives before us in shaping and designing new
lifestyles and a harmonious human race?

V

Fortunately, there is nothing final about the educational
crisis and the impending doom of the human race. If there are
killers of freedom, there are also the champions of choice and
peace—rather hopeful voices. We have another way of looking
at the crisis, a larger and more inward view. We have thinkers
like Teilhard de Chardin, Arthur Koestler, Lewis Mumford,
Julian Huxley, Lecomte du Nouy, Rabindranath Tagore and
Sri Aurobindo who are speaking of a new direction in evolutionary process had we the vision to see and the ear to listen
to them.

It is fascinating to note that the entire body of literature
on education handed on to us from ancient times to the present day describes education in terms of the evolutionary

growth of the individual, development of the total individual potentialities—biological, ethical, intellectual and spiritual. This will become apparent if we briefly look at the goals and objectives of education. Howard Bowan says that "Instruction —both in and out of the classroom—should be directed towards the growth of the whole person through the cultivation not only of the intellect and practical competence but also of the affective dispositions, including the moral, religious, emotional, social and aesthetic aspects of personality." Plato quotes Socrates as saying, "And we shall begin by educating the mind and character, shall we not?" In our time Neviti Sanford writes: "Our goal is to expand both the intellect and the area of motive and feeling and to bring [them] together in a large whole." Kenneth Keniston states: "The critical components of education attempt to expose students to multiple and conflicting perspectives on themselves and their society in order to test and challenge their previously unexamined assumptions. It strives to create conditions that stimulate students' intellectual, moral and emotional growth, so that they may ground their skills in [a] more mature, human framework of values." Faure states: "The physical, intellectual, emotional and ethical integration of the individual into a complete man is a broad definition of the fundamental aim for education." According to Bertand Russell, the aim of education is to develop minds sensitive enough to perceive, to feel the shock of tragedies taking place thousands of miles away and communicate a feeling to the heart. Tagore writes that the highest mission of education is the realization of an inner quality of man, a realization that places human life in harmony with all existence. Aldous Huxley expects education to build bridges between art and science, between man and nature and between objectively observed facts and immediate experiences. Both Teilhard de Chardin and Sri Aurobindo believe that education should facilitate the process of evolutionary breakthrough of consciousness, the noosphere and the supermind respectively. Sri Aurobindo's equation of yoga with evolution opens up a new horizon.

"What is needed is a radical change of the whole basis of our life and consciousness, motive and method, a yet untried balance between the past and the present, between biosphere and noosphere." This is not the place to analyze in depth the evolution of human consicousness but the point which I intended to make is that the present fluid situation is the result of our inability to achieve a balanced development between unique scientific and technological breakthroughs and the growth of human consciousness. In such a situation, can education correct this imbalance by enlarging our areas of awareness and opening the new potentialities of our mind?

We are at a crucial point in human history and cannot afford to be bogged down in an endless controversy of specialized education curricula versus liberal education curricula, general education versus vocational education, and modern education versus the classical, but what is needed is the building of bridges between various kinds of fragmentations and divisions. Not only should we probe our educational curricula in depth but look forward to an alternative integrated curricula with a sense of greater urgency. We must begin to think about a world where basic human values are widely recognized and where the future is more than merely indulgence in selfish pursuits and fleeting pleasures. Man, values and cosmos: our lifestyle depends on a balancing of the three. To be precise, the source of our widest and most abiding motives centers in the cosmic man, transcendent values and the unlimited community. Here is the dynamics of the inner man and the new society. Here, as Plato would say, is the vision of the city laid up in heaven, the pattern for him who wills to see, and seeing, to found a city in himself. The soul is a society. Is there any ground for this faith in the future? Somehow, we must activate the pattern-making function of the mind, the pattern hidden in the heart of every man, as in the most ancient traditions, especially Upanishadic and tantric Buddhism.

It is striking to note that recent researches have unfolded enormous possibilities of the evolutionary growth of the human mind that lie ahead. In human or psychosocial evolution man is an unfinished intermediary creature and must be surpassed and completed. Perhaps no one knows about the total potentiality of the human minds and our awareness of human nature (including the natures of human systems) is selective, shaped by our symbolic and presymbolic images. True, man is the product of millions of years of evolution from the first unicellular organisms; evolution has produced a race that has been able to put a few of its members on the moon. Spectacular though his development has been, there is no valid reason to assume that human consciousness is the final product of evolution. Indeed, a strong case can be presented on the basis of a variety of writings to show that there is a distinct possibility of a new leap in evolutionary consciousness.

One even perceives a new trend towards convergence between the perennial philosophy and recent researches in biology, pedagogy and psychology, if not social reconstruction. It is not for us to speculate on the nature of the convergence and integration; but perhaps the hope of mankind lies in this direction. Our loyalty to this emerging idea will be the measure of our responsibility to the race and reality; that will determine the fate of mankind and the curve of culture. There may be a new definition of man, reality and consciousness; some unachieved unified field lies before the dreamer, the enquirer, the lover of mankind.

VI

If revolution by consciousness is the model for tommorow, perhaps the time has come to reaffirm and recommit to the concept of an integral education and to common core curriculum. If man has to grow towards the future, then the focus of educational curriculum would have to be on the attainment of creative, evolutionary, planetary, environmental philosophy. In many ways, it will have to be open-ended, multifaceted, experimental and innovative. Cutting across the extreme specialization and artificial barriers which divide humanity into races, religions, and sexes, the new educational system will strive to create a climate of opinion in favor of only one earth, one planet, one globe and one world to curb the arms race, to improve the human environment, to defuse the population explosion and to supply the required momentum to developmental efforts. While taking adequate care in preserving and enhancing cultural pluralities and identities, the new educational system will be directed towards the realization of the goal of planetary consciousness. Let us not reject the hope as an impossibility.

Before this can be attempted, there must be change in our educational methodology, our teaching-learning process and the setting and structure that surround and often support it. It should not be overlooked that the teaching process is inextricably linked up with curriculum development. It is either explicitly or implicitly determined and shaped through the teacher's behavior in the classroom as well as by the material that the student reads.

Before dealing with the problem of curriculum development, it would be appropriate to look briefly at the crucial issue of the teaching-learning process. There is something which is most important beyond the facts of knowledge, beyond books or examinations, which can be described as the inner relationships or love affairs between teachers and students. Teaching is a creative art; it should be what Koestler would call a biosociation, a bringing together of the formally unconnected, thus forming a wholeness.

It is only when the teacher becomes a creative person that he or she enters into true friendship with a learner without presenting any facade. A bond of love is established between the teacher and the learners and he or she starts appreciating their feelings and privacy, and helps them in the process of their self-actualization. In this process of mutual trust and confidence, the teacher is unfolding his or her own personal self and also helping the learners in their voyage to self-discovery.

Very little is known about the modes of learning and whatever is known about them, opinions are sharply divided, the pendulum swinging from one extreme to another. Different basic kinds of learning processes may be distinguished. One way of distinguishing them would be by physiological features (e.g. membranes, neurons, neuron networks, the cortex in evolution). Since the major thrust of this paper is on the development of an integrated value and enlarging the areas of awareness of the student community, it would be appropriate to follow Laszlo's (1972) categorization of natural systems by the type of consciousness they bring into play. Ontogenetic learning processes may then be characterized by the way which system consciousness unfolds in them.

Some of the popular modes of learning which have currently been discovered by educational thinkers to meet the challenge posed by scientific and technological breakthrough and the alienation of human life are: (i) virtual learning; (ii) functional learning; (iii) conscious learning; and (iv) superconscious learning. Time and space do not permit us to examine these modes of learning in detail. However, the major questions before us are: How to improve educators' attitudes and beliefs in the teaching-learning activity? How to introduce elements of authenticity and integrity in the teaching-learning environment for the actualization of the maximum potentialities of students? How to produce holy, healthy and happy individuals? How to create an educational milieu in which the teacher and student feel more integrated and less split, are open to experiences and pereptual awareness, fully functioning, more creative and ego-transcending and independent of their lower needs? When I speak of authenticity, I am thinking of uniqueness, that is the experience of becoming a more autonomous, more confident person. It is the experience of learning to be. Nelson Foote and Leonard Cottral use the term interpersonal competence while referring to the idea of authenticity. Abraham Maslow, a humanist-psychologist, conceives of authenticity, or self-actualization, as the inner potential of all people.

Let us not go into these questions at the moment; but the point which I intend to make is that very few people, on both the Eastern and Western scene, know that our ancient and modern seers and thinkers have had a clear perception of the quality and kind of education needed for the actualization of latent human potentialities. Dimly or clearly, they could foresee the possibility of an open-ended evolution in which man could participate in making himself. If this ideal is not utopian then we must state in categorical terms the core curriculum needed for the attainment of an ideal education. While identifying new components and viable units of a new educational system, we must take into account the relationship between nature and nurture. If we start with this problem and make it central, we can bring together information from a large number of isolated disciplines. It is only by developing an atti-

tude of love in the individual towards nature that we can unveil
the basic fact that a living organism exists in balance. As
Huxley puts it: "We need the aesthetic, an organized sensibility which will polarize our feelings and thoughts in an artistic
way towards the world."

Here is an insight from Wordsworth:

One impulse from a vernal wood
May teach you more of a man
Of moral evil and of good
Than all the sages can.

And he speaks in "The Excursion" of being:

Rapt into still communication that transcends
The imperfect offices of prayer and praise.

Wordsworth felt strongly about the spiritual relationship
of man and nature. He was convinced that in nature man could
discover his own deepest mind, "that in his relationship with
nature, he could discover his spontaneity and an immediate
unsophisticated experience of life."

The core curriculum must contain sufficient learning material to awaken our love, understanding and curiosity about
natural phenomena. To counteract the forces of dehumaniza-
tion and mental illness, like neuroses produced by our fragmented and highly specialized knowledge, we must structure
in our courses the ancient educational practices like *Yogic* exercises and physical postures, meditation and exercises in
dhyanas and mental disciplines for sharpening our intuitive
awareness. For this we have to begin at the beginning. The
choice of the self, the self as freedom, is man's hardest and
ultimate choice. The business of being aware of everything
within and without has been explicitly stated in Buddhist
texts, Upanishadic writings and Zen psychology. There is a
text, for example, which is introduced by a dialogue between
Shiva, the great god, and his wife, Parvati. Parvati asks Shiva
the secret of her profound consciousness of *Tatvami Asi*, of
Thou Art that, the consciousness that the *Atman* is identical
with the *Brahman*. Shiva proceeds to give her a list of 118 ex-

ercises in awareness which he says are all extremely helpful toward achieving this ultimate consciousness. They are exercises in awareness in every life situation, from eating one's dinner to sneezing, from going to sleep to making love, to having dreams to daydreaming.

Another identifiable major component of education curriculum could deal with the training of perceptions. Those people whose perceptions are trained experience love and joy and know the meaning and purpose of life. Following a phrase of Blake's, if "the doors of perception were cleansed, everything would be seen as it is: infinite", through proper training in perception we could cleanse the doors of our perceptions, and we could certainly look forward to a kingdom of values, a new heaven and a new earth, where the matter shall be the spirit's willing bride. It is not distorting history to say that, coming from entirely different backgrounds, yet united in aim and effort, marches an army of souls; in our midst are morning voices of the future, a new planetary culture. "There is in the world today," Kenneth Boulding has written, "an invisible college, people in many different countries and many different cultures, determined to devote their lives to contributing towards its successful fulfillment. Membership in this college is consistent with many different philosohical, religious and political positions." Auroville is another experiment in international living where the entire focus of education is on the awakening of consciousness in the individual, leading to new designs for an integral living and harmonious society.

Can there be anything more beautiful and necessary than the remaking of man and society? As Wagner has pointed out, civilization itself is obsolete and humanity is ready for apotheosis. It is our date with destiny to be civilized beyond civilization.

> And if that is all meaningless, I want to be cured
> Of a craving for something I cannot find
> And of the shame of never finding it.

UNESCO: Adventure in Evolution of Consciousness

Although I have come here to listen and learn, to obtain your opinions and pass them on to my UNESCO colleagues, who follow your activities with increasingly fervent attention, may I say how gratified we are to see that the problems mentioned in the introductory note to your seminar (which we received) mirror the imperatives which constantly guide the action of the Director General of UNESCO and the activities in the program drawn up according to his instructions. Need I call to mind the special emphasis which you lay on the problem of the links between the individual, the community to which he belongs and mankind as a whole and, even more so, between technical progress and the importance of human consciousness in the historic and natural universe. You doubtless share the anxiety of the twentieth-century predicament of man continually being wrecked by the schism between science and universal ethical imperatives. Some maintain that this anxiety is groundless. But how can this be so, seeing that it has become the most tangible factor in our time, so tangible that it is becoming more real than any real object?

Man's scientific adventure is central to your discussions, and rightly so. You are profoundly justified in pointing out to those in whom familiarity has bred indifference and blind unconcern that the realm of a nature which is every day more and more subjugated and deprived of its human significance, is necessarily taken over by forcible possession and violence, with whom alone the truth can be seen to lie. It is heedlessly said that only the balance of terror maintains world peace, without weighing the full horror of these words; whether owing to cynicism or mental insensitivity, we do not know.

So the awareness which you evoke is not easy to evoke. It is not, as is said, the result of direct apprehension; for what is at present known of the conscious mind reveals to us our ignorance, naivety and lack of consciousness. In the 1920s, when criticism of violence was developing precisely in this country [India], whose intellectual traditions prepared it for this particular task, a Western philosopher, as if echoing Indian thought, wrote, "I see that we are promised chemical warfare, and even biological warfare. Man will destroy Man, in much the same way as he destroys bugs and rats." We have since acquired the unenviable power to engender even more superhuman forces. In fact, not only more superhuman, but altogether too gigantic for our ecological sphere, for the planet as a whole is too small to withstand the damage they can inflict. Those names which evoke the extreme violence of the most terrible divinities, those who devoured their own children, are but pale shades alongside the terrible weapons which our all-powerful science has enabled us to make. The path to peace has recently been blocked by more and more formidable obstacles. At the same time, it has become the only possible path to follow.

This path UNESCO is endeavoring to identify and mark out by formulating the strategy for a "New International Economic Order" such as will meet the requirements inherent in the triangle whose verities—"human rights", "peace" and "development"—define our field of action. By virtue of its activities directed along these threefold lines, UNESCO is engaged in a continuous effort to bring about the conditions most conducive to the future age of justice which everyone has the right to hope for and the duty to promote. And it was Sri Aurobindo's dearest desire to pave the way for this glorious future by inducing in the consciousness of men the psychological change without which it cannot come into being or maintain itself. Without a new international order, all genuinely human existence remains an unfulfilled aspiration, a pious hope; but without psychological change a union of free, fully mature people remains a mirage. Individual ethics is thus, in the words of Sri Aurobindo, "a means of fulfillment for the individual and of perfect harmony for the community".

The individual must be taught to respect humanity in man, for himself and for others, but the community also must be made aware that in this respect tolerance at the international level is something which is difficult to conceive and put into practice—a concept and a way of acting which we must reformulate for ourselves if the language of consciousness is to regain a vigor worthy of reality itself. So it is not merely a question of understanding others: humanity must also understand itself. It must conceive of itself not only in terms of the adage, "whatever is human commands respect," but in terms of a still more categorical imperative, namely, that the world in which it is given us to live also commands respect, respect which compels the establishment of a new order for human relations, at the individual, community and international level: a new order for the world as a whole.

Consciousness and Culture

For Sri Aurobindo, at once radical and tradition-based, altered states of awareness, its levels, are both a fact and a value, the supreme fact and value, "for if these did not exist, the liberation of the embodied being would have been impossible" (SY, II, xix). The assertion of a higher than the mental life is the very foundation of Indian culture as of yoga (SY, Introduction). All the same, he is not a *sannyasi* or a "Hindu orthodox idealist" (HC, Ch. I). His philsophy of culture is not static, past-oriented or other worldly. On the contrary, it is emphatically futuristic, holistic and evolutionary: "A new power and powers of consciousness would be an inevitable consequence of its evolution passing beyond mind to a superior cognitive and dynamic principle" (LD, II, Ch.28). In terms of their evolutionary future, *all* cultures are but "half achievements". For, "If we define civilization as a harmony of spirit, mind and body, where has that harmony been entire or altogether real?" (FIC, I).

As Sri Aurobindo sees it—in terms of man's "deeper psychological elements" (HC, Ch. I), "the depths upon depths of our inward being" (FIC, III, ii)—"the imperative of his awakened consciousness" (IAP) points toward an alternative culture. This will fulfill—beyond the infrarational, rational, regimented, religious, ascetic, typal, spiritual—what he thinks to be "the living aim of culture . . . the realization on earth of the Kingdom of Heaven" (FIC, I).

The hope is based, clearly, on an ontological view, or "inter-view", an astounding release of visionary-expository energy. Consciousness is seen as the very stuff of Reality: "The world is real precisely because it exists only in consciousness," and, "It is a Conscious Energy one with Being that creates it." (LD, I, iii). Again: "The Being is integral and unifies many states of consciousness at a time; we also, manifesting the nature of Brahman, should become integral and all-embracing" (LD, I, iv).

What makes the Aurobindian metapsychology so unusual, positive and optimistic is the powerful social correlative, the application of a wholly "novel formula of self-determination" (IHU, Ch. 33). The recovery of a lost secret (FIC, Appendix) enables him to recast our worldly prospects "here,in life, on earth, in the body" (SY, I, ii). *Brahmateja*, soul-force, about which he had written to his wife during his political days, finds, in the later years, a cosmic annotation. "But all power is in the end one, all power is really soul force" (SY, IV, i). His tools have become more sensitive and inward; also no doubt more elitist.

Inwardness is not inactivity, but a shift of levels, effective consciousness-force. Against the crisis of civilization-cum-evolution, Sri Aurobindo projects the perilous "passage" (a Vedic idea matched by the Mysteries everywhere) from plane to plane. But what is a plane? It is the poise or the working out of a general relation which an existence or consciousness has created between itself and its powers of becoming, between self and nature. Since to exceed the self is inherent in nature or evolution, the traffic between the planes has to be opened once more and freedom founded in the context of the total, boundless, self-determining all-consciousness. Using the Vedic and Vedantic classification, Sri Aurobindo speaks of the *anna-maya, praṇamaya, manomaya vijñāna* and *ananda purusas* or *kosas*. It is only when, moving through the lower triplicity, the lower three worlds, we reach—that is, the few that do—the level of gnosis (*vijñāna),* self-luminous, supramental, that a reversal of consciousness can take place and we begin to assume the nature of the divine. After the Knowledge-Self comes the Self of Bliss, the original creative principle. A Bliss Science, not in-capable of world-play nor the monopoly of the world-negating ascetics. The bliss-freedom alone knows how to unite conflicting values and relations, outer no less than inner, and can create a culture in which "the perfected internal figures in a perfected external living" (HC, Ch. 13).

The moral is not hard to guess. "It is a spiritual, an inner freedom that alone can create a perfect human order" (HC, Ch. 20). The ideal of brotherhood, of which we hear now and then, exists only in the soul (IHU, Ch. 33). Only by the energies of the soul and self can man and society be saved. Here is the radical cure of a worldwide "essence-blindness" (Heidegger). A therapist of sick souls and societies, Sri Aurobindo does not believe in the stereotyped separation between life and yoga. According to him: All Life is Yoga (SY, epigraph). Though, truth to tell, all yoga is not Integral Yoga.

With his all out subjective approach, Sri Aurobindo's social insights—for instance, about the myth of the state and about Germany's false subjectivism that confused the life and body with the soul, about the failure of organized religions and the incompleteness of the French revolutionary slogans—are proof and offshoots of his world-view that is not innocent of the ways of the world. Man is not merely a rational or a religious animal. Both ideas suffer from almost similar limitations and lead—though through different routes—to an authoritarian, static order: in one case it is mundane, in the other transmundane. Neither makes for the total man or an achieving society and both ignore our integral possibility. But what is possible must one day be.

Certain conclusions follow. As contrasted with the rational and the religious regimentations, the spiritual society—careful to avoid the tyranny of systems—will not make the mistake of forcing men to be free. Hence, even in its early stages, before it has become a reality, two conditions are essential, two that are really one: first, awakened individuals who have remade themselves in the image of the spirit and who can communicate the idea-force to the masses, the group-mind; and, secondly, a mass or group-mind able and willing to fulfill the inexorable conditions of the higher living or transcendence. This means the transference of our will, or central being, to a higher consciousness-force above the vital and mental will, a change that has not happened on a large scale.

The "twice-born", realizing God, unity and freedom in

himself, will not be a Teutonic, Nietzschean Superman, beyond good and evil, an *Asura* armed with the latest science. Rather, seeing God in all, such a person will gladly serve all, his individuality realized in the universality. Such a person will live neither for the individual nor for the collective ego, neither for the State nor for society. His only loyalty will be to the divine. For him the only thing essential will take precedence: the conversion of the whole life to the lead of the dynamic, unitive spirit. That is, only deeper and wider truth of being, or self-vision, can cure the malaise or discontents of civilization.

The search for a planned, perfected society, a just socio-economic order, has its place in the totality. But as an end in itself it is not without danger. In any case, no change from without, no social machinery, however well-intentioned, can cut life and mind to perfection. The protest and affirmation has to be individual though; hopefully, it might spread. It is likely that in the One World, to which Nature and history have propelled us, the like-minded might come together in a common pursuit of a higher group life. The signs of such workshops of the future are not wanting, East or West.

There are bound to be problems and difficulties during the transition. These need not be stressed or denied, but "it is precisely the difficult thing that has to be done, if man is to find and fulfill his true nature" (HC, Ch. 22). Its values grounded upon eternal verities, the aim of the coming civilization will not be to create a new type of imperfect, superior mental being, but beings of another order, the supramental. The mind cannot foresee—or manipulate—the shape of supramental things to come. Much that is normal to our ways of seeing and doing will no doubt disappear: war, injustice, commercialism, uglification.

The emerging life will not be a monotone, cast into a single, fixed type; it will not necessarily be one of ascetic spareness. An evolution in the Knowledge will be more beautiful and glorious, vivid and fulfilled than any evolution in the Ignorance. Poised on the freedom of the heights, beyond reason, religion and revolution, the play of the evolved consciousness and culture will be a constant miracle: a "complete manifestation". It will be the last of things for which the first was made. "Part of the collective Yoga of the divine Nature in the human race" (SY, IV, i), it is this that will turn the child-soul into "an adult in the divine culture" (SY, I, ix). To the unity of being and the unity of culture, Sri Aurobindo has given a vigor and value that will inspire a new cycle of civilization, a most radical sociology in terms of the most ancient psychology.

Never was Sri Aurobindo more relevant than when he appeared to be remote.

The abbreviations in the text refer to these works of Sri Aurobindo:

SY *The Synthesis of Yoga*
HC *The Human Cycle*
LD *The Life Divine*
FIC *The Foundations of Indian Culture*
IAP *Ideals and Progress*
IHU *The Ideal of Human Unity*

Toward Culture and Consciousness Symbiosis: A Contemporary Challenge

It is necessary to understand the content of culture in the broad and comprehensive sense. This in itself is a challenge because no exact definitions are possible, even desirable, in the case of such an emotional and intellectual complex as the culture of a specific society. Culture like love will always elude definition and remain an awareness beyond words and concepts, a precious belonging that is within us and also around, linking us to a whole expanse of life, retaining its own uniqueness in time and space. For each one of us, it will have a special meaning and significance.

In general, the culture of a particular society comprises three distinct elements: *ideas*, *aesthetic forms* and *values*, largely molded by past traditions and future aspirations. Ideas give rise to habits and beliefs, thereby perpetuating themselves through social institutions that provide stability; aesthetic forms reflect the artistic expression of a culture in its visual arts, music and poetry as well as the sense of beauty manifested in the day-to-day living of individuals and social groups; and the values of a culture are formed by the interplay of both ideas and aesthetic forms and provide norms of conduct, standards of behavior, and sources of faith and vision. Of these three elements of culture, the values are of the greatest importance; values develop the precious assets of wisdom and discrimination in a specific culture, and they also provide the dynamism for action and change, and impart vitality and quality to the life of the people.

The understanding of a particular culture requires a correct comprehension of the ideas underlying it and a measure of intelligent appreciation of its aesthetic forms; it is, however, the values of a culture that contain its essence and offer the best way of understanding it and participating in it. A living and vital culture is rooted in authentic and healthy traditions, has the capacity of continuous renewal and adaptation, and is developed by new aspirations and bold innovations; in this way the past, the present and the future are reflected together in that life of the mind and the spirit that is the indefinable complex of culture. The humanities and the arts, the sciences and the technologies, the network of communications and relationships, the magic of poetry and the transcendence of religion, all these spheres of action and speculation form the pattern of a culture. The rich and fascinating diversity of these patterns is a precious heritage of mankind that needs to be preserved and developed. The participation of all and not only the privileged elite in the culture life of a community, and the increasing cooperation among cultures to renew and enrich all cultural patterns and to evolve a new sense of universality and more harmonious and cooperative world order, these are the two great needs of our times. The fantastic growth of knowledge and the rapid pace of change in all spheres of life make it necessary to initiate deeper reflections on the content of culture, the role of cultural values and the nature and methodology of cooperation. Such reflections should take place both inside each living culture and among them together in a spirit of cooperation and friendship. Those concerned with action and implementation should be able to forecast trends and innovate programs of relevance to the future. The need for cooperative and interdisciplinary research and meaningful dialogues is obvious and urgent.

Never before the emergence of this age was it possible to consider consciously, systematically and synthetically the challenge to man and his larger society from a cosmic point of view. Contemporary man has to seek his salvation along with the salvation of his society and apart from his local and national homes, his global habitat is now a reality. Both his scope of action and responsibility of choice have taken a universal dimension of possibilities and consequences. In the past thoughtful persons living beyond the prison of the passing moment and seeking some unattainable vision have speculated over the future of their own life spans and the mystery beyond life and death; but never before have they probed into the living problems of all humanity or even their own civilization or culture in order to find solutions and plan for appropriate action.

This has been achieved by the growing awareness of man about his own personal nature, about his larger society and culture and about the whole of humanity. We partake of many diversities in an overall unity of similar concerns and a common bondage. The interdependence of nations and the solidarity of mankind are sensed far more keenly and seen in so many more tangibles by contemporary man than by his forebears of the past.

In addition to this shrinkage of space in the mind of man and his daily concerns, contemporary man has established a new relationship with time. Different cultures have viewed the phenomenon of time in diverse ways, but all men and women of our time, sharing the universal advance of science and technology and the explosion of knowledge, can confidently feel that man is now, more than ever before, a maker of his own destiny, a conscious and masterful agent in the process of evolution. The fulfillment of this destiny calls for new capacities, responsibilities and duties, which are now not beyond his grasp and performance.

We must now move towards a greater synthesis of life by a wise and orderly convergence of its many parts and seek the wholeness of man in the integration of his inner being and his outer environment. The union of science and spirituality poses a challenge which is both enormous and exciting. The dominance of the economic man which still persists in the habits and institutions of our industrial, money-making and power-grabbing past can now give way to the shaping of a more integrated man, preferring the richness and wholeness of the quality of life to the mindless production and consumption of material goods in a debasing spirit of acquisition and greed, leading always to tension and conflict.

The challenging implications of these contemporary developments, deeply concerning the inner man and his outer environment of people in his time and space, call urgently for accurate knowledge and deep wisdom in order to act together for the creation of a new man and new world order. Many challenges face us. To my mind three great challenges loom large and continually gather force; for me, the third of these, the making of the inner man in his moral and spiritual entity, is the most crucial problem.

The three great challenges confronting man and his societies can be briefly stated as follows.

MAN'S PHYSICAL SURVIVAL

This is perilously endangered by a trinity of evil forces that are not unrelated. The three forces are: (a) the terrible consequences of the armaments race and man's mad and increasing investment in the powerhouse of death and destruction —which draws an enormous part of his intellect and wealth; (b) the dangers of unbridled consumerism which leads to waste, the pillage of nature, and the decadence of man's moral and spiritual nature; (c) the persistence of poverty and sheer starvation among large sections of humanity when some optimum well-being is clearly within the reach of all if we can only act wisely in a spirit of sharing together and mutual cooperation.

MAN'S MORAL INTEGRITY

Here too the challenge to man's moral integrity assumes three important forms: (a) care for human dignity by battling against misery and wretchedness and recognizing the innate worth of all living beings; (b) promotion of and defending freedom, which is the birthright of all and also an essential condition of any worthwhile civilization and culture; (c) attaining a large measure of equality and social justice within each society and among all societies of both the so-called developed and developing nations.

MAN AS A SPIRITUAL ENTITY

The overriding factor in the making of civilization is always the spirit of man, which is now unfortunately depressed and threatened by the technology and institutional network of power and vested interest. More than anything else we need now to assert the primacy of man's immortal spirit and his precious spiritual entity by exploring and developing the inner man which is the source of creativity and transcendence. For me the foremost challenge of contemporary man is the discovery and affirmation of man's spirituality and bringing it into full play in the marvelous drama of life and for the attainment of some new leap forward in creation and transcendence. Only such an affirmation and transcendence can solve the numerous problems that bedevil us in the process of temporal life, and threaten man's essential moral nature and even his physical survival.

How can we go about meeting this supreme challenge of affirming and generating man's spirituality for a greater quality of life, a new civilization of order and beauty and the best refinements and creative sparks of culture?

At this point I wish to present a statement on *Toward Creativity and Transcendence in Search of the Inner Man* which I wrote for myself during an obscure period of my life. I present this here because it is relevant to the overriding challenge to contemporary man.

When things go wrong in the normal working of human affairs and the business of day-to-day living becomes sour and bleak to the taste and the eye, it is good to think of the larger dimensions to existence. They are always with us but tend to fall into oblivion in the passion and frenzy of living and in the rush of the "grab and get" tempo of daily life, inspired by the rather low pursuits of power and acquisition.

Beyond the dimension of the present moment of temporal existence filled by the needs of the body and its earthly drives of flesh and lucre, there are always two other dimensions, the cosmic and the elemental, to which we belong, deeply and irrevocably, and in a sense more intensely and relevantly than the seeming immersion in the temporal. To ignore and forget these realities of our external home in the cosmos and our origins in the elements of nature and heredity is to invite disaster to the integrity and wholeness of the human person. The lure of temporal existence, dominated by the pursuit of power and the might of technology, and obsessed with the needs and desires of life experienced in moments and fragments, deludes us into such a condition.

Let us think of the larger dimensions of the cosmos and of the elements of our being beyond the plight of the temporal in the present moment.

The cosmic dimension of my life relates me to the vast totality of awareness received through the mind and the senses from all the known wonders of the sciences, the arts and the humanities, and the warmth of sheer living and human relationships experienced in an evergrowing sensitivity of the spirit. It also includes the consciousness of the ultimate mystery, which may remain distant and unfathomed, but can never disappear or become insignificant. In fact, the more we know and experience the greater is the consciousness of the mysterious, and the best perspective of life often emerges from the living reality of the mysterious, felt and experienced vividly alongside the luminosity of knowledge and the intensity of sensual awareness. The cosmic dimension, therefore, comprehends both reason and faith, science and poetry. My cosmos is truly a world of greater wonder and greater mystery in which I can sense the infinitely larger whole of which I am a tiny fragment and thus feel in this keen sense of belonging what one may call the sancity and unity of life. The cosmic dimension brings experience of timelessness in love, worship and beauty. It calls for several ways and moods for its revelation, the ways of reason and faith, the moods of active strife and patient waiting, depending upon one's condition, choice and temperament. Each one develops his own way and style of transcendence in the pursuit of the same urge for reaching beyond the self and its present predicament to higher dimensions of awareness and vision.

For me the daily offering of solitude and meditation is always an attempt at merging into the cosmic; the passing events assume their true proportion and meaning only in the awareness of the cosmic, which relates the trivial and the transitory to its inner care of meaning and timelessness; and the day's brief passage flows into the endless stream of history by the magic touch of the cosmic which is always with us but is seldom recognized and employed in the busienss of daily living. Now it is time to turn to the cosmic dimensions of life and brood over its mystery in wonder, enjoy the marvel of its contemplation, and probe into its essence.

The elemental dimension is also a reality to be reckoned with, an essential part of existence. While the cosmic partakes largely of the world of the mind and the spirit, the elemental dimension is comprised of the seed and sap of life and the essence of the life-force. I mentioned above that the main components of the elemental are nature and heredity. Nature is the larger environment of our earthly habitat from which we derive our biological origins and our sustenance through life. Heredity conditions within certain limits our individual makeup and offers participation in the life of the past—the past of our tribes and societies and, indeed, of the entire species, the past of man which each man shares. The elemental dimension of existence, highlighting as it does our identity with nature and our origins in the past, is also an experience of a larger whole than the moments and patches of the temporal present. The two dimensions of the cosmic and the elemental are in a way similar, though the former extends far beyond the nature and scope of the latter. We are citizens both of our lovely planet pusating with life and the beauty of nature and of the larger cosmos spread in the infinity of space and time. The awareness of this dual citizenship is for me the highest achievement of the human person and the most precious element of the quality of my life. The extension of this personal awareness to a larger awareness shared by my society enriches the social life and adds an essential element to all progress and development. Both the cosmic view and the awareness of the nature and origins of life by individual persons as well as by the larger socieities afford the two objectives.

But in the alienation from the temporal state of which I am so acutely now aware these two dimensions are powerless to create except in the realm of the mind and the spirit, and even such creations remain incomplete, often irrelevant. I can relax and ascend, but I am cut off from a certain reality that lives essentially in the moment and finds expression in the routine and strife of daily life. I fear escapism and the irrelevance of personal satisfaction derived from the cosmos and from the elements divorced from the reality of the present moment. No, the temporal present is all-important because it is the only habitation of the cosmic and the elemental that is given to mortals. It is the only moment of consciousness, the past having ceased to be and the future still unborn. The temporal present should always comprehend the point of revelation of the cosmic vision and the awareness of the elemental reality. Any sense of alienation from the temporal present clouds the vision of the cosmos and undermines the relevance of the elemental. We are made to live in all three dimensions at the same time and in some balance and harmony that joins all three. This balance and harmony is the product of human creativity. Therefore, the fullness of life is given to creative persons living harmoniously on all three dimensions of the cosmic, the elemental and the temporal.

Creativity, then, is the power to balance, harmonize and integrate, to be aware of all the parts that make a whole without losing sight of the whole that is far more than its parts, and to be able to live in the intensity of fullness at least in the moments of creation. A sense of harmony, the wholeness of integration and the intensity to know, express and transcend are the three essential hallmarks of creativity. All three operate together, in periods of long labor or prolonged waiting, or in moments of sudden flashes of luminosity, emanating spontaneously from some kind of simmering that had gone on both consciously and unconsciously. The apparent manifestations of the birth of creativity vary widely, depending upon the nature of the creating agent, the object of creation and the integrity and equality of the final creation itself. The achievement of creation is marked by three elements of discovery, uniqueness and communicability.

Some sense of discovery always enters into the creative process. The creator is impelled by an itch or urge to know the unknown and to build what has never existed before. The sense of discovery leads to the creation of something special and unique. The creatio may be small and familiar; it is never commonplace and trivial.

The uniqueness of creation lies in the quest of the creator who brings into play the entire uniqueness of his personality, harnessing all its resources in the fullness of the creative effort. Ordinary, routine and commonplace living expresses moments of thought and action in time and space. Creative living is always in search of transcendence, groping towards meaning and synthesis, defying the limitations of time and place, always achieving some measure of expansion or flight of the spirit in success or failure. A creative act cannot be repeated because its uniqueness has given it a form and a meaning which were born out of circumstances that will never again be the same.

Communicability is the third element of creation. By its very nature the product of creativity is intended for a larger sharing, or the striving to be universal. It is, as it were, an offering of the creation to all creation. That is how God created the universe and the spirit of such a divine creation can be left by all created things. For us mortals of the human species on a tiny speck of the universe the measure of our creation is infinitely small and insignificant; but the quality and thrust of the creative act partakes of that spirit of the divinity from which we ourselves emanated. An element of universality enters into all creation.

THE BASIC PROBLEM

The main point is the problem of finding the ways and means of achieving creativity or fullness of life by harmonizing the temporal, which cannot be renounced, with the cosmic and the elemental, which should not be forgotten. Man's frequent sloth and faintheartedness, and his abiding fear and greed, often employed in the pursuit of false gods of power and worldly values, have so far condemned him to a track of history which has projected prominently only his lower nature, hiding the few beautiful creations of saints, sages and artists among the vast ocean of meaningless, forgotten deeds. Can we reverse this process? Instead of being so sparse and exceptional, cannot creativity be the normal manifestation of human life? I believe such a leap of transcendence to be not only possible, but inevitable if we have to survive as a species and avoid the temptation of committing suicide by senseless violence or sheer decadence. The enormity of the danger and the supreme challenge to human life now posed to all mankind may generate that rare spark of creativity and the upsurge of moral and spiritual resources to keep it alive, which are necessary to the blossoming of wisdom, compassion and courage for the attainment of transcendence in an ever-ascending perception and experience of life's meaning and quality. We are moving towards that moment of man's destiny when the choice is narrowed to the shooting at the stars by mobilizing fully the power and potentiality of the inner man and harnessing his physical, intellectual and spiritual energies for a new creation of conscious transcendence or perishing in confusion, selfishness, greed and fear with a bang or a whimper.

The Future of Consciousness

Human consciousness did not all of a sudden evolve like Venus Aphrodite. It came through millions of years of long and tortuous evolution. This may be debatable as to whether it is the answering reflection of an all-pervasive divine consciousness or simply a function of matter in evolution, but it is now widely recognized that human consciousness is not something alien to this planet but has emerged from the very heart of earthly evolution over the eternal time continuum. What is not yet adequately realized is that human consciousness, rather than being the *summum bonum* of evolution, may be just another stage in the evolutionary adventure which will ultimately be transcended, much in the manner that human consciousness itself marked a transcendence over mineral, vegetable and animal forms of awareness. If one thinks about it, there is really no justification for us to assume that human consciousness is the end result of the evolutionary thrust. If the dinosaurs who dominated this planet for millions of years had been asked whether they were the high point of evolution, they would have no doubt, if their brains had been larger, growled the question aside as that of an impertinence. And yet they disappeared from the face of the earth, leaving only fossil remains that the puny but imaginative homo sapiens recreated into their likenesses.

This *species megalomania* is not surprising, and yet the sharpest minds among our race have, ever since the dawn of recorded history, questioned the assumption that man as we know him today is the highest that evolution can achieve. In many of the great civilizations that have flourished over the last five to seven thousand years there is to be found a thin but distinct stream of thought running like a golden thread across the centuries that postulates the further growth of man into something greater than himself. I am referring here not to the mass of beliefs regarding after-death states found in all religions, but to the conviction that here on this planet itself it is possible for man to evolve into a superior being, superior not merely in physical and mental capacities but in a sense that expresses a qualitatively higher form of consciousness. Ancient texts of many civilizations, including our own Vedas and Upanishads, are replete with references to this evolution of a higher consciousness from the present texture of human awareness, veiled under a variety of myths and symbols. The tradition of superior beings who have transcended their human limitations and yet remain on earth to sweeten the bitter sea of sorrow for their fellow men is to be found in most of the great cultures of mankind. In recent times some of the most penetrating minds have paid special attention to the question of evolution of consciousness. Thus Sri Aurobindo among the Eastern and Teilhard de Chardin among the Western thinkers have devoted a great deal of their remarkable talents to studying in great depth the modalities of evolution, the difficulties in the path and the nature of the next evolutionary plateau.

The fact is that man is the first species on this planet to be *self* conscious, in other words conscious of being conscious, and therefore the first to have to grapple with the implications, at once profoundly disturbing and endlessly fascinating, of the possibility of transcending himself. What will the next step on the evolutionary ladder be? It would seem that physically there is little possibility of major changes in the foreseeable future, except that with better nutrition and public health facilities the future human being may perhaps be larger and better nourished. It is essentially in the sphere of the brain that changes may be expected, and here again it would appear that what will be involved is not so much a growth of the brain itself but a fuller utilization of its existing capacities. It is a strange fact, often mentioned but seldom analyzed, that we are at present utilizing only a small fraction of our brain cells as far as our waking consciousness is concerned. Estimates vary, but few experts put the utilization above ten per cent, which means that nine-tenths of our brain capacity remains unused. Could it be that the next evolutionary thrust would involve a progressive dawning into our waking consciousness of these unutilitized areas of darkness?

It is in the words of the mystics that some hints are available as to the possible nature of the new consciousness. Throughout human history mystics of every age and clime, every culture and religion, have sung of a wondrous new way of seeing, a qualitative leap in the text of consciousness itself. Thus William Blake spoke of holding infinity in the palm of one's hand and seeing eternity in an hour, while Francis Thomson lamented:

> The angels keep their ancient places,
> turn but a stone and start a wing,
> 'tis ye, 'tis your estranged faces
> that miss the many splendored thing.

What is this many-splendored glory of which the mystics sing? What did the seer of the Svetashevatara Upanishad mean when he proclaimed in ecstasy: "I know that great being shining in splendor like the sun beyond the darkness"? Could it be that these flashes prefigure a mode of consciousness that could one day become the common heritage of the entire race and not remain confined only to a handful of remarkable men and women?

The question of evolution opens out a vast field of fascinating enquiry towards which some of the best minds of the race are now beginning to turn their attention. More and more men of science are turning their minds towards a most fundamental question facing mankind as we move towards the end of the second millennium after Christ. It is the question as to whether we are destined permanently to remain in our present largely unsatisfactory state of consciousness, or whether we can move onwards up the evolutionary ladder, this time not obliged to wait for millions of years until mother nature nudges us gently upwards but with the capacity to actively cooperate with the evolutionary force and thus telescope into a comparatively few centuries what might otherwise take another billion years.

The question is not as theoretical as it might appear at first hearing. In the last four decades since nuclear power was harnessed and the space barrier broken, our race has entered a new and potentially extremely dangerous phase of its long and tortuous history. The old chasm between knowledge and wisdom has widened dangerously. There has been a fantastic, exponential growth in knowledge. In almost every field of human endeavor science and technology have worked and designed revolutionary changes. And yet with all this progress, indeed because of it, the human race is for the first time in real danger of nuclear annihilation. There is enough fissionable material already circumambulating the earth to destroy mankind several times over, waiting only for a neurotic leader to push the fatal button. Despite phenomenal economic progress in the developed world the problems of mankind do not seem to get permanently resolved, and many of the old phobias and neuroses which were supposed to have been banished long ago are returning to plague the race and shatter its smug illusion of endless material growth leading to a new golden age. Knowledge grows, but wisdom atrophies.

Perhaps the problem of the human being cannot be solved at all until we emerge into the light of a new consciousness. But if so, how can this be achieved, and how long will it take? Is man, as Arthur Koestler has postulated, essentially a self-destroying mechanism, so that all his technological ingenuity will inevitably end in self-annihilation? I am endlessly fascinated by the ancient myth of Atlantis, that great civilization with its unparalleled material glories which one night sank beneath the waves forever, unable to develop the wisdom necessary to match and tame its knowledge. Are we now witnessing the neo-Atlantis, or will some benign turn of destiny enable us to stave off disaster? If the latter happens it must surely involve the evolution of a new, higher mode of consciousness that cuts across the barriers of race, religion, nationality and ideology, and knits the entire human race into a unified whole.

Communicative Consciousness with Built-In Control

This paper attempts to discuss the following topics:

1. An effective system of practicing communicative consciousness;

2. Exercising self-control with mutual/collective recognition; and

3. Actualizing supranatural breakthrough to achieve balanced insight.

Man at present is having difficulty with his own conscience, that is the consciousness within oneself which shows that growth of the elements out of which human consciousness is composed is improper and imbalanced, which in turn justifies the fear that the stability of the existence of man may be at stake. Man is already losing his faith in the possibility of maintaining security and welfare in the future. We realize nowadays that man's world is shocked by conflicts and challenges that are in themselves manmade or caused by nature. Apparently man has lost his identity in the sense that he has lost his focus on the spiritual will that could give him consciousness of the source and purpose of life. Therefore, he would only live physically or partially without any knowledge of the full scale of life which is based on a pleasing harmony of all the elements of human consciousness.

It is the spiritual will in man that endows him a full and clear conscience, and makes him awake, aware, attentive, realizing, having knowledge and understanding about his origin, his life-plan in the present as well as in the future life. It is the state of consciousness in man that provides him with the key to all perceptive qualities which may be adapted for this life as well as for the eternal life. Completeness of conscience or full consciousness within oneself will provide a person with a feeling of stability in his faith which means that he has identified himself for being the innerself.

Partial consciousness on the other hand exposes a trend of producing intellectual scientists whose conscience is dominated by a strict causal thinking which has brought about the present high level of science and technology. It has however been perceived that with all this advanced progress in thinking it has become more and more difficult for man to create and to maintain peace and understanding. It seems almost that those philosophers and scientists are misused to support the forming of concentrated power-centers which confront each other. Apparently cultures that are mainly based on the special power of thinking and reasoning have been unable to resist the temptations of improper human desires which are in conflict with principles of humanity and social justice. Man has been increasingly worried by the confrontation of power-centers which have been supported by technologies that can be sold for the sake of a "partial living world" to satisfy the "partial conscience of man".

The problem indicated above is not how to suppress the progress of man's intellectual power or of his technological capacity, but how to manage such power and capacity growing within the containment of man's full consicousness. Imbalanced knowledge has been developing increasingly because of the mistake of letting intellectual powers and capacities grow outside the structure of man's conscience. In that way the power of the brain has been developing separately from the other elements of conscience, while arts and ethics have been developing also their own values in the partial way.

Thus the need for "recreation" came into existence when problems of thinking caused signs of stress; of course this is the result of the partial use of conscience. Also came into existence the need for "confessing and relief of sins", being full of regret-repentance when man's thinking went astray when tempted by improper desires.

Completeness of conscience does not only mean having a thinking force, an artistic feeling, and a strong will side by side. There should be also a horizontal lively communication between those elements. From the flow of communication will arise a conscience which envelopes a highly ethical and artistic thinking power and high moral standards.

This full conscience indicates man's inner self and serves as an inner instrument to monitor dynamic thinking, aesthetic feelings and proper desires. If the three monitored parts are aligned and free from conflicts, so the nature of man's action will be. Here then we see the first stage of practicing communicative consciousness, that is to develop the fullness of conscience inside man individually. Thereafter, the system will link this developed conscience of man among individuals collectively. In this way, we will be able to develop social conscience or collective consciousness.

At this stage of consciousness people are each for themselves caring for their pure conscience, pure in body and mind, the conscience of the inner self, which may induce a mutual flash of conscience between them for better recognition and understanding of each other. In this very position man is practicing introspection and self-control, while at the same instant he is also able to certify the very same position of his fellow human beings. Man is practicing self-control with the ability of mutual and collective recognition.

These inward- and outward-link attitudes of consciousness open the door for a social behavior towards self-correction which will enforce the forming of stable and efficient social habits and of an honest community with high moral standards. At this stage the cultured man and the man's culture develop on the foundation of a balanced consciousness. The balancing interaction of physical and mental powers guided by the inner self guarantee the growth and the maintenance of man's dignity and of national and world cultures. A culture that has only physical outer values and that has no lively inner backing of human consciousness is poor of resistance and is certainly doomed to die.

Thus the balanced personal consciousness has integrated all existing inner elements of human conscience, and so it has opened the door for communication between persons in all physical and mental aspects, as well as the full inner self. Man, who has reached the stage of inner self at the same time, will establish the bridge to other people's inner self, and thus develop the proper foundation of social life. This should be performed or at least practiced with a strong conviction so that it doesn't stop with daydreaming. In fact, the practice is not too difficult because man has only to be honestly willing to probe his inner self and meet its identity.

The inner self is the seat of the complete consciousness which will affect all factors concerning factual life. In this way, development of technologies would take by itself aesthetic feelings and moral standards into account. The inner self will monitor all developments inclusive of one's faith towards the higher true self, so it turns out to be a self-developing force.

To get an insight in one's inner self, one should try to lift his consciousness to a level from where he could observe the movements of thoughts, feelings, and desires without being directly involved in those movements themselves. From that level he will notice the driving force and also the restraints that exist because of the partial functionality of the diverse elements. Such movements will slow down and settle themselves into an equilibrium which coincides with the mood of relaxation of each element. Thought, feeling, and desire communicate in the mood of relaxation, and a state of bliss will result as if one experiences the existence of a continuous stream of life. It is this bliss of continuous stream of life that indicates the inner self identity, the spiritual will.

If one has once experienced the process mentioned above, further on, in either integrated or in partial functional position, his humane properties will always function, well-balanced in the monitoring towards total and continuous life, and thus keep man's actions away from conflicts and frustrations. Similar experiences of many individuals will lead to the growth of a social consciousness.

This social consciousness in fact connects two or more individuals who are each of themselves in an inner-self position, while flashes of pure conscience are exchanged which are felt physically as well as spiritually. In other words, a common social consciousness has conceived the individuals or connected them in a strong bond of life without losing the condition of balanced conscience each for themselves. It is the balanced social-individual conscience that has the power to create the knowledge and understanding about optimum common individual wants.

The notion and practice of consciousness indicated above open the way, directing to super/supranatural dimensions. While the natural life is based on human desires supported by reasoning and feeling, supranatural life is guided by conviction based on divine indications, which will light the way for achieving the true self as being a product of eternal life.

In this setting, man is given the opportunity to remain protected in the well-balanced position of factual life. The more people practice this supranatural breakthrough in order to gain experience and knowledge of divine indicators, the more the natural life of humankind in general will be protected in factual life. Man in general will achieve balanced insight.

The practice of supranatural consciousness as a breakthrough experience of the inner self towards the complete true self can be witnessed, certified and acknowledged by people who have settled their horizontal alignment as mentioned before, and thereafter have started to develop a vertical evolution. The achievement of their inner self and their balanced social behavior have been accomplished by the horizontal alignment, while their vertical evolution has been working on the improvement of the inner self towards the identification of the true self. Therefore, the vertical evolution has the nature of the purifying evolution or the divine evolution.

The vertical process is needed to purify our monitoring faculty for actual life purposes which explains the practical aspects of the system. It is sincerely hoped that world consciousness equilibrium will be monitored at ever increasing levels of purity and well-being.

As a conclusion, it is wished that man and community be aware of:

1. the existence of an effective system for achieving a fair level of communicative consciousness;
2. the existence of a method to practice introspection/self-control while being witnessed one by another in a group; and
3. the existence of the opportunity to achieve a level of consciousness at which human conscience and supranatural

guidance will meet within the framework of an endeavor to monitor and contain the world's physical and mental life into a more balanced and solid growth so as to guarantee a true welfare for man and his environment.

The learning of the sytems indicated above has been obtained by individual experience, practicing and exercising, and not merely by reasoning or intellectual research, within a life period of more than forty years. The system has been verified thoroughly wthin a social group consisting of at least five thousand active members.

Atom and Self

For a physicist, it is not enough to understand physics and mathematical advances, one must have some acquaintance with the history of science and philosophy. During my formative period of growth, I was fortunate enough to be exposed to a number of books in this area including Oliver Lodge's *Pioneers of Science* and Will Durant's *The Story of Philosophy and The Mansions of Philosophy*, under the able guidance of Prof. Meghnad Saha. The study of these works unfolded a new vision of reality and a number of strange questions disturbed my consciousness, especially the question relating to the problem of *mind-body interaction*. Another question which posed a riddle relates to identifying the happiest and saddest thought in one's life. Most people, except the highly creative, would find it very difficult to identify a single thought as the "happiest" of their life. For Einstein, the "happiest thought" of his life came in 1907 at the age of 28, as he has himself recorded. It was the thought that "the gravitational field has similarly (like the electric field produced by electromagnetic induction) a *relative* existence. For, if one considers an observer in free fall, e.g. from the roof of a house, there exists for him during his fall no gravitationl field at least in his immediate vicinity." (G. Holton, *The Physics Teacher*, March 1979.)

What fascinated me most in the realm of philosophy was the issue of "self". There is no more profound problem, nor one more fundamental and more puzzling than the interaction between "atom" and "self". Another name for it is the brain-mind or body-soul problem.[1]

If we use a word such as "soul", we should not mix this profound concept with naive, puerile descriptions which contradict science or reason. To do so is to kill the concept right at the start. This is emphasized forcefully in the *Upanishads* and the *Gita*.

The awareness—for me—of the brain-mind problem is largely a result of renewed interest among physicists in the foundations of quantum mechanics, and the writings of Sherrington, Schroedinger, Wigner, Eccles, and Popper—to mention a few who come immediately to my mind. But what an irony! At a time when even the remotest idea that there was a problem of the "self" did not strike most people doing physics in the homeland of the *Upanishads*, there was Schroedinger, in distant Berlin, writing an essay in 1925 on the *Vedanta*. And this at the very same time he was fully absorbed in the discovery of the epoch-making wave equation for the electron. How formidable is the gap between Indian higher education and our philosophical-ethical thought!

In an oft-quoted statement (1951) Schroedinger says: "I consider science an integrating part of our endeavor to answer the one great philosophical question which embraces all others, the one that Plotinus expressed by his brief *Who are we*? And more than that: I consider this not one of the tasks, but *the* task of science, the only one that really counts."

In other words, the ultimate goal of science and of all moral and spiritual striving is the same. There is no difference. "*Who am I?*" is what Nachiketa asks in the *Katha Upanishad*. The question "*Who am I?*" is, on close analysis, no different from the question, "What is the abode of *Truth*?" Does *Truth* reside in space and time or is it outside both space and time? More about this later. Many may not go as far as Schroedinger, but all would agree that the grave dangers facing mankind today —think of the mounting probability of an all-out nuclear war— cannot be met unless earnest attention is paid to an understanding of the self, the human being.

The search for "Who am I?" is the foundation of all true morality and religion. While "What is an electron?" is a question which relates to the external world,"Who am I?"belongs to the internal world.

Mankind's very survival is at stake.[2] That we need to know more about the atom, about the external world of space-time and matter-energy, is certain. But to ignore altogether the knowledge of the self can in the end only invite disaster. The foundation of duty and reverence is self-knowledge, and not the atom, not the external world. Even to decide to dedicate oneself to Science, this decision is not a part of Science. It is outside science. It is akin to some kind of religious faith. It is, perhaps, no exaggeration when E. F. Schumachar (1977) says: *"The modern experiment to live without religion has failed,* [italics his] and once we have understood this we know what our "post-modern" talks really are." A. N. Whitehead said some years ago that the future of civilization depends on the degree to which we can balance the forces of science and religion. And in describing the aims of education, he tells us that the essence of education "is religious . . .which inculcates duty and reverence" (A.N. Whitehead, *Aims of Education,* 1962.)

It has been my belief from student days (ever since I read the *Gita* in Annie Besant's translation) that foundations of relativity and quantum theory provide highly suggestive analogies and ideas for an appreciation and understanding of Indian spiritual thought. This has been, of course, immensely reinforced by the inspiring writings of Einstein, Bohr, Schroedinger, Heisenberg, Wigner and others. Also, for a quest of the *foundations* of modern physics, Indian philosophic thought can be very stimulating and suggestive. No longer can the problems of the *nature of reality* be evaded in physics. An occasion to speak on *"Atom and Self"* has for me therefore a special interest.

TWO REALITIES

Two things are important. First, *the duality of the two worlds,* and secondly, *the question of interaction between them.* The "external world" and the "internal world", that is to say the "atom" and the "self" should be accepted as equally significant for human life, the two equally real. Cyril Hinshelwood (1962) observes: "To deny the reality of the inner world is a flat negation of all that is immediate in existence; to minimize its significance is to depreciate the very purpose of living, and to explain it away as a product of natural selection is a plain fallacy."

The external world (E-World) is public, *objective*. The E-World includes, of course, the body. The internal world (I-World) is the world of the *psyche*—"I", self, spirit, soul, mind, or whatever we may call it. It is private, *subjective*. Thoughts, feelings, emotions, pleasure and pain, purpose, goals, all these belong to the I-World. Psychology, to the extent that it investigates the I-World by methods appropriate for the E-World, can be called science, strictly speaking. But then it is hardly a study of the I-World. The amazing reliability and strength of science lies in its *objectivity*. Within science there is no place whatsoever for questions such as: To what purpose? To what ends or goals? Why the starry sky so beautiful? These are moral questions. These are not questions *within* science. *The exclusion of subjectivity, that is, "I", from natural science is total.* This has come about gradually since the time of Galileo and Newton. *Brain* belongs to the E-World, *mind or consciousness* belongs to the I-World.

If we insist on holding one of the two, the external world (matter) and internal world (mind), as the only reality, or the one as the more fundamental of the two, two options are open to us. We may take matter *above* mind, or mind *above* matter. The choice is not at all an easy one. We may be inclined to believe that matter is primary, and mind an appearance, an epiphenomenon, of matter. It accords with the usual presentation of the theory (or rather the doctrine) of the Darwinian organic evolution. But then there is this difficulty. The *belief* itself that mind is an "appearance" of matter belongs to the mind. This belief, therefore, can be no more than an appearance. It loses its reliability, its reality. Recall Hinshelwood's statement quoted earlier. If then a choice has to be made at all, it seems prefereable to take mind as the primary reality, and matter as secondary: *chetan* as primary and *jada* as secondary. This is in keeping with the teachings of the great *Upanishads* which emphatically declare the primacy of *chetan*.

Everything that exists is either chetan or for the chetan (mind)
[see e.g. Hiriyanna (1973)]. The very idea of something existing
implies the existence beforehand of an entity to which the idea
can belong. In recent years, strong support for the primacy of
the *chetan* has come from a totally unexpected quarter. Many
scientists, notably theoretical physicists such as Schroedinger
and Wigner, hold that the mind, as distinct from the brain, is
the primary reality. Wigner (1964) says: "There are two kinds
of reality or existence—the existence of my consciousness and
the reality or existence of everything else. This latter reality
is not absolute, but only relative. Excepting immediate sensations, the content of my consciousness, everything is a construct; but some constructs are closer, some farther, from the
direct sensations."

The views about the primacy or otherwise of mind, by
their very nature, are not a part of physics, not within physics.
These go beyond physics. To say "beyond-physics", is not to
imply antiphysics, or contradiction of physics. Not at all. Antiphysics, or antiscience, should be ruthlessly denied any place
whatsoever in human thought and affairs. One must remember the distinction clearly, in principle even if in practice it be
difficult to apply, between *antiphysics*, *physics*, and *beyond-
physics*.

It is of the utmost importance to grasp the fundamental
distinction between "atom" and "self", or, what comes to the
same thing, between brain and mind. Atom or brain belongs to
the external, objective world of space-time and matter-energy.
Self or mind belongs to the internal subjective world. The subjective (mental) world is not describable in terms of space-time
and matter-energy concepts. *Self or mind, therefore, lies outside
natural science.* When I say that the "self" is outside the domain of space-time, many great recent writings which lucidly
and convincingly expound the theme immediately come to
mind—for example, Sherrington (1940); Schroedinger (1958);
Penfield (1975); Greidanus (1975); Popper and Eccles (1977),
and Wheeler (1977). (Notice that the title of the great book by
Poppler and Eccles is *The Self and Its Brain*, and *not* The Brain
and Its Self.)

Let me content myself with one quotation from Penfield.
He writes (1975): "Throughout my scientific career, I, like other

scientists, have struggled to prove that the brain accounts for the mind. But now, perhaps, the time has come when we may profitably consider the evidence as it stands, and ask the question, *Do brain mechanisms account for mind?*" And he concludes: "Because it seems to me certain that it will always be quite impossible to explain the mind on the basis of neuronal action within the brain, and because it seems to me that the mind develops and matures independently throughout an individual's life as though it were a continuing element . . . I am forced to choose the proposition that our being is to be explained on the basis of two fundamental elements." It reminds us forcefully of the *Sankhya Darshan*; and especially the *Sankhya Karika* of Ishwarkrishna, a fifth-century text and a psychophysical classic of all time.

As the brain is *within* natural science and the mind outside natural science, the problem of comprehending the brain-mind interaction becomes the riddle of riddles—the greatest mystery of all. What little light modern physics can throw on the problem we shall consider presently. In passing, we may note a suggestive analogy between atom and self. When an atom makes a transition, or a "jump", from one stationary state to another, the actual process cannot be visualized or even imagined. There are no intermediate stages. We cannot break down the process into its components: the entire process of transition from one state to another is a nonvisualizable, unanalyzable unity. *It is indivisible.* Its parts cannot even be imagined. It is a "quantum jump", as we call it. The interesting thing is that there is an analogous situation for *thought processes*. As we "think"—in any sequence of thoughts—there is always a sudden, discontinuous jump from one thought to the next. We are not aware at all of any intermediate stages. If we were so aware, no thinking would be possible. There would be an almost infinite sequence of "sub-thoughts" between two thoughts, like an infinity of points between the two ends of a line. *Quantum jumps for thought appear to be as much a necessity for the conscious self as these are for the atom.* This analogy between the self and the atom—*and it is no more than an analogy*—suggests some interesting possibilities for the mind, but these will not be pursued here.

Einstein remarked that "the most incomprehensible thing about the universe is that it is comprehensible." Perhaps, even more incomprehensible is it that one mind can comprehend another mind, though the two are totally isolated, separate from one another. How does it become possible that we understand one another, at any rate in some measure, whether we talk about the external world or about ourselves? Is it that in reality there are not many minds, but only *One Mind*? This is the assertion of Vedanta. There is a penetrating discussion of the problem by Schroedinger in *My View of the World* (1964). This remarkable book, of no more than 29,000 words, and which for Schroedinger was "really the fulfillment of a very long cherished wish," contains two essays: one, "Seek for the Road", was written in 1925, the year of his fundamental discovery of wave mechanics; and the other, "What is Real?", was written in 1960. "Seek for the Road" is an enquiry into "*who am I?*" Schroedinger, fully occupied in 1925 in elucidating the wave nature of the electron, is responding, as it were, to the reciprocal question of the electron: "*who are you to know me?*" Maybe his deep preoccupation at the time with both the electron and the psyche led him to the symbol *psi* for the electron wavefunction rather than *phi* (Greek *Phusis*, Nature). The two essays were published for the first time in 1961. Why this long wait to publish the 1925 essay? Perhaps (as he says), the thoughts expressed were far too strange, far too daring—at any rate for the Western World—to be published but in old age. Schroedinger writes: "A hundred years ago, perhaps, another man sat on this spot; . . . Like you he was begotten of man and born of woman. He felt pain and brief joy as you do. *Was* he someone else? Was it not you yourself? What is this self of yours? . . . What clearly intelligible *scientific* meaning can this 'someone else' really have? . . . Looking and thinking in that manner you may suddenly come to see, in a flash, the profound rightness of the basic conviction in Vedanta . . . that sacred, mystic formula which is yet really so simple and so clear; *Tattvam asi*, this is you. Or, again, in such words as 'I am in the east and in the west, I am below and above, *I am this whole world* . . . It is the vision of this truth (of which the individual is seldom conscious in his actions) which underlies all morally valuable activity. It brings a man of nobility not only to risk his life for an end which he recognizes or believes to be good, but—in rare cases—to lay it down in full serenity, even when there is no prospect of saving his own person."

To understand the physical world, ever since Galileo and Newton, mathematics—the most powerful and penetrating expression of human reason—has been the indispensable key. As mathematics advances, so does our understanding of the external world. This is well illustrated by the theory of relativity and quantum mechanics. Newton held that there are two Books of God, one the Holy Bible and the other the *Book of Nature* which is the language of mathematics.

Mathematics, and experiments, unravel the secrets of the atom. On the other hand, self-control and "moral experiments" lead to self-knowledge and self-liberation. *Moral experiments have the same place for the internal world, as physical experiments have for the external world.* Without continuing experimentation and assessment, there can be no advancement either of the individual or of society. Recall that Gandhiji called his Autobiography *"The Story of My Experiments with Truth."* He writes: "[*My Experiments with Truth*] will of course include *experiments* (italics added) with nonviolence, celibacy and other principles of conduct believed to be distinct from truth. But for me, truth is the sovereign principle, which includes numerous other principles. This truth is not only truthfulness in word, but truthfulness in thought also, and not only the relative truth of our conception, but the Absolute Truth, the Eternal Principle, that is God . . . I am prepared to sacrifice the things dearest to me in pursuit of this. Even if the sacrifice demanded be my very life, I hope I may be prepared to give it . . . Though this path is straight and narrow and sharp as the razor's edge, for me it has been the quickest and easiest."

And in his ceaseless quest, he heard the "Voice of God". "I can say this that not the unanimous verdict of the whole world against me could shake me from the belief that what I heard was the true Voice of God . . . For the voice was more real than my existence."

He concludes his *Story of My Experiments* with the words: "To see the universal and all-pervading Spirit of Truth face to face one must be able to love the merest of creation as one-self . . . I must reduce myself to zero. So long as a man does not of his own free will put himself last among his fellow-creatures, there is no salvation for him. Ahimsa is the farthest limit of humility."

Einstein said (1939)[3] of Gandhi that "generations to come will scarce believe that such a one as this ever in flesh and blood walked upon this earth". Very significant is Einstein's observation: "Revolution without the use of violence was the method by which Gandhi brought about the liberation of India. It is my belief that the problem of bringing peace to the world on a supranational basis will be solved only by employing Gandhi's method (*Satyagraha*) on a large scale. And how spiritually close are these two unquestionably greatest of human beings.

When asked (during a serious illness) whether he was at all afraid of death, Einstein said, "I feel such a sense of solidarity with all living things that it does not matter to me where the individual begins and ends." And he added, "There is nothing in the world which I could not dispense with at a moment's notice." (Born, 1971.)

The *Katha Upanishad* declares: "When every desire that finds lodging in the heart of man, has been loosened from its mooring, then this mortal puts on immortality; even here he tastes God in this human body." (Sri Aurobindo's translation, II-3-14.) It was about this stanza that Paul Deussen said that no nobler, profounder words had been ever uttered by human lips. It speaks of God realization *here* and *now*.

There is unambiguous testimony for God realization "here and now" by seekers of the highest integrity and spiritual attainments in all ages and countries. The evidence is far too significant to be evaded or ignored.[4] It would not be in keeping with the temper of science to do so. William James (whose writings had no negligible influence on Niels Bohr, has given an illuminating discussion of mystical experience in his Gifford Lectures on *Varieties of Religious Experience*. Sri Ramakrishna speaks of his actually "seeing" God; of "talking" to him. ". . .God is beyond the power of reasoning . . . I do actually *see that whatever is, is God*."

It is apparent that soul or God cannot be *proved* by reason or logic. Nor can it be *disproved*. This is beyond question. Any logical reasoning must start from some unproved postulates and some undefined terms. Any postulate (axiom) that we may presuppose to prove (or disprove) God would be in effect tantamount to our withdrawing from that position. We may take God and Absolute Truth as identical concepts—undefinable, unprovable. Though reason is indispensable for moral quest, the concept of morality rests ultimately not on reason but on faith in God in some form or the other. The distinction between "right" and "wrong", between "good" and "evil" is not a scientific distinction. It goes beyond science, beyond reason. Anti-reason has no place in beyond-reason. Bertrand Russell says in *Wisdom of the West* (1959): "We cannot give scientific justification for the goals that we might pursue, or for the ethical principles that we adopt. We can begin to argue only if we admit, from the outset, some ethical premises . . . Most of the principles which make for civilized living are of this ethical character. No scientific reason can be given why it is bad to inflict wanton cruelty on one's fellows. To me it seems bad . . . [but] I am not sure that I can supply satisfactory reason." In the end, it is the "small voice" within a *pure* heart that alone can tell what is right and what is wrong.

If "self", mortality, and God are beyond science, what contribution can science make to self-knowledge and moral behavior? The answer is the contribution is extraordinarily large. It is most far-reaching, and rapidly increasing. We can divide the discussion under a few headings, somewhat overlapping. It will include the problem of *interaction* between self and atom.

SUPERSTITIONS ABOUT OUTER AND INNER WORLDS

Nothing has done more than science to loosen the hold of magic and superstition on the minds of men. When there is no framework of objective knowledge as provided by science, everything seems possible. For example, a bird sitting on yonder tree may be what it seems to be or it might be something else under the spell of magic. *Science limits the possible.* By continually deepening our understanding of nature, science tells us more and more of what is permissible in nature and what is not. Where can we find a more inspiring account of the impact of science on superstition than in Charles Sherrington's *Man on His Nature*. Writes Sherrington: "[Before Galileo and Harvey] Magic and sorcery were part of the belief not merely of the common folk but of the cultured, especially those of 'progressive' view. . . Cultured liberal opinion was inclined to medical astrology as the climax of scientific medicine. . . [Today] our insight into nature is of a different order from theirs of yesterday. . . The half-gods are not only vanished, they are by nigh forgotten; matter for labels and a museum shelf." And he continues: "Today man can go out into the natural world without carrying the distortion of monstrosity with him. We can interrogate the natural world with a confidence drawn from riddance of misunderstanding no less than from extension of understanding. . . The position for reading from Nature's lips what she may have to say of Godhead never yet in the past was what it is for us today." (Chapter II—*Nature and Superstition*.)

Science education, in countries where it is widespread, has gradually banished to a large measure magic and superstition about the external world. But there still remains, as strong as ever and possibly stronger, the far more dreadful "Superstitions" of the inner world: *Greed, Hatred and Delusion*. These are the roots of all violence and wars. And though there is no war *for* science, yet science-based technology has amplified beyond measure the cruelty and destruction of wars. Greed, Hatred and Delusion (GHD) cannot be conquered except by knowledge and self-control. There is no other way, no Royal Road.

Nuclear weapons and uncontrolled GHD cannot coexist. They can only lead to a total collapse of civlization. It is a sad thing, a fault of public education, that not enough people are aware of the global danger facing mankind. The very survival of the human species is at stake, nothing less than that. And the only hope lies in the common people becoming aware of the unprecedented danger that faces them and their children. Remarkably, in the very same century in which men deployed nuclear bombs against fellowmen, th expanding knowledge of the natural world has disclosed an unexpected relatedness and pervading harmony in an amazing diversity. It seems that the emergence of man from the lower primates has probably its roots in cooperative and altruistic behavior. This brings us to our next point—man and his kinship with all living beings.

MAN'S KINSHIP WITH LIVING BEINGS

The recent work of Konrad Lorenz and others has shown that in Nature, harmony is the normal rule and conflict an exception. Members of the same species rarely kill one another. Their fights are either sport or ritual. There are a few species which deviate from the rule, one of which is the human species (which calls itself Homo sapiens—man and wise). Homo sapiens torture and murder one another in war and peace, with an abandon, wantonness and brutality that has no parallel in Nature. It is Man's gift to Nature. Within a span of 40 years, two World Wars killed many tens of millions of people. How deep and pervasive are the effects of GHD? More than 60 per cent of all the world's research and development work in science and technology is directed to military ends; and $400 billion a year is the global military expenditure (300,000-*crores* of rupees), and still increasing. Some 700 million human beings are living today in absolute poverty—hungry, illiterate, and disease-ridden. The link between the two is apparent. Total comprehensive disarmament and elimination of global poverty go together.

The food problem of poor countries has been aggravated by the large increase in recent decades of consumption of animal protein by people in rich countries. A third of the world's yearly total output of cereals is used as animal feed to produce animal protein. About 5-20 kilo of vegetable protein goes to produce a kilo of animal protein. This is done by industrial animal-breeding methods of unspeakable cruelty. We cannot be cruel to animals and expect that it will not harden human sensibility towards fellow human beings. In the long run, cruelty is indivisible; so is compassion. Alfred Kaestler (of optical pumping fame) at a UNESCO roundtable in June 1978 observed that since animals are our "biological brothers", the time has come that, in the interest of man's own future, "this relationship is legally recognized". The suffering of animals and of man is in the end not separable. No longer is the rigid *Cartesian Partition* between human beings and other living creatures scientifically tenable. We need to get away from it completely. It is totally unreasonable.

SCIENCE AND FAITH

The pursuit of science rests ultimately on our *faith* that nature is understandable by the human mind. The faith is reinforced by the advancement of science itself. Einstein says: "Certain it is that a conviction, akin to religious feeling of the rationality or intelligibility of the world, lies behind all scientific work of a higher order. This firm belief, a belief bound up with deep feeling, in a *superior mind* [italics added] that reveals itself in the world of experience, represents my conception of God." Ten years later (1929) he wrote: "I cannot conceive of a genuine scientist without that profound faith (the universe is comprehensible to reason). The situation may be expressed by an image: *Science without religion is lame, religion without science is blind.*" This reminds us of Heisenberg's view that science points to some Central Design, some purpose in the Universe (Heisenberg, 1971).

The extraordinary beauty, power, and fertility of mathematics has a profound influence on a sensitive mind. Mathematical results are communicable. These can be discussed and criticized. This is very different from transcendental or yogic experiences. These are ordinarily not communicable. Perhaps no path takes us closer to *communicable* Truth than abstract mathematics at its best. Plato declared that none enter his Academy if he had no love for mathematics. Why does mathematics provide *the key* to the physical world? In truth we do not know, cannot know, the answer. James Jeans said many years ago, "God is a pure mathematician." And more recently Dirac (1964) said that "[God] used very advanced mathematics in constructing the universe . . . [and] as we proceed to develop higher and higher mathematics we can hope to understand the universe better. It may well be that the next advance in physics may come about . . . [by] people first discovering the equations and then . . . the physical ideas behind the equations." This, of course, is an expression of faith, and not logic. In oversimplified terms, we may say that as mathematics is the golden key to *communicable* Truth or Reality, the key to *noncommunicable* Truth is mystic experience, that is, yoga. The highest yogic state is possible only when *all* desires lodged in the heart have been dissolved. In a state of "I" reduced to zero, "insights" may be permissible which are ordinarily inaccessible, going beyond physical limitations of space-time. These may be partially communicable. There are accounts whose authenticity cannot be doubted. We may assume that the ultimate source of yogic insights and other creative insights is the same, by whatever name we may call it, for the simple reason that both belong to man.

Transcendental experience goes beyond science. But, as we have emphasized, beyond-science is totally different from a contradiction of science. To admit contradiction in a realm which belongs to science is not only a violation of our scientific experience, but much more is at stake. And let us note that the cumulative scientific experience is extraordinarily wide-ranging, and extraordinarily coherent and deep, going to the very heart of Nature—and extending to the farthest limits of the universe in space and time. A violence to science is a violence to our cosmic religious feeling, to our most precious and cherished faith that Nature is understandable.

PHYSICS AND PHILOSOPHY

Moral and spiritual thought is not a part of Natural Science. Terms like "spiritual energy", "mind energy", or "moral force" are nonsensical, if energy and force are conceived as having semblance to the terms energy and force as used in science. A lot of confusion is caused on this account in the popular mind. On the other hand, science, especially modern physics, provides suggestive analogies which can help better understanding of moral and spiritual thought. But the analogies should be treated as no more than analogies. Take the famous *Santi-Sloka* of the *Ishvasyopanishad*. It says that the Supreme Whole (Isvara) is such that it remains Whole even if Whole is taken out of it, or Whole is added. It reminds us of the concept of the *mathematical infinity*, developed for the first time in the 19th century. An illustration from physics is of the velocity of light. A fundamental postulate of the theory of relativity is that whatever velocity we add to or subtract from the light velocity, it remains unchanged.

As the language of science becomes richer with advancement of science, it enriches possibilities for better appreciation of deep metaphysical concepts such as self, soul, or God, concepts that inevitably involve contradictions. For an analogy from mathematics, recall Goedel's celebrated theorem on the "incompleteness" of mathematics. He *proved* that in mathematics, the most precise part of science, there is no escape from concepts with latent contradictions. The contradictions are latent in the infinity of integers which are the foundations of mathematics. This most astonishing discovery has for both science and philosophy consequences of the greatest significance, yet not clear.[5]

Concepts like *Self, Time, God* are embedded in the deepest core of our language. Take these away and language collapses utterly.

A word about Time. The mysterious and self-contradictory nature of Time is apparent on a little reflection. On the one hand *Past* and *Future* extend to infinity and, on the other hand, these are contained in the single moment, *Now*, for otherwise these would not exist at all. Goedel(1949) is of the view that Einstein's relativity theory by its deep and surprising insight into the nature of *physical time* provides "an unqualified proof for the view of those philosophers who, like Parmenides, Kant, and the modern idealists, deny the objectivity of change and consider change as an illusion or an appearance due to our special mode of perception."

Another major development in modern physics with far-reaching philosophical and ethical implications is Bohr's *Principle of Complementarity*. No longer can we keep physics and philosophy, or atom and self, apart. Max Born goes so far as to say that theoretical physics today is actual philosophy. Recall Shroedinger's statement on the aim of science. As we probe more deeply into the nature of the atom and the universe, it is becoming increasingly clear that physics and philosophy have much to learn from each other.

In the present century, physics has undergone its greatest revolution since Galileo and Newton. The theory of relativity paved the way for de Broglie waves and quantum mechanics. In the preface to his great book, *The Principles of Quantum Mechanics*, Dirac writes: "The new theories, if one looks apart from their mathematical setting, are built up from physical concepts which cannot be explained in terms of things previously known to the student, which cannot even be explained adequately in words at all. Unlike the fundamental concepts (e.g., proximity, identity) which everyone must learn on his arrival into the world, the newer concepts of physics can be mastered only by long familiarity with their properties and uses."

The philosophy of modern physics has a special relation to Upanishadic and Buddhistic thought. Ernst Mach's critical analysis which brought to light deep flaws in Newtonian mechanics exercised a profound influence on the young Einstein. Mach, as he himself acknowledged, was deeply influenced by Indian philosophic thought. *This important aspect of the history of modern physics is still largely an unexplored chapter* (Kothari, 1979).

The starting point of relativity theory is a completely unbiased examination of the nature of time and space in physics, free of all preconceived notions no matter how deeply rooted in common sense or philosophy. It demands a renunciation of the concept of absolute time which was the foundation of Newton's dynmics. The constancy of the velocity of light, independent of the state of motion of the observer, requires inevitably that there is no *absolute time*: that is, there is no common time for all systems.[6] On the other hand, each physical system has a *time* of its own which depends on the state of motion of the system. Suppose the velocity of a system, in motion with respect to us, approaches the velocity of light. All physical and biological processes occurring in the system, as *observed by us*, will be slowed down more and more. These will come to a *dead stop*, if the velocity of the system were exactly that of light. There is no flow of time for a system moving with the speed of light. For such a system there is no ageing whatever, that is, there is "immortality". A direct consequence of Einstein's theory is the following. Suppose a person traveled with nearly the speed of light to a near star and returned to earth without stoping on the star. For *him* the time elapsed would be no more than a few seconds or so. But here on earth he would find everything older by many years. This is tantalizingly paradoxical for common sense, but so much the worse for common sense. We must accept as inescapable the reality of the relativity of time and the unreality of absolute time. It is required by fundamental physical theory and unambiguous experimental evidence.

Speaking about time in physics, there are as it were a *hierarchy of time*, "levels of time", in the words of Prigogine (1974, 1978) who has made a far-reaching contribution to the problem. For a purely dynamic system, an atom, for example, there is no distinction between past and future. This means that from the behavior of a purely dynamic system, we cannot determine the arrow of time. This holds both in classical and quantum mechanics. But for a thermodynamic system, on the other hand, time is not reversible. A hot body left in the open always get cooler with time till its temperature is that of the surroundings. Past and future are not interchangeable for thermodynamic systems. Thermodynamic systems are large systems. A large system is one which consists of a large number of small systems. We will discuss what a small system is later.

The next level of time is time associated with evolution or history. This applies to nonlinear thermodynamic systems far removed from thermodynamic equilibrium. Prigogine's work has brought out a suggestive complementarity between dynamics and theormodynamics, in the sense of the wave-particle complementarity.

We may also mention the *two* times of Dirac, the *atomic time* and the *cosmological time*. The concept of *two* times leads to a continuous creation of matter.[7] At the highest level of time, we may think of an "absolute time of the universe". When the object of investigation is the whole universe, there is no other physical system to which it could be related. There arises no question of relativity of time, and we have an *absolute* cosmological time.

We have been speaking so far of the physical time or clock time. This is time for physical systems, not time for a *self*. The psychological time, *the time as experienced by a self*, has little *direct* relation to physical time. What may be no more than a few seconds of physical time, the time as experienced by a self —call it psychological time— could be very large. In certain critical situations it could be near eternity, but we do not know.

What about the concept of beyond-time? It is envisaged, for example, in the *Sankhya Darshan*. Kant recognized such a possibility. He says: "Those affections which we represent to ourselves as changes in beings with other forms of cognition, would give rise to perception in which the idea of time, and therefore also of change, would not occur at all."

To ask the question *what is truth?* (whether about atom or self) is to raise the problem of time. For truth, if the concept means anything at all, implies continuity, survival in time. A *partial truth* must contain some grain of everlasting truth. As we learn more about "levels of time", there will emerge a more unifying vision of Nature.

THE PRINCIPLE OF COMPLEMENTARITY

Einstein wrote in 1951: "All these 50 years of conscious brooding have brought me no nearer to the answer to the great question 'What are light quanta?' Nowadays every Tom, Dick, and Harry thinks he knows it, but he is mistaken" (Banesh Hoffmann, 1973).

Light quanta, electrons, and atoms, are small objects. An orange is a large object. But in comparison to the earth an orange is very small; as small as an atom is compared to an orange. *What the new physics does is to give an absolute meaning to the concept of "small" and "big" objects.* An object is *small* in the absolute sense if the effect of the *"disturbance"* which inevitably accompanies an act of observation is not negligible. A certain indeterminate disturbance is inevitable even under *ideal* conditions, that is, observations made with "perfect instruments" supposed free of all limitations except what are inherent in the very nature of things. If the disturbance has a negligible effect on the state of the object, the object is said to be *big* in the absolute sense. The moon is a big object, because looking at it, observing its motion, has no effect on the motion of the moon. An electron, or an atom, is a *small* object in the absolute sense, because the unavoidable disturbance (inherent in an act of observation) drastically alters the state under observation. Note that a perfect observation is an imaginary observation with ideally "perfect" instruments. It is a kind of "thought experiment": the only requirement for it is that it should be theoretically permissible. It should conform to the laws of physics. *Ideal experiments are useful tools of thought.* A certain indeterminate disturbance accompanying an observation, totally unpredictable, is inherent in the very nature of things. Nature is made that way. It is a direct consequence of the existence of Planck's constant. *To appreciate the absolute distinction between big and small systems is the gateway to modern physics.* (Where such an absolute distinction is not called for, we shall continue to use the words big and small in their everyday sense.)

Permit me to present a brief description of something so well known. Think of a beam of photons (light quanta) starting from a light source and falling on a distant target; say a photographic plate. On the way, before reaching the target, the particles pass through two or more narrow slits in a screen. On the photographic plate a certain pattern of fringes is observed. These intereference fringes can only be explained on the basis that each photon passes undivided through all the slits at the same time. This is an imperative requirement. It seems impossible! How can a photon pass through a number of slits at once? But there is still more to it.

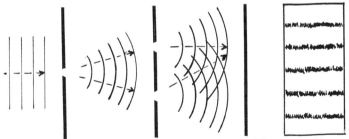

A beam of particles travels from left to right, and forms a pattern of interference fringes on the plate at the extreme right. To explain the *observed* interference pattern it is imperative that *each* particle passes, at the same time, through both the holes (A and B) in the middle plate. This sounds impossible—crazy beyond words, and so it is.

A similar experiment with a beam of electrons, requiring great sophistication, was first made a little over 50 years ago. The light experiment is nearly two hundred years old. The electron beam forms an interference pattern on the plate, essentially no different from what is obtained from a beam of light. The interference pattern can be accounted for only on the assumption that each electron goes through all the slits in the screen it meets on its way to the photographic plate. It is not as if some electrons go through one slit, some through another, and so on. No, not at all. *Every electron goes through all the slits* . . .The situation is altogether unimaginable, inconceivable. How can an electron, the same electron, cross through a number of slits at the same time? Impossible! How can the same electron be at two different places at the same time? You and I cannot pass through two doors at the same time; and yet the photons and electrons do that as if it were a normal thing for them. What is the reason? It is none other than the fact that photons, electrons, atoms, are *small* objects—small in the absolute sense; and you and I are big objects in the absolute sense. The small objects, judged by the behavior of big ones, literally perform miracles (Heisenberg 1958, pp. 157-160).

Consider an electron on its way from its source to the target plate. Quantum mechanics tells us that the (unobserved) electron is not moving as a "particle". A particle could not pass through two or more holes at the same time. The electron is moving in the form or guise of a "wave"—a wave of *probability amplitude*. These waves are not in physical space, not in our everyday space, but in an abstract mathematical space that can have many dimensions. (If the electron wave were in physical space, we could see it—but we don't. A photon, or an electron, has a *dual* aspect, a wave aspect and a particle aspect.) The two aspects are complementary. The one aspect excludes the other aspect. That is why the two aspects are not contradictory. A contradiction between them could arise only if the two aspects could be observed at the same time. But this never happens; and we have compelling theoretical arguments that this could not happen. *The wave and the particle aspects are complementary and not contradictory.*

New developments in quantum mechanics and gravitation, leading to a possible unification of the two, are likely to bring to light "higher levels" of complementarity not yet envisaged.

Speaking of the wave-particle duality of the electron, it is interesting to note that whereas *thermal* ionization brings out the *particle* aspect of the free electron gas (*nondegenerate gas*), *pressure* ionization brings out the wave aspect (*degenerate gas*). *Thermal* ionization and *pressure* ionization are comlementary. The theory of pressure ionization requires that the large planets consist mostly of metallic hydrogen; and that there cannot be a "cold body" bigger in size than Jupiter. It appears probable that *metallic hydrogen* has been recently produced under pressures of a few million atmospheres (*Science*, 4 August 1978). It could be superconducting even at room temperatures, but we do not know.

Theoretical physics enables us to calculate the wave functions for simple atomic systems. In principle these can be constructed for any system, whether small or big. For a big system this is unnecessary because we can use for it the much more familiar Newtonian mechanics. Wave functions give the *probabilities* of every possible result obtainable on observation of the system under consideration. It is inherently impossible to predict with certainty what a particular result is going to be in the case of a particular observation. This is because of the inevitable, uncontrollable, indeterminate disturbance inherent in an act of observation. When an electron, or as a matter of fact any small system, is not under observation, its course of development, that is, the change in its state of motion, cannot be conceived in our everyday space. It takes place in an abstract mathematical space. An act of observation throws the system into our ordinary space, the manifest space. This all looks so bizarre. Ordinary language—but not mathematics—fails to describe the situation without introducing absurdities. This is understandable for ordinary language has not evolved to deal with *small* objects. It is based on our everyday experience with large objects. Expressed in ordinary language, the behavior of small objects is desperately anticommonsense, exasperating. The world of small objects, small in the absolute sense, is built that way. *Large objects behave according to common sense but not small ones.*

We shall not go here into the famous Einstein-Bohr controversy about the probabilistic foundations of quantum physics. The famous Einstein-Podolsky-Rosen paper of 1935 on the "incompleteness" of quantum mechanics was answered by Bohr; but not to Einstein's satisfaction.[8] The debate led to many interesting developments (Max Jammer, 1974) in suggesting experiments on the role of "hidden variables" in quantum theory.

Einstein could not reconcile himself to this probabilistic world of atoms. It was repugnant to his intuition, to his cosmic religious feeling. "*Gott wurfelt nicht,*" Einstein often used to say in various ways. This may be naively rendered as "God does not play dice."

Fundamental discoveries which go deep into the nature of things are the result of uncommon intuition and faith, not cold logic. And what we witness here is a difference in faith, a difference in the cosmic religious feeling of Einstein and Bohr. It reminds us of the difference in the faith of Newton and Leibnitz. In a sense, Einstein's philosophy emphasizes "Being" and Bohr's emphasizes "Becoming".

We now go back to the distinction between small objects and large objects. Any experimental setup for small objects must necessarily consist of large objects, otherwise the setup will not be unambiguously describable. It will, therefore, be not repeatable. If not repeatable, it is not an experiment.

To fix our ideas, think of a large number of identical experiments to determine the velocity of an electron, which at the start of the experiment, let us suppose, is located at some specific point, say the zero point of the scale. The results of the velocity measurement in these identical experiments will be widely different. This is because of the uncertain disturbance in the motion of the electron caused by the act of locating it, at the zero of the scale, at the start of each of the identical experiments.

If we desire to measure not the velocity but the position of an electron, the experimental setup required for the purpose will be totally different. But this is not so far a large object. The different experimental setup required for the measurement of different variables can, in principle, be joined together into one comprehensive apparatus. This one apparatus will measure everthing measurable in principle for a big object. There is no objection to this procedure because observations do not disturb the state of a big object under observation: all possible meassurements can be made without interfering with each other with the aid of a single superinstrument. But this is impossible for a small object. Why? The measurement of one variable for a *small* system, because of the nonnegligible accompanying-disturbance, disturbs the values of the other variables to be subsequently measured. We must, therefore, make a definite choice as to what variable we desire to measure for the system. For example: the setup required for a measurement of position of an electron and that required for a measurement of velocity cannot, in any circumstances, be combined into a single superinstrument. (This is the essence of Bohr's argument for rejecting the EPR thesis.)

An all-comprehensive instrument is impossible in quantum mechanics because, in general, *measurements are not compatible with one another for small objects*. It is important to grasp this radically new situation.

At the root of the wave-particle duality *is the principle of absolute indistinguishability, absolute identity, of particles of the same kind*. All electrons in the universe are absolutely identical, absolutely indistinguishable from one another. What does it mean?

Think of two *identical* particles. If these are to be *absolutely identical*, it should not be permissible to precisely define their trajectories, for otherwise their separate trajectories could be used to distinguish one particle from the other for all time. One particle riding one trajectory and the other a different one would be distinguishable by their different trajectories. Absolute identity of particles demands that there cannot exist for them *sharply* defined trajectories. This leads to the wave aspect; and hence the wave particle duality; and with it the Heisenberg uncertainty relations. The periodic table of elements, and nearly all chemistry and biochemistry, is a direct product of the *absolute identity of electrons*. How? The identity principle introduces a fundamental and exceedingly simple symmetry in the wave functions of electrons. In response to this symmetry, chemical compounds are formed.

Think of the total wave function of all the electrons in a piece of metal. We may in principle do the same for all the electrons in the Universe. In this total wave function, the identity of the individual electrons is completely, absolutely lost. Not a trace of their separate individuality is left. One electron has absolutely the same role in the total wave function as any other electron. *The electrons have submerged themselves, as it were, in one "brotherhood" of electrons.* The many have become *ONE.* Note that as stated earlier, the wave function exists in an abstract mathematical space, not in physical space. The individual electrons can be observed, if we so choose, but then the act of observation would project the electrons from mathematical space into our everyday space. The observation would drastically alter the state which was there before the observation.

When we speak of the total-wave-function or the field, and the many identical particles incorporated in the wave function, it is not a sort of aggregate, a sum of the MANY. In an aggregate, the ONENESS is no more than a euphemism for the MANY that are still visible, maybe dimly, in the aggregate. The concept of ONENESS in quantum mechanics is a totally, fundamentally new concept. It has no analogy, no parallel whatsoever in classical physical physics or in everyday experience. Common sense fails utterly to be of any aid. *The ONE is in an abstract space, the MANY in physical space.* The two aspects are complementary. All this is a consequence of Planck's constant. *We may say that Nature (or God) created the Planck Constant so that particles of the same kind in the Universe could be absolutely identical.*

There is an interesting analogy between the behavior of an atom and the self regarding disturbance caused by an act of observation. The stage of an atom is disturbed if it is observed. In psychological investigations of a conscious subject, or during introspection, the act of investigation disturbs the mental state under investigation. Suppose one wants to find out how he actually goes to sleep. So long as he is alert (awake, so that he can find out how sleep comes to him), the very fact of alertness prevents him from going to sleep. We can never know how we *actually* go to sleep. That is impossible in the very nature of things.

THE ROLE OF CONSCIOUSNESS IN QUANTUM MECHANICS

We spoke of the *absolute* indistinguishability of particles of the same kind, e.g. electrons, in quantum mechanics. We have a most remarkable, thought-provoking analogy drawn from modern physics for the great *Upanishadic formula*: the different individual selves on the empirical plane are ONE AND THE SAME on the transcendental plane: *Tat tvam asi.* Perhaps, there is a little more here than mere analogy. For it is important to recognize that in *quantum mechanics consciousness or self has a significance which has no counterpart in classical physics.* This was emphasized by von Neumann, and further developed by many others, notably Wigner. We have seen that an act of measurement, even an ideal one, inevitably and unpredictably disturbs the state of the dynamic system under observation. But what precisely is a measurement and when can it be completed? It would take us too far to discuss this question adequately. Even after more than 50 years of quantum mechanics there is no unanimity of views on this point. It is still a "live issue". We may state the following considerations, partly overlapping, which are relevant to the role of consciousness in quantum physics.

(a) An act of measurement in quantum mechanics requires a *choice* between incompatible experimental arrangements. An act of choice implies a conscious subject or self to do the choosing. *A choice is neither determinism nor is it chance.* It implies a certain freedom to elect between possible alternatives. Consciousness and freedom of choice or free will go together. This is crucially important. A computer has no choice of its own: the choice belongs to its programmer. That is the fundamental distinction between a computer and its programmer.

(b) An act of measurement is not completed until the result of the measurement has been noticed by some subject, noticed by some self. In the oft-quoted words of E. P. Wigner (1964): "The measurement is not completed until its result enters our consciousness . . . [this] last step is, at the present state of our knowledge, shrouded in mystery and no explanation has been given for it so far in terms of quantum mechanics, or in terms of any other theory." However, it has been argued by others that a measurement is effectively completed if the result is recorded in some instrument. An "entry into consciousness" is not necessary. What is necessary is an irreversible thermodynamic change resulting from the measurement action. (This is the answer to the "cat paradox" of Schroedinger.) We shall not go further into this subtle question. It is enough to note that the very concept of a measurement process in quantum mechanics demands an irrevocable choice between incompatible setups. And choice demands a conscious subject to exercise the freedom of choice.

(c) Suppose for a moment that electrons possess some kind of self-awareness. This, as we shall see in a moment, leads to a *reductio ad absurdam*. It is obvious that if the electrons have their own *separate egos*, they cannot be absolutely identical. Under these circumstances, there can be no wave-particle duality. Therefore, to be consistent with modern physics, we require that *self-awareness cannot arise in small systems*. It is interesting that such a significant conclusion follows directly from quantum mechanics. Self-awareness can appear only in a large system. As self-awareness carries with it an "arrow of time", the large system must be a thermodynamic system far removed from thermodynamic equilibrium.

Notice that the property of self-consciousness relevant to quantum mechanics is its freedom of choice, or free will. And it is this property, and this alone, which unambiguously distinguishes consciousness from matter, or self from atom. For matter there is necessity and chance, but no choice or freedom, and freedom is the basis of all moral activity.

I feel within myself—and we all do the same—absolutely certain that I am free to write this sentence or not write it. But what does it all mean? How can my consciousness or mind exercise its choice of writing or not writing this sentence, except by interacting with my body, that is, by interacting with matter? Everything we do, everything without exception, is a direct expression of brain-mind interaction. Yet science provides not the faintest clue as to how such an interaction could occur. It is totally beyond explanation, totally beyond understanding. It is the supreme mystery; for it is an interaction between one element (brain), which is within space-time and another element (mind or self) which is *outside* space-time.

Despite the earlier, rather lengthy discussion, we may still feel uneasy to admit a reality other than matter, a reality outside the framework of space-time or matter-energy concepts. How can we physicists admit any *reality* outside physics. It may appear more satisfying, more comforting, to hold that matter or atoms are everything—that besides matter there is nothing, and that sooner or later every thing would be accounted for in terms of atoms and subatomic entities. But, pray, *who* is this entity about whose satisfaction and comfort we are so worried? *Why not ignore who*: Has this *who* any reality or is it only an "appearance" not worth bothering about? We are now back at the beginning: *who are we*? Science cannot, and must not, evade its task and its responsibility. Developments in physics in the present century have clearly brought out the need and urgency in this respect. And, of course, science cannot contribute meaningfully to the great moral challenge facing mankind today, the greatest in man's history, unless it recognizes its obligation to the problem of the "self", and not merely that of the atom.

At this point there may arise the doubt that if the *objectivity* of science excludes totally the "I" from it, how can science tell us anything at all about the "I", and the nature of the self? The answer is: It can. But how?

Firstly—that developments in mathematics and physics in the present century have demonstrated convincingly that science is, by its very nature, "incomplete". There can be "reality" not encompassed by science. The "incompleteness" is not in the ordinary, expected sense that there will be always far more to discover than discovered so far: science is an "endless quest". We are not here speaking of "incompleteness" in this obvious sense, but in the extraordinary and totally unexpected sense that there are fundamental truths, about which we are intuitionally certain, but which must always remain outside the domain of science. (Recall Goedel's theorem.) As the work of Tarski and others has shown, the concept of *truth* is itself a telling example of this. To quote M. Delbruck (Nobel Address, Dec. 1969): "Thus, even if we learn to speak about consciousness as an emergent property of nerve nets, even if we learn to understand the processes that lead to abstraction, reasoning and language, still any such development presupposes a notion of truth that is prior to all these efforts and that cannot be conceived as an emergent property of it, an emergent property of a biological evolution. Our conviction of the truth of the sentence, 'The number of prime numbers is infinite,' must be independent of nerve nets and of evolution, if truth is to be a meaningful word at all."

This reminds us of Einstein's remarks on Scientific Truth and his conception of God. He said (1929): "This firm belief [in the intelligibility of the world], a belief bound up with deep religious feeling in a superior mind that reveals itself in the world of experience, represents my conception of God. In common parlance this may be described as 'pantheistic' [Spinoza]."

Secondly—Science, especially psychology and the neuronal sciences, can be used to explore the *objective aspects* of the mind and self—whatever these may be.

Thirdly—as our knowledge of mathematics, physics, and the neuronal networks increases so also, by exclusion and comparison, our understanding of the self gets richer. On the analogy that consciousness enters into quantum mechanics, a deeper study of yoga and mystic experience may reveal some reciprocal aspect. But we do not know.

Fourthly—the specific and formidable problem of brain-mind interaction needs investigation from both ends, from brain to mind, and mind to brain, with increasing use of sophisticated techniques and refinements.

Fifthly—The foundations of quantum mechanics need deep and critical examination. As the brain is subject to the laws of physics, the freedom exercised by the mind in brain-mind interaction can take place only within the confines permitted by the indeterminacy which is an integral feature of quantum mechanics. *For the operation of free will, quantum indeterminacy is necessary but not sufficient.*

There is also need for a better understanding of the concept of probability. This may require radical developments in mathematics.

We may note in passing that the role of individual consciousness in quantum mechanics has a certain obvious analogy to the role of Cosmic Consciousness in relation to the Universe; but we shall not go into it here.

Sixthly—scientific study of what Jung calls the phenomena of *Synchronicity,* that is, meaningful "coincidences" of events, are inexplicable phenomena not merely because the cause is unknown, but because for them the "cause is not even thinkable in intellectual terms". The course of our lives is paved with such meaningful coincidences.

The book, *The Interpretation of Nature and the Psyche* (Routledge and Kegan Paul, London, 1955), contains two essays, one by C. G. Jung ("Synchronicity, a Causal Connecting Principle") and the other by W. Pauli ("The Influence of Archetypal Ideas on the Scientific Theories of Keplar"). Jung says that the synchronicity principle advanced by him throws light on the body-soul problem. He says (p. 124): "*The absolute knowledge* which is characteristic of synchronistic phenomena, a knowledge not mediated by the sense organs, supports the hypothesis of a self-subsistent meaning, or even expresses its existence. Such a form of existence can only be transcendental, since, as the knowledge of future spatially distant events shows, it is contained in an irrepresentable space-time continuum."

It has been noticed for quite some time that there are certain remarkable "coincidences" among the physical constants. It seems that were it not for these apparent "coincidences", there would be no life, no man on the earth: in fact, there would be no earth. (B. J. Carr and M. J. Reec, *Nature,* 12 April 1979).

Why these coincidences? Is it a case of some kind of cosmic "Synchronicity", or lack of physical knowledge, or both? We do not know.

Seventhly—Psychosomatic medicine is directly related to mind-brain interaction. As a challenging speculation it could be argued, in the light of the dual reality of mind and brain, that *whatever is possible physiologically is also possible, within obvious limits, psychologically.* With the growing appreciation of the *two* realities, the role of psychosomatic health care and psychosomatic medicine is likely to be increasingly important in the future.

Eighthly—Study of the "thought process", and "thought noise". *Thought noise* may be defined as random, uncontrolled, distracting thoughts, pleasant and unpleasant, that come to us from nowhere, as it were: from the subconscious mind, as we say. The degree to which thought noise can be reduced by meditation practices (yoga) could be explored—to a certain extent quantitatively.

Conscious thoughts largely are *determinate*, that is, determined by past thoughts, memory, and so on. This reminds us of something like an "equation of motion" for a dynamic system. The question arises as to what extent thoughts are *free* and under control of the individual self, and to what extent these are not free. Here, analogies and models from quantum physics could be helpful in suggesting interesting lines of new investigation, theoretical and experimental. There is also the question of the relation between thought noise and *creativity*.

The question also arises: on what basis, according to what principle or "framework", does my mind or your mind exercise its freedom of will and action?[9] What guides it? If freedom of action is entirely uncontrolled, unguided, then the choice made by the mind between possible alternative courses of action is all a matter of pure chance. It will be an entirely random choice, and that is not freedom; no moral responsibility can be assigned to such random operations of the will.[10] On the other hand, if the mind is guided in its choice, how does this come about? Who guides it? And if there is guidance, the mind is no longer free in its choice between alternative actions. Maybe the freedom is there to enable the individual to link himself with the great "Central Design of the Universe": to realize ultimately the *Kaivalya* state of being. The freedom of the mind which is *real* at the human level is perhaps an illusion at the metaphysical level. (We may suppose that an individual mind is always in "contact" with the Supreme Mind; and this is especially close during creative experience.)

Ninthly—The "fact" of the exclusion of "I" from the realm of science needs to be constantly reviewed critically in the light of new developments in science and philosophy. It is important to examine how compelling are the arguments, derived from the "incompleteness" of mathematics and fundamental physics, which require the existence of a *reality outside science*. The role of consciousness in quantum mechanics discussed above is one such example. Another inspiring example is Schroedinger's Epilogue on Determinism and Free Will in his book *What is Life?*

CONCLUSION

As I conclude the Lecture, I realize how feeble, jumbled up, and how manifestly superficial has been my attempt to describe the relation between Atom and Self. The simple truth is that we can hardly comprehend the value, harmony, and grandeur of the one without knowing something of the other. One thing is clear, reinforced by recent developments in science. At the human level, *both* Atom and Self are equally real, equally true. It is the *Sanyoga* of the two which is the human mystery. If the atoms were to declare that we are everything, the only reality, this assertion itself would be meaningless unless there is a Self to believe in it. This is what the *Sankhya* philosophy described long ago. This is what Democritus said. once the fundamental need for the *two* realities, the external world and the internal world, is grasped, it is but a small step to the concepts of Cosmic Consciousness. (See, for example, Schroedinger, *Mind and Matter*, 1958.)

We have seen that as far as present knowledge goes, and in keeping with the spirit of quantum mechanics, the mind (self) cannot interact directly with matter. Again the mind for its adequate manifestation needs a large, extraordinarily complex apparatus, namely, the human brain. Notice that my mind or your mind cannot directly influence (as far as we know) the motion of a single electron or an atom, which is outside a living brain. But for atoms constituting a living brain, bound to a brain, nothing is more common than mind-brain interaction. That I speak to you and you understand me are—both of these things—a direct demonstration of the mind-brain interaction. This mind-brain *Sanyoga* is the greatest of all mysteries.

What is mind, or rather, what is self-conscious mind? It is not easy to define. To define "mind" we have to employ the mind. Mind becomes both an *object* and a *subject*, and a precise definition therefore is inherently impossible. If you use the entire mental apparatus to define mind, then there is hardly anything left of what is to be defined. On the other hand, if you make nearly the entire mind the *object* to be defined, then there is little mental resource available to provide the thinking required to do the defining. The situation reminds us of the complementarity we have discussed before. But let us leave out a precise definition of mind. What is really important is the recognition that *mind is an entity, a reality, apart from matter.* If mind is separate from matter then there could be, and might even need to be, different paths, not totally exclusive, leading to them: namely, science in one case and meditation or yoga in the other. Once we recognize the separate reality of mind, the concept of "supreme mind", "one mind", is in a sense a natural extension.

Mind is not a thing. In the sense in which we speak of mind, it stands for thought, consciousness, preception, memories, reasoning, feelings, emotions, willing, and so on. Mind stands for "self", for soul. Its most significant characteristic is an unambiguous feeling of freedom to elect between alternative courses of action. At the human level, this feeling is undeniable, incontrovertible.

Equally, we recognize, as the great lesson of science, that the behavior of matter is, in all its aspects, fully explicable on an objective basis. To understand matter needs no direct reference to mind or self, and/or supernatural agency. *In the realm of natural science, reason is supreme.* Therein lies its extraordinary strength. We believe this will hold for, and will be reinforced by, future advancement in our understanding of the natural world.

As far as our experience goes, mind always occurs in association with matter, the brain. It is, therefore, apparent that the freedom exercised by the mind, and the influence of the mind on the course of physical and biological events, just operate *without* violating the laws of nature. In other words, we believe that the physical laws, as explored by the mind, must involve a certain inherent *inderterminacy*. It is within the limits of this indeterminacy that the ind could exercise its freedom of *interaction* with matter. Quantum indeterminacy is a case in point, though how far it is indeed relevant for the mind-body problem is a matter for future investigation. As the brain is a large system, the role of quantum indeterminancy, it would seem, cannot be anything more than negligible. But against this, we have to remember that the mind-brain interaction is likely to be extremely *nonlinear,* and as such the effects could be noticeable even though triggered within the limitations of quantum indeterminacy. Also, it should be remembered that though the brain is a large system, the "thoughts" are discreet, and (as discussed earlier) furthermore the transition from one thought to another in a sequence of thoughts is sudden, and the transition process is unanalyzable. This is not quite the characteristic of a large system. It seems that when we approach from the side of the mind, the brain does not appear to have the characteristics of a "large system". This we should expect, and it is at the root of the mind-brain mystery. The indeterminacy we have spoken of with reference to the mind-brain interaction permits influence of one kind on another without the mediation of other brains. It also allows for possible influence of the Cosmic Mind on individual minds.

It seems certain that with a deeper understanding of *space-time*, the mind-brain interaction mystery is likely to become richer, and open new possibilities for human experience, both in relation to the external world and the internal world.

Be that as it may, it is beyond question that for human advancement we need to pay attention to *both* the knowledge of the atom and the knowledge of the self. The universal knowledge of the atom has placed in man's hands, for the first time in man's history, *means* which, if *wisely* used, can bring prosperity for all. Otherwise the very survival of mankind is at stake.

It is a challenge for our education. What the Buddha proclaimed about the imperative need to *know* the mind, to *shape* the mind, and to *liberate* the mind has been never more true than in the Age of the Atom.

"Truth and Love—*Ahimsa*—is the only thing that counts," said Mahatma Gandhi. It binds men together, and it binds Man and the Cosmos.

NOTES

1.   Unfortunately, I did not come across books on Indian philosophy until very much later.

2.   As the SIPRI Yearbook (1978) points out, the total explosive power of nuclear weapons in the World's arsenals is equivalent to about one *million* Hiroshima-type atomic bombs. Even if a significant fraction of these weapons were used, most of the cities in the Northern Hemisphere would be utterly destroyed; and the genetic damage might decimate the human species itself.

3.   Quotations from Einstein are from A. Einstein, *Ideas and Opinions*, New York: Crown Publ., 1954); O. Nathan and H. Norden, *Einstein and Peace* (Methuen, 1963); and K. Brecher, *Nature*, 178 (15 March 1979).

4.   C. G. Jung has written much on religious experience. He says: "Religious experience is absolute. It is indisputable. You can only say that you have never had such an experience and your opponent will say, 'Sorry, I have.' And there your discussion will come to an end.

No matter what the world thinks about religious experience, the one who has it possesses the great treasure of a thing that has provided him with a source of life, meaning, and beauty and that has given a new splendor to the World and to mankind. He has *pistis* and peace. Where is the criterion by which you could say that such a life is not legitimate, that such experiene is not valid and that such *pistis* is mere illusion? Is there, as a matter of fact, any better truth about ultimate things than the one that helps you to live?" [*Psychological Reflections, An Anthology of the Writings of C. G. Jung*, selected and edited by Jolande Jacobi (Pantheon Books, 1953, XLVI, 188 [B, 113f.])].

5.   Goedel's work has established that any logical system, which at least includes ordinary arithmetic, necessarily contains statements that can be neither proved nor disproved within the system, but which are nonetheless intuitively true—that is there are statements which are "obviously" true but are not provable. *Thus even in mathematics we must admit truths that are not provable.* That there is no escape from this has been conclusively demonstrated by Goedel. He also proved that the *axioms* of any logical system which depends on ordinary arithmetic cannot be guaranteed to be consistent, that is, free from hidden contradictions.

6.   The concept of *absolute space* implies the idea of *absolute rest* and absolute velocity. Galileo showed that the idea is meaningless. With the concept of an all-pervading luminiferous ether in the nineteenth century there was a return to the concept of absolute space. *Absolute time*—the time which characterizes Newton's equations of motion—is founded on the idea that *absolute simultaneity* of events at different places as a precise, well-defined meaning. Einstein showed this to be a mistaken theory. Both *absolute space and absolute time* were demolished by Einstein's theory of relativity. Time and space were reduced from the status of *noumena* to *phenomena*, that is, "ap-

pearances" dependent on the state of motion of the observers. Interestingly, the ether is again reappearing in a totally new form, *the quantum ether*, a result of an interaction between general relativity and quantum theory. (See Bryce S. Dewitt, "Quantum Gravity: the New Synthesis" in *General Relativity, An Einstein Century Survey*, edited by S. W. Hawking and W. Israel, Cambridge University Press, 1979.)

7. Dirac has presently modified his theory of *two* times so as to incorporate conservation of matter in the visible universe (*Proc. R., Soc.*, 365.A [1979]: 19-30).

8. Einstein writing to Schroedinger (9 August 1939) says that he is as convinced as ever that quantum mechanics does not give a complete description of reality. "The mystic [meaning Bohr] . . . forbids, as being unscientific, an inquiry about something that exists independently of whether or not it is observed, i.e. the question as to whether or not the cat [reference is to Shroedinger's 'cat paradox'] is alive at a particular instant before an observation is made." (Bannesh Hoffmann, *Albert Einstein, Creator and Rebel*, 1973.)

9. This question is generally ignored. An exception is Schroedinger's discussion of the problem (see the Epilogue to his *What is Life?*).

10. In *The Human Mystery* (1979), J.C. Eccles says: "The *self-conscious mind is a self-subsistent entity* that is actively engaged in reading out from the multifarious activities of the neuronal machinery of the cerebral cortex according to its attention and integration and interest, and it integrates this selection to give the unity of conscious experience from moment to moment. It also acts back in a selective manner on the neuronal machinery. Thus it is proposed that the self-conscious mind exercises a superior interpretative and controlling role upon the neuronal events by virtue of a two-way interaction between World I and World II that is the External World and the [Internal World] . . ."

REFERENCES

Born, M. *Born-Einstein Letters*. New York: Walkers, 1971, p.151.

Brecher, K. *Nature* (15 March 1979): 178.

Burgers, J.M. "Causality and Anticipation." *Science*, 189 (July 1975): 194-98.

Cohen, P.J. and Hersh, R. "Non-Cantorian Set Theory." *Scient. Am.* (1967): 104-116.

Dewitt, B.S. "Quantum Gravity: the New Synthesis" in *General Relativity, An Einstein Century Survey*, S.W. Hawking and W. Israel (eds.). Cambridge: Cambridge University Press, 1979.

Dirac, P.A.M. *The Principles of Quantum Mechanics*. Oxford: Oxford University Press, 1958.

Eccles, J.C. *Facing Reality*. New York: Springer, 1970.

_____. *The Human Mystery*. New York: Springer, 1979.

Einstein, A. *Ideas and Opinions*. New York: Crown Publishers, 1954.

Goedel, K. "Albert Einstein: Philosopher-Scientist" in *The Library of Living Philosophers*, E. A. Schilpp, ed. (n.p., 1949), pp. 557-562.

Greidanus, T. A. *Psycho-Physical Theory*. Netherland Academy Series B 78, pp. 1-37.

Heisenberg, W. *Physics and Philosophy*. London: Allen and Unwin, 1958.

_____. *Physics and Beyond*. London: Harper and Row, 1971.

Hinshelwood, C. (Quoted from J. C. Eccles, *Facing Reality*, 1970).

Hiriyanna, M. *Outlines of Indian Philosophy*. India: Allen and Unwin, 1973, p. 363.

Hoffmann, B. *Albert Einstein, Creator and Rebel*. 1973.

Holton, G. *The Physics Teacher* (March Nr. 1979).

Jammer, Max. *The Philosophy of Quantum Theory*. New York: John Wiley, 1974.

Jung, C. G. *Psychological Reflections, An Anthology of the Writings of C. G. Jung*, selected and edited by Jolande Jacobi. Pantheon Books, 1953.

Kothari, J. N. *Biographical Mem. Fellows. R. Soc.* 5(1960).

_____. *J. N. Tata Memorial Lecture*. Bangalore: Indian Institute of Science, 1979.

Nagel, E. and Newman, J. B. "Goedel's proof." *Scient. Am.*, 194 (1956): 71-86.

Nathan, O. and Norden, H. *Einstein and Peace*. Methuen, 1963.

Penfield, W. *The Mystery of Mind*. Princeton: Princeton University Press, 1975.

Popper, K. R. and Eccles, J. C. *The Self and Its Brain*. New York: Springer, 1977.

Prigogine, I. "Physics and metaphysics." *Bull. 1. Academic Royale de Belgique* (Special issue 1974).

_____. "Time, structure and fluctuations." *Science*, 1 (Sept. 1978).

Rosenfeld, L. *Phys. Today (October Nr. 1962)*.

Sherrington, C. S. *Man on His Nature*. Cambridge: Cambridge University Press, 1940.

Schroedinger, E. *What Is Life?* Cambridge: Cambridge University Press, 1948.

———. *Science and Humanism*. Cambridge: Cambridge University Press,1951, pp. 4, 51.

———. *Mind and Matter*. Cambridge: Cambridge University Press, 1958.

———. *My View of the World*. Cambridge: Cambridge University Press, 1964, pp. 20-22.

Schumachar, E. F. *A Guide for the Perplexed*. London: Jonathan Cape, 1977.

Sri Aurobindo. *The Upanishads*. Pondicherry: 1972.

Tarski, Alfred. "Truth and proof." *Scient. Am.* (1969):63-77.

Wheeler, J. A. *Physics Today* (October 1963).

———. "Genesis and Observership," in University of Western Ontario series in the *Philosophy of Science* (R. Butts and J. Hintikka, eds. Boston: Riedel, 1977.

Whitehead, A. N. *Aims of Education*. London: Ernst Benn, 1962, pp. 22-23.

Wigner, E. P. "Two kinds of reality." *The Monist*, 48 (1964): 248-264.

The Turning Point: A New Vision of Reality

The new concepts in physics introduced at the beginning of
this century and still being elaborated in our current theories
of matter have brought about a profound change in our world
view: from the mechanistic world view of Descartes and Newton to a holistic and ecological view, similar to those of mystics
of all ages and traditions.

The new view of reality was by no means easy to accept
for the physicists of the early twentieth century. The exploration of the atomic and subatomic world brought them in contact with a strange and unexpected reality. In their struggle
to grasp this new reality, the scientists became painfully aware
that their basic concepts, their language, and their whole way
of thinking were inadequate to describe atomic phenomena.
Their problems were not merely intellectual but amounted to
an intense emotional and, one could even say, existential crisis.
It took them a long time to overcome this crisis, but in the end
they were rewarded with deep insights into the nature of matter and its relation to the human mind.

Today our society finds itself in a similar crisis. We can
read about its numerous manifestations every day in the news-
papers; high inflation and unemployment, the energy crisis,
a crisis in health care, pollution and other environmental disasters, a rising wave of violence and crime, and so on. I believe
that these are all different facets of one and the same crisis,
and that it is essentially a crisis of perception. Like the crisis

in physics in the 1920s, it derives from the fact that we are trying to apply the concepts of an outdated world view—the mechanistic world view of Cartesian and Newtonian science— to a reality which can no longer be understood in terms of these concepts.

Today we live in a globally interconnected world in which biological, psychological, social, and environmental phenomena are all interdependent. To describe this world appropriately we need a new paradigm, a new vision of reality—a fundamental change in our thoughts, perceptions, and values. The beginnings of this change, of a shift from the mechanistic to the holistic conception of reality, are already visible in all fields and are likely to dominate the entire decade. The gravity and extent of our global crisis indicate that the current changes are likely to result in a transformation of unprecedented dimensions, a turning point for the planet as a whole. The mechanistic view of the world was developed in the seventeenth century by Galileo, Descartes, Newton, and others. Descartes based his view of nature on a fundamental division into two separate and independent realms: that of mind and that of matter. This Cartesian division allowed scientists to treat matter as dead and completely separate from themselves, and to see the material world as a multitude of separate objects assembled into a huge machine.

While Descartes postulated the fundamental division between mind and matter and outlined his mechanistic vision of reality, Galileo was the first to combine scientific experimentation with the use of mathematical language. In order to make it possible for scientists to describe nature mathematically, Galileo postulated that science should restrict itself to studying the essential properties of material bodies—shapes, numbers, and movement—which could be measured or quantified. Other properties such as color, sound, taste, or smell he considered subjective mental projections which should be excluded from the domain of science.

Throughout the history of modern science, this strategy has proved extremely successful, but it has also extracted a heavy toll. A science concerned only with quantity and based exclusively on measurements is inherently unable to deal with experience, quality, or values. Indeed, ever since Galileo, scientists have evaded ethical and moral issues and this attitude is now generating disastrous consequences.

The conceptual framework created by Galileo and Descartes was completed triumphantly by Newton, who developed a consistent mathematical formulation of the mechanistic view of nature. From the second half of the seventeenth century to the end of the nineteenth, the mechanistic Newtonian model of the universe dominated all scientific thought. The natural sciences, as well as the humanities and socials sciences, all accepted the mechanistic view of classical physics as the correct description of reality and modeled their own theories accordingly. Whenever psychologists, sociologists, or economists wanted to be scientific, they naturally turned toward the basic concepts of Newtonian physics, and many of them still hold to these concepts, even though physicists have now gone far beyond them.

Present day economics, for example, remains fragmentary and reductionist, like most social sciences. It fails to recognize that the economy is merely one aspect of a whole ecological and social fabric. Economists tend to dissociate the economy from the fabric in which it is embedded, and to describe it in terms of simplistic and highly unrealistic theoretical models. Most of their basic concepts (e.g., efficiency, productivity, GNP) have been narrowly defined and are used apart from their wider social and ecological context. In particular, the social and environmental costs generated by all economic activity are generally neglected. Consequently, current economic concepts and models are no longer adequate to map economic phenomena in a fundamentally interdependent world, and hence enconomists have generally been unable to grapple with the major economic problems of our time.

Because of its narrow, reductionist framework, conventional economics is inherently antiecological. Whereas the surrounding ecosystems are organic wholes which are self-balancing and self-adjusting, our current economies and technologies recognize no self-limited principle. Undifferentiated growth—economic, technological, and institutional growth—is still regarded by most economists as the sign of a "healthy" economy, although it is now causing ecological disasters, widespread corporate crime, social disintegration, and ever increasing likelihood of nuclear war.

The situation is further aggravated by the fact that most economists, mistakenly striving for scientific rigor, avoid explicitly acknowledging the value system on which their models are based. In doing so, they tacitly accept the highly imbalanced set of values which dominates our culture and is embodied in our social institutions

The new paradigm now emerging consists not only of new concepts, but also of a new value system, and it is being reflected in new forms of social organization and new institutions. It is being formulated largely outside our academic institutions, which remain too closely tied to the Cartesian framework to appreciate the new idea. To describe the new paradigm, I shall begin with the view of matter that has emerged from modern physics, and then discuss the extension of this view to living organisms, mind, consciousness, and social phenomena.

The material world, according to contemporary physics, is not a mechanical system made of separate objects, but rather appears as a complex web of relationships. Subatomic particles cannot be understood as isolated, separate entities but have to be seen as interconnetions, or correlations, in a network of events. Subatomic particles are not made of any material substance: they have a certain mass, but this mass is a form of energy. Energy is always associated with processes, with activity; it is a measure of activity. Subatomic particles then, are bundles of energy, or patterns of activity. The notion of separate objects is an idealization which is often very useful but has no fundamental validity. All objects are merely patterns in an inseparable cosmic process, and these patterns are intrinsically dynamic, continually changing into one another, in a continuous dance of energy.

Thus, the world view presented by modern physics is holistic and ecological: it emphasizes the fundamental interrelatedness and interdependence of all phenomena, and also the intrinsically dynamic nature of physical reality. To apply this view to the description of living organisms, we must go beyond physics and turn to a new conceptual framework which seems to be a natural extension of modern physics: systems theory. Actually, the term "theory" may be somewhat misleading, since systems theory is not a well-defined theory, like that of relativity, but rather a particular approach, a language, a perspective.

This approach is concerned with the description of systems, defined as integrated wholes that derive their essential properties from the interrelations between their parts. The systems approach, therefore, does not focus on the parts, but rather on the interrelations and interdependencies between the parts. In the systems view, all structure is seen as a manifestation of underlying processes, and living systems are described in terms of patterns of organization.

Examples of systems can be found both in the animate and nonanimate world. Every living organism, for example (a cell, plant, animal, or human being), is a living system; however, living systems need not be individual organisms. There are social systems, such as a family or a community, and then there are ecological systems, or ecosystems, in which networks of organisms are interlinked, together with various inanimate components, to form an intricate web of relations involving the exchange of matter and energy in continual cycles.

All living systems exhibit similar patterns of organization. One important aspect of living systems is their tendency to form multi-leveled structures of systems within systems. For example, the human body consists of organs, each organ of tissues, and each tissue of cells. All these living systems consist of smaller parts and at the same time, act as parts of larger wholes. Living systems, then, exhibit a stratified order, and there are interconnections and interdependencies between all systems levels, each level interacting and communicating with its total environment.

Nobel Prizewinner Ilya Prigogine has posited, in collaboration with researchers in a variety of disciplines, that every living organism is a self-organizing system, which means that its order in structure and function is not imposed by the environment but is established by the system itself.

Self-organizing systems are "always at work": they must maintain a continuous environment to stay alive. This exchange involves processes such as metabolism, self-renewal, self-healing, regeneration, adaptation to environmental changes—in sum, the processes of self-maintenance. What makes living systems unique (and uniquely interesting) is the fact that they not only have a tendency to maintain themselves in their dynamic state but, at the same time, tend to transcend themselves—to reach out creativiely beyond their boundaries and limitations to generate new structures and new forms of organization.

In living systems, the principle of self-transcendence manifests itself in the processes of learning, development, and evolution. Thus, according to the new systems view, the Darwinian theory of evolution represents only one of two views, both of which are necessary to understand the phenomenon of evolution. The other view sees evolution as an essential manifestation of self-organization which leads over time to an ordered unfolding of complexity. The two complementary tendencies of self-organizing systems—self-maintenance and self-transcendence—are in continual dynamic interplay, and both contribute to the phenomenon of evolutionary adaptation.

In order to apply the systems view of life to higher organisms and, in particular, to human beings, it is necessary to deal with the phenomenon of mind. Gregory Baterson proposed a definition of mind as a systems phenomenon characteristic of living organisms, societies, and ecosystems, and listed a set of criteria which systems must satisfy for mind to occur. Any system that satisfies these criteria, he theorized, would be able to process information and develop various phenomena which we associate with mind-thinking, learning, memory, etc. In Baterson's view, mind is a necessary and inevitable consequence of a certain complexity which begins long before organisms develop a brain and a higher nervous system.

Baterson's criteria for mind turn out to be closely related to the characteristics of self-organizing systems. Indeed, mind is an essential property of living systems. As Baterson put it, "Mind is the essence of being alive." From the systems point of view, life is seen not as some substance or force, and mind is not an entity interacting with matter. Both life and mind are manifestations of the same set of systemic properties —a set of processes which represent the dynamics of self-organization.

Thus, drawing on Baterson's work and systems theory, I would define mind as the dynamics of self-organization. This concept of mind should, I feel, be of tremendous value in our attempts to overcome the Cartesian division. Mind and matter need no longer appear to belong to two separate categories, but can be seen to represent merely different aspects of the same phenomenon. The relationship between mind and brain, for example, which has confused scientists for centuries, now becomes quite clear: mind is the dynamics of self-organization, and the brain the biological structure through which this dynamics is carried out.

While adhering to Baterson's concept of mind, I would also use slightly different terminology in order to remain closer to conventional language. I would use the term "mentation", meaning mental activity, to describe the dynamics of self-organization at lower levels of living systems and reserve the word "mind" for organisms of higher complexity. Every living system (a cell, tissue, or organ, etc.) is engaged in the process of mentation, but in higher organisms an "inner world"—including self-awareness, conscious experience, conceptual thought, symbolic language, etc.—unfolds which is characteristic of mind.

The fact that the living world is organized in multileveled structures means that there also exist levels of mind. In the human organism, for example, there are various levels of "metabolic" mentation involving cells, tissues and organs, and then there is the neural mentation of the brain which, itself, consists of multiple levels of human evolution? The totality of these mentations constitutes what I would call the human mind, or psyche. In the stratified order of nature, moreover, individual human minds are embedded in the larger minds of social and ecological systems, and these are integrated into the planetary mental system—the mind of "Gaia", if you wish—which, in turn, must participate in some kind of universal or cosmic mind. Clearly, this systems view of mind has radical implications for our interactions with the natural environment —implications which are fully consistent with the views of spiritual traditions through the ages.

The systems view of life has many important consequences, not only for science but also for society and everyday life. It will influence our ways of dealing with health and illness, our relation to the natural environment, our social and political structures.

All these changes, of course, are already taking place. The paradigm shift is not something that will happen some time in the future, it is happening right now. The philosophical, spiritual, and political movements generated in the 1960s and '70s all emphasize different aspects of the new paradigm and all seem to be going in the same direction—though, so far, most of these movements still operate separately and have not yet recognized how their purposes interrelate. Thus, the human potential movement and the holistic health movement often lack a social perspective, while spiritual movements tend to lack ecological and feminist awareness. However, coalitions between some movements have recently begun to form—as in the "ecofeminist" movement, for example. Indeed, in that it presents what is perhaps the deepest challenge to the old value system, the feminist movement can be expected to continue to act as an important catalyst for further coalescence.

I believe that during the coming decade the various movements will recognize the communality of their aims and will flow together to form a powerful force of social transformation. This may seem an idealistic picture, in view of the current political swing to the right in the United States. However, if we look at the situation from a broad evolutionary perspective, these phenomena become understandable as inevitable aspects of change and transformation.

Cultural historians have often pointed out that the evolution of cultures is characterized by a regular pattern of culmination, decline, and disintegration. The decline occurs when a culture has become too rigid, in its technologies, ideas, or social organization, to meet the challenge of changing conditions. This loss of harmony inevitably leads to the outbreak of social discord and disruption. During this process of decline and disintegration, while the cultural mainstream has become petrified by clinging to fixed ideas and rigid patterns of behavior, creative minorities appear on the scene and transform some of the old elements into new configurations which become part of the new culture.

This process of cultural transformation is what we are now

observing in our society. The Democratic and Republican parties, the Chrysler Corporation, the Moral Majority, and most of our academic institutions—all are part of the declining culture. They are on their way down, in the process of disintegration. The social movements of the '60s and '70s are the rising culture. While the transformation is taking place, the declining culture may refuse to change, clinging even more rigidly to its outdated ideas; nor will the dominant social institutions willingly hand over their leading roles to the new cultural forces. But they will inevitably go on to decline and disintegrate while the rising culture continues to rise; eventually, it will take the lead. As that turning point approaches, the realization that evolutionary changes of this magnitude cannot be prevented by short-term political activities provides our strongest hope for the future.